Indy 500 Memories

Indy 500 Memories

AN ORAL HISTORY OF "THE GREATEST SPECTACLE IN RACING"

Art Garner & Marc B. Spiegel

4/25/16
Hi Doron
Hope you like Memories!
— Art Garner

ISBN-13: 9781530313242
ISBN-10: 1530313244

For Mathew and Scott, always in our memories.
- Art

For my mom and dad, who always enjoyed a good race, but liked the hospitality at the track even more.
- Marc

"After I say, 'Gentlemen Start Your Engines,' I feel
like I just pulled the pin on a hand grenade."

Tony Hulman

Contents

Mario Andretti

Preface

***Mario Andretti** was born in Italy and immigrated to the U.S. after World War II with his parents and twin brother Aldo. He won the Indy 500 in 1969 and Formula One World Championship in 1978.*

The first time I set foot at Indy was in 1958 when my brother and I went to watch the race with my Uncle Louie. I was 18. When I got home I thought about nothing else for days. In fact, for decades.

I'm still thinking about Indianapolis. I love that place. Now that might seem odd since I raced there 29 times from 1965 to 1994 and only won once. I actually had terrible luck. But here's the thing, every driver still loves Indy, regardless.

We love the battle of man and machine to the finish. And we respect the historical significance of the Speedway. It's not only a shrine of monumental importance to our sport – in Indianapolis, racing is religion. The Speedway is our temple. That's the best way I can explain my worship for Indianapolis. The Indianapolis Motor Speedway is my Mecca.

When I won in 1969 it was the most exhilarating experience and it remains my personal favorite memory. Fame came suddenly – a thunderclap, a bolt from the blue. Indianapolis changed my life.

Just like that.

Introduction

The premise was simple. Ask race car drivers, crew members, car owners, officials, media, celebrities, fans and others for a personal memory about the Indy 500.

The idea came during the launch of my previous book, *Black Noon, The Year They Stopped the Indy 500.* I was struck by how often I was approached by people, many with tears in their eyes, with their own story about what the 500 meant to them. Those stories, I thought, could fill a book.

Marc B. Spiegel, one of the best in the business of sports marketing and public relations, agreed to help in gathering and editing the memories. Our initial goal was 100 memories (for the 100th running of the race) of about 500 words (for the obvious reason). It didn't take long to realize we would exceed both those targets.

While the question seemed simple, narrowing it down to a single memory often proved difficult. After all, how do you ask A.J. Foyt to pick a single memory from 35 consecutive years of driving in the 500? You don't. And who wants to tell Bobby Unser they have everything they need after two hours of stories and the memories are still flowing? Not me. One more story please, Uncle Bobby.

Our job turned to editing our discussions down to 500 to 1,000 words, normally what can be covered in 10 to 20 minutes of conversation. We still didn't always hit our goal. But when you've won the 500 four times like Foyt, Al Unser, Sr. and Rick Mears, you're allowed a few extra words.

The memories are full of surprises. It's amazing how many drivers, including Juan Pablo Montoya, Eddie Cheever and Scott Goodyear, took their first lap around the track in a tour bus after paying their way into the Speedway Museum. Those who have won the race typically – but not always – cited their victory. For drivers from the '60s and '70s, when 50 to 100 cars were often entered in the race, simply qualifying for the 500 was often a standout memory.

Some people, especially those with journalism backgrounds, but also fans, drivers, and others, wrote and submitted their own memories. Most required very little editing. We never put words in anyone's mouth, just edited their words for brevity and clarity.

All the memories included are from post-World War II races. In a few instances we've drawn from biographies, news articles and videos to include a key memory from someone who is no longer with us.

In the end, we weren't able to include all the memories in this book, not even close. But they're too good to put away in a file cabinet and instead will be shared on our Facebook page, https://www.facebook.com/Indy500Memories/. Please check it out and feel free to post an Indy 500 memory of your own.

The Pagoda

CHAPTER 1

First 500

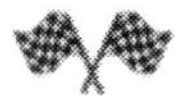

Nearly everyone recalls their first trip to the Indianapolis Motor Speedway when discussing their Indy 500 memory. Many talked about how watching the race as a spectator, whether as a child or someone already in the sport, affected their life and their career. For most everyone, their first trip to the Speedway had a lasting impact.

Eddie Cheever *started 132 Formula One races, more than any other American driver, before racing in his first Indy 500. He competed in 14 500s, winning with his own team in 1998.*

Both my parents were American and even though I was raised in Italy from the age of five, our home was an American home. My father liked racing and he always talked about Indianapolis, (A.J.) Foyt and the Unsers. He'd actually been to the 500 with my mother the year I was born.

Somewhere in the mid-1980s – I think I was going to Detroit for the Grand Prix – I stopped at Indy. I got in that little bus to go around the track. Every now and then the driver would stop and show the tire marks where a car had spun and hit the wall. He must have thought this was very entertaining and I'm sure most of the people on the bus found it entertaining. I thought it was terrifying.

Two of the drivers that I admired the most when I was a younger driver in Europe were Jochen Rindt and Alan Jones. Both of them had went to Indy and then decided they weren't going to do it – it was too dangerous. Those guys were, in my mind, brave as you can be. So when I put those two things together, how there was no room for error and that drivers like Rindt and Jones decided not to race there, it made me sit back and scratch my head. That was my first touch with Indy.

I knew I wanted to eventually race at Indy, but it wasn't first on my list. I was a Formula One driver and we didn't race on ovals. I'd have to learn ovals and it wasn't on my agenda. It wasn't until (Chip) Ganassi called and said he wanted to start a team. I thought it would be a great experience, not just for me, but for my family, to come and live in the U.S. It also was a continuation of an open-wheel racing career and the second best place to go. Formula One has been, and will always be, the pinnacle of racing. But for me as an American, Indy was a great challenge.

Indy has always been an enigma for me. I was still learning on the last lap I did, probably as many things as on my first lap. It's alive and it changes every hour. If the car's not working, it's really difficult. But when you get it right, it is the most magical place in the world to drive a race car.

Feeling that you're in control – because you're never really *in* control at the speeds we were going in the middle '90s, about 260 mph on the straight – and being about to get around the track without lifting your foot off the throttle was an unbelievable experience.

I felt like I was at the point of an arrow being hurled forward by a hurricane. It was so violent, so much inherent violence, that to be able to control it for 500 miles and finish a race, I thought was a miracle. And I had the luck of winning it. I can't sit back and say I drove incredibly well that day or I was on my game that day. It's such a team sport that so many things have to fall into place.

It's very hard to explain what the Indianapolis 500 is to a driver that hasn't seen it and hasn't actually felt the thrill of driving a car around there. Once you have raced there, see what the grandstands look like to the field, go through all that pageantry and start to find your place in the history of it, it becomes addictive. When I was racing there I would dream of the 500, I don't know, 50 percent of the time. It's such an intricate puzzle and such a difficult riddle to solve, it just consumes you. It was a business decision to race there, but in the end, it became much more of a passion than a business.

***Townsend Bell** has competed in nine Indy 500s heading into the 2016 race with a best finish of fourth. He also is a motorsports commentator for NBC Sports.*

My strongest Indy memory would be at the very beginning of the adventure for me. I was 10 years old in 1985 and watched Danny Sullivan spin and win on television. That was pretty cool.

Growing up in San Francisco, my dad had a deal with me and my two brothers that when we turned 10 years old he would take us on a trip anywhere in the United States. My other two brothers had picked New York and Alaska.

So the following May I decided I wanted to go to the Indy 500. We flew out from California on Friday night after dad was done working. It was pretty hard to get a ticket back then. We were seated just off the front straight in the grandstands and I sat totally mesmerized by all the hype and the marching bands and "Back Home Again in Indiana" and the whole deal.

I have two very vivid memories. One was being on Georgetown Road – I couldn't believe the amount of empty beer cans on the street. I've never seen anything like that.

The second was in the bathroom. I'm standing at the urinal and a pretty tall guy walked in next to me. I'm naturally fairly intimidated – this guy was 6'4" and I'm 10 years old. I look up and it's Michael Knight from *Knight Rider,* David Hasselhoff. He was a VIP co-partner of Arie Luyendyk. *Knight Rider* was far and away my favorite show in the world and I was frozen at the thought that, 'Oh my god it's Michael Knight.' Standing next to me at a urinal no less.

Just before the engines were to start, it started raining and it kept raining and unfortunately they cancelled the race, until not the following day, but the following weekend. So we flew back to California.

With a little encouragement, my dad agreed to fly me back to Indianapolis the following weekend to see my first Indy 500. With the additional seven days of unexpected build-up, the anticipation was even greater as the rows of three came racing down for the start. I was totally addicted from that point forward with the sport of Indy car racing and the fantasy that someday I would get a chance to do it. And exactly 20 years later in 2006 I made my first Indy 500 start. It was a pretty cool feeling.

When I think back to that trip, the crazy thing is that I didn't even think it remotely possible that I would ever get a chance to drive in the Indy 500. That seemed like such a far-fetched ambition. It wasn't even a dream.

That made the reality all that much more powerful, to be standing there on the grid for my first Indy 500, literally 200 feet from where I sat as a kid 20 years earlier. It's a profound moment when it all sinks in that you've made something happen that at first seemed so ridiculous, I would never have even dreamed it was possible.

***Dan Cotter** is a longtime Indy car team owner who captured the checkered flag in the 1983 Indy 500 with driver Tom Sneva and the Bignotti-Cotter Team.*

Some might think that owning a car that won the 1983 Indianapolis 500 would be my most vivid memory of the Indianapolis Motor Speedway. It was not. My most vivid and best memory of Indy was my first visit to the track.

In 1949 my father gave me the most outlandish gift of my then young life. For my eighth grade graduation present he invited me to go with him to the Indianapolis 500. For many years we had listened to this famous race on the radio each Memorial Day.

That year he was going to take me to see it in person. I was beside myself with excitement and could not wait to leave. In those days there were no expressways between Chicago and Indianapolis. So we left a day early and spent the night in Danville, Ill. My father was in the hardware business and we visited some hardware stores on the drive. All I wanted to do is get to the Speedway, so that was a long day.

Early on race day morning we drove to Indianapolis. I can remember parking near some railway train cars that had brought in people from Chicago to see the race. I thought that would be a pretty neat way to travel. I had never before seen this many people in one place in my life. Everyone seemed to be in a rush to get into the track. I also remember that our seats were on the inside of the track behind the pits. I can still see the multitude of colors and hear the excitement all around me. And the race hadn't even started.

I have several standout memories of the race itself. The roaring noise at the start and the clouds of dust kicked up on the first lap absolutely amazed me. The man sitting in front of us actually started pounding his head with both of his fists in excitement. During the race Duke Nalon crashed one of the Novis and it caught on fire. I can remember seeing it and being scared by the huge smoke cloud rising from the north side of the track. Later on in the race, I noticed that one of the drivers was racing down the straightaway and his tee shirt had blown up almost to his shoulders exposing his stomach and chest. I thought that was wild!

Back then, I did not realize that this trip with my dad would foster an ever increasing interest in car racing – one that would see the Bignotti-Cotter Team and our driver Tom Sneva in Victory Lane 34 years later.

Michael Davis *is from South Bend, Ind., and has been to every Indy 500 since 1965.*

My first venture to the Indy 500 was in 1965 when I was 13. I have other good memories, but the first 500 still sits in my heart. It seems like yesterday.

My mom and dad took me and we actually went the night before and stayed in the North 40 lot just outside the track between turns 3 and 4. We spent the night in a 1965

Ford Galaxie that was a demonstrator from the Ford dealership in Plymouth, Ind., where dad was the service manager.

I was amazed at all the cars lined up in the lot the night before the 500. When the cannon went off, if I remember right at 5 a.m., dad made a mad dash to Turn 1. Mom had breakfast and lunch packed up for us and dad made breakfast on the green Coleman stove. We had our blanket laid out in a pretty good position in Turn 1.

When the race finally started I managed to make my way up to the fence several rows ahead of our blanket and that's where I stayed for the whole race. I was a diehard Jimmy Clark fan and to this very day the green 82 is still my favorite car. I can still vividly remember that car and also the gold 98 of Parnelli Jones. Little did I know that day would make such of a big impact on my life that I've never missed a 500 since.

Chuck Fawcett *lives in Southern California.*

I can't remember when the Indianapolis 500 wasn't a central interest in my life. My earliest memories are of the family gathered around the radio on Memorial Day, listening to Sid Collins, Luke Shelton, Howdy Bell and the other commentators painting a word picture of "The Greatest Spectacle in Racing." The first broadcasts I recall are from 1947, '48 and '49 when the Lou Moore Blue Crown cars dominated.

The year 1953 was a milestone for Bill Vukovich – and me. My dad had done some work at the Kurtis Kraft shop in Glendale, Calif., and got tickets for the race. We drove across country in my dad's '52 Hudson Hornet.

For a young kid seeing his first major sporting event, this was sensory overload. There were more people than I had ever seen in one place. The infield was full of scaffolding with fans perched atop them. The pageantry of the Purdue marching band, aerial bombs, balloons and Morton Downey signing "Back Home Again in Indiana" was all exciting stuff.

And of course there was the race. The brilliant colors of the cars coupled with the staccato of their racing engines was an indescribable experience for me. The race was run in near record heat. Relief drivers were the order of the day, but Vuky was victorious without relief.

My dad took shelter in the shade of the grandstand and encouraged me to do the same, but I wouldn't budge from my seat until Seth Klein waved the checkered flag. I had seen my first Indy 500 – and had the sunburn to prove it.

College, military, marriage, a daughter and a career all conspired to keep me from attending the 500 after 1959, and living 2,000 miles from the Speedway didn't help. As

2003 approached, I decided to make the pilgrimage to Indiana on the 50th anniversary of my first visit to the Brickyard.

Much had changed in 50 years. The Speedway was a gleaming modern edifice and the cars were light years beyond Vuky's roadster. But the history and the tradition were as pervasive as ever. Walking through the main gate at 16th and Georgetown gave me goose bumps. The ghosts of Ray Harroun, Tommy Milton, Wilbur Shaw and Louie Meyer were all around me. No matter where you live, if you are a race fan, you know you are back home again in Indiana when you walk through the gate.

There is no other place like it.

***Bob Gates** is a longtime Indy 500 fan from Greenwood, Ind.*

For kids passionate about auto racing and growing up around Indianapolis, the month of May was like a second Christmas. Three daily newspapers competing for scoops, four local TV stations loaded with Speedway coverage and radio stations with quarter-hour track reports brought Christmas Eve-like excitement with each day.

However, all that scrutiny made it difficult to endure the routine drudgery of higher education on those cloudless, blue-skied, Indiana May days, knowing the cars were on the track.

When doodling race cars on a notebook and daydreaming about the roar of Offys and Novis in math class just wasn't enough to satisfy those racing longings, something drastic was needed. So skipping school for a day at the track became an essential springtime rite for many Hoosier kids.

I had one memorable close call. I'd convinced a friend to join me on a classroom escape and all was going well. We'd made a foray into the Snake Pit and hung around Gasoline Alley to check out the cars and stars up close while wrangling autographs.

With plenty of stories to tell our friends the next day, we were delightfully satisfied with our *Ferris Bueller's Day Off* escapade.

Then disaster.

We bumped smack into our assistant principal.

'Well, hello boys,' was his sugar-coated greeting. 'Are you young men enjoying yourselves?'

Stunned, we stuttered and stammered out a couple of, 'Yes sirs.' Having to speak to any authoritative adult in a social setting was enough to cast tongue-tying fear into any kid with 1960s sensibilities. But a principal? At the Speedway? When we'd skipped school?

We were paralyzed with paranoia and excused ourselves. For days we lived in dire dread, anticipating a call from school and a confrontation with our parents about just who had forged the names on our sick notes. In our era, the only thing worse than being in trouble at school was having your parents find out about it.

But that never happened. We never knew why. Didn't ask.

Possibly our principal understood the near magical pull of the Speedway. Or maybe he also skipped school for his jaunt to the track.

Either way, the experience left another one of those indelible memories that wove the Indianapolis 500 into the fabric of our lives.

***Bill Jansen** grew up in Illinois, attended Michigan State University and worked as an FBI agent for 24 years. He earned a law degree from Drake University and served as a Judge in the Las Vegas county criminal court for 27 years, before retiring in 2012.*

I started going in 1949 and I have attended roughly 47 500s.

I grew up in the town of Pekin, Ill., and had an uncle who was a car nut and a race nut. He used to pick me up to go to the midget car races around Illinois – in Peoria and Lincoln and Springfield. He had a daughter and no sons – so he sort of adopted me and my brother as his sons. That's really what got me interested in racing.

I remember sitting in the den at home with my dad listening to the Indy 500 on the radio in 1947 or '48, and I said to my dad, 'Let's go.' In 1949, my dad, my brother, my uncle, two of my uncle's friends and I got tickets – and that's how I got started going to the Indy 500.

That first year I was 13 and we made the trip to Indianapolis for the race. My Uncle Herb had a 1948 Packard and he drove us. It was about 200 miles from Pekin to Indianapolis, and we left early in the morning. There was a creek with two boards over it and we parked on the other side of this creek. Two boys were charging a nickel for every person going over that "bridge" to the other side and I remember thinking they were very business-like at a young age.

My first impression of the Speedway was that it was awesome. It was big. It was something you heard about on the radio, but really didn't fully understand until you were there to see how huge it was. They had good crowds that were sellouts at that time. I don't know what the estimate on attendance was, but I would say it was at least 100,000, if not more.

We sat in Section C – which at the time were some old wooden grandstands. I didn't know too many drivers. My favorite was always Tony Bettenhausen because I saw him drive in the midgets, and he was from Tinley Park, Ill.

After the race, I remember my brother and I went out on the track. The front straightaway was brick and it was like you were on ice. You'd slide along the brick because of all the oil and grease on that track.

The Indy 500 is a sporting event that in order to really enjoy and understand it, you have to attend one. I guarantee you if you attend one, you'll want to come back and see the race again.

It's a tradition. You have to go there and be there to witness it. "Back Home in Indiana," and the Purdue band and all the balloons. All traditions. As they say, "The Greatest Spectacle in Racing."

***Dan Layton** has been working in motorsports public relations for American Honda for more than 20 years.*

Although I've been most associated with Honda throughout my Indy car career, my first Indy 500 came in 1994, working for a small, month-of-May team called Pagan Racing.

At the time, I was trying to support a young family by scratching out a living handling PR for the Toyota Atlantic and Pro Sports 2000 series and working as a racing school instructor. I was like hundreds of others, stitching together different jobs in the various support series and schools to call ourselves, however barely, professional.

But in April, the phone rang. It was John Barnes, team manager at Pagan, saying he needed a PR person for Indy, couldn't pay me much, but the driver would be Roberto Guerrero. That was good enough for me.

Coming together late, there was a lot to organize in a short time, starting with finding a place to stay in Indy. I ended up crashing on an air mattress at a friend's apartment. There were a series of late, late nights building up a mailing list for news releases, etc., putting together an activity schedule for Roberto, getting to know the IMS staff and procedures, etc., etc., etc. It was a steep learning curve, and I was starting at the very bottom.

But it also was a month of meeting cool people, learning a ton, and enjoying every minute. Indy veterans on the team like Mike Griffin, engineer Ian Ashdown and engine builder Ed Pink were incredibly helpful, as was Roberto, who had a ton of patience with a newbie PR guy.

It also was the year of the Penske/Ilmor pushrod Mercedes-Benz engine and the year of Honda's failure to qualify. Our garage was directly across from the Rahal/Honda units, and the constant shuffle of engines, personnel, and eventually (ex-Penske) chassis was eye-opening, to say the least.

The month just flew by. Roberto qualified the Lola-Buick in the middle of the seventh row in a year where 16 cars failed to make the show, including the likes of Gary Bettenhausen, Geoff Brabham and Buddy Lazier. The night before the race, I was so paranoid about traffic coming into IMS that I slept in the team's hospitality unit.

Then I was standing on the grid in a fire suit, watching Chuck Yeager lead the fly-over, and feeling the hair on the back of my neck stand at attention. Our race ended all too quickly – on just the 20th lap. Roberto got caught out in midfield traffic, spun and slapped the wall in Turn 1 – and our day was done.

One year later, I was back at Indy for my second 500, but now a full-time PR rep for American Honda's Indy car program. You could write a book about that year – but 22 years later I'm still with Honda, still in Indy car racing, and still learning something new every day.

I'm not much of a souvenir collector. But I still have my silver badge number 7764 for the 78th running of the Indianapolis 500 on a shelf in my office.

Paul Page *is a longtime television and radio broadcaster of the 500.*

I listened to my first Indy 500 in 1953, in Stuttgart, Germany on the Armed Forces Network. My stepdad was stationed there and I was seven years old. It registered as really something great to listen to. There were all these different voices and they were reporting all these different things and it was very exciting.

We moved around quite a bit and our last duty station was Fort Sheridan, Ill. I had a great uncle in Indianapolis, Harry Gisel. I never knew my father, so the first six years of my life I was raised by Harry. He was a fascinating human being, an American League baseball umpire who retired in 1946 and knew all the greats. He was also interested in showing me things that I otherwise hadn't seen and invited me to come down to see the Indy 500. That was in 1960.

During those seven years I was kind of keeping track of the radio broadcast. Keeping real track of the Indy 500 in those days was impossible. It wasn't in the newspaper or anything. I got on the train and came down to Indianapolis and saw the '60 race. It was the perfect race to see.

It was all roadsters. I liked it in those days because you could see the driver up close and he's fighting at the wheel. The battle toward the end of the race, the Dick Rathmann and Rodger Ward duel, where they were literally changing position on every lap, is still one of the great all-time finishes. I was infected with the crowd screaming and cheering their person on.

We were in our seats, like an hour before the start, and some of the marching bands were still in the area. I remember there was a track crossover point at the entry to the first turn and they had group of safety patrol workers with vacuum cleaners out, vacuuming up after the crowd.

One of the things that really struck me was the P.A. and the dramatic way in which it was done. I was sitting up in D grandstand in the first turn. Tom Carnegie often started an interview with the words, 'Here at the starting line we have…' From my seat I knew they were half a mile or more away, but I knew where they were. For some reason that whole thing impressed me.

Years later, 2003 or so, it was the first time I didn't have to be part of the pre-game broadcast for the Indy 500. So I was free to walk around until the time came to start the engines and I had to be up in the booth. It was such a thrill for me because I had never been able to do it before. So that was pretty exciting for me, exciting in that my son – who was a race engineer at the time for Andretti Green – I could talk to him and be next to his car on the starting grid.

So I'm wandering around and I see Carnegie sitting at his little stand. Tom and I were very, very good friends and he says, 'Paul, come here.' So I walk over and he picks up his mike and says, 'Now at the starting line, Paul Page.'

I was shocked. I had no idea. I thought, my god, I'm gonna be *that* guy.

***Bobby Rahal** won the 500 in 1986 and won the CART series championship in 1986, 1987 and 1992. He competed in 13 Indy 500s and is currently a team owner fielding entries for his son Graham.*

I remember going to do rookie orientation in 1982. I think it was the first year they had it. In fact, the day we did my orientation it was snowing. It was so cold, there were actually snowflakes flying on the track, although nothing was sticking. It was a very gray day with all those gray grandstands. Everything was just gray. It was a very intimidating experience.

We were a brand new team. Nobody on the team had any oval track experience and I had never driven an oval. Steve Horne, the team manager, he'd never been an oval racer. None of the mechanics had ever done an oval. You want to talk about baptism by fire – that was it.

All during practice, I was never that comfortable. Of course, we were learning something new every day. The setups were something new. We had Lee Dykstra come on board because our first race that year in '82 at Phoenix was a total disaster. We all knew we needed to do something because it was not going to end up well. We actually skipped the second race at Atlanta to get our act together and Indy was the third race.

In the race, it's just like everything clicked. We were running fifth. I was fighting with Al Unser, Sr. I think we were fourth and fifth. Then, with about 20 laps to go, my engine broke. But in the race, it just all seemed to come together, the comfort level or whatever we were doing.

I suppose that one of the highlights was later on Gordon Johncock, who won that year, had said to one of his mechanics, 'Who was that guy in number 19?' Al and I were running with Rick Mears and Gordon, but we were a lap or two down at that stage. The guy that I least expected to get accolades from was Gordon Johncock because he wasn't a really talkative guy. But after the race, he talked me up to people. He said, 'That guy really can drive.' I was shocked. We didn't finish, I think we ended up 11th just because in those days the reliability of those cars was not very good.

That year, I don't think any of us on the team were really prepared to go there. I don't know if anybody is ever really prepared the first time. As the month went on, the light bulb that's over our head started getting brighter and brighter and in the race it started to shine pretty brightly. While we didn't finish, we left there thinking, 'You know what, that was not too bad.'

***Mark Reuss** is the executive vice president of Global Product Development, Purchasing and Supply Chain at General Motors and the son of Lloyd Reuss, former GM president.*

The memory of my first trip to the Indy 500 as a young boy is as vivid in my mind now as it ever was. My dad took me and we sat low in Turn 1. When it started, I had just never seen anything start like that before.

I'd seen kickoffs and opening pitches. But this was something else entirely. The roar of the engines filled my ears, and vibrated in my chest as it bounced off everything around me. I could feel the air move in the whole area, the wind and draft as they rumbled by us. I was blown away. And I knew right then and there, without question, that I wanted to be a part of it. It was the mid-1970s, and there were different engines with a wide range of distinct sounds – the turbo Buick V6s, the Chevy stock block V8s, the Cosworths – and my dad pointed out the differences and how to discern them. I was wide-eyed and fascinated, and totally 100 percent hooked.

I've had a lot of fantastic memories of Indy since that first time. Often in those first few years we'd have tickets to Roger Penske's suite. I'd be the only child there and Roger's wife, Kathy, would go out of her way to take care of me and make sure I was fed and happy. To this day we still talk about it. And she'll still make sure I've had a sandwich.

In 1983, my dad took me for a hot lap in the Buick Riviera convertible pace car. He didn't pace the start of the race – that honor went to the legendary Duke Nalon – but he was able to take me out on the track for my very first time and that's another vivid, terrific memory that will stick with me for the rest of my life.

As an adult, I've certainly had many memorable and successful trips to Indy, especially after working with Roger to reestablish Chevrolet's presence at the Brickyard. It was incredibly special to see Chevy return to Victory Lane once more. Just as it was incredibly special for me, given what I experienced as a boy, the first time I took my own son to the race. And there's something special about every single trip I take to Indy, even now.

But they'll never quite outshine the memory of that first time in Turn 1. It opened my eyes and ears and heart to it all, and helped shape the rest of my life.

Ryann Rigsby *works in public relations for Andretti Autosport.*

To the world it's just another month. Thirty-one days of rainy and stormy springtime, preparing to kick off summer.

But to those of us who call Indy racing home, it's much more than just another month. It's *the* month – the only one that counts. It's seven straight days of practice. Two days of qualifying. Countless driver appearances. Two solid weeks of hard work and high emotions for drivers and their crews.

I remember my first Indy 500 in 2008. I had never been to the race before I started working in the sport. In fact, I wasn't even a race fan. It was back when it really was a *month* of May. Four weeks of practice, two weekends of qualifying and pretty close to the same number of driver appearances (just more time to do them). It was 31 days, but it felt like 100. The emotions were just as high – but lasted twice as long.

Then came race day, a day unlike any other.

After a month of controlled chaos, race day is eerily calm. You're in the gates before 5 a.m. to beat the traffic. No driver appearances. No garage tours. No interviews. Just a nap in your car, breakfast and a wait that feels endless. Then it's time for the walk – the trip from the garage to the track.

This is my most memorable moment of May. I walked out of the garages that first year and down the famed Gasoline Alley with one of the most legendary families in racing. I was trailing right behind not one, but three Andrettis, which may not mean much at the mall, but at the Indianapolis Motor Speedway and to its crowd, it means everything.

They close the garages before the race, so what is usually an area packed full of fans feels almost abandoned and forgotten. Silent. And then you turn the corner into a literal wall of people. They line the sides, they fill the catwalk above the Alley, they hang out of every door and window. They are everywhere, and they are loud. It gives you chills. It's a true moment of, 'Holy #*@%!' as you realize just how massive Indianapolis Motor Speedway is – and how tiny it can feel when the empty stands become a sea of faces.

From the troops marching down pit lane to the command to start engines, the opening ceremonies leave a lasting memory. It gives you a new appreciation for that day – that 100th day of May – and for every day before it. You made it and you'll forever see the race in a whole new way. You'll see a whole new race track. You'll see history and innovation – laughter and tears.

And maybe, just maybe, you'll see your hard work become the glow in the eyes of a little boy as he begins his journey to 500 miles of memories.

***Tony Stewart** started on the pole in his first Indy 500 in 1996 and competed in the race five times. He moved to NASCAR in 1999.*

I came with my father. We were in some bus that had a luggage rack. You had to get up at 0-dark-30 to get on the bus to ride up to Indy for race day. They threw me up in the luggage rack. Somebody gave me a pillow and everybody started throwing their jackets on top of me to keep me warm. The ride home wasn't nearly as cool, because after a long day at the track, everybody but my dad and I were kind of rowdy.

I was probably five years old. We sat between turns 3 and 4 and we were two rows up, right in the middle of the short chute. You could hardly see anything. The cars were so fast. They were a blur. But to see those cars under caution and smell the methanol fumes and everything, it was still pretty cool.

I didn't care how much homework I had. It was the last priority when the month of May was going on and whatever coverage was on TV, you were just glued to it. I rode my bike to school every day and your parents beat it in your head to stop at stop signs and wait for green lights before you cross the road. Well, I played Frogger going home, trying to get home as fast as I could, trying to get the TV on. That's my biggest memory, just growing up and watching, loving the opportunity to get home. There wasn't any one particular moment. It's just been something that's been a huge, huge part of my life.

A.J. Foyt, Jr.

CHAPTER 2

Foyt

NO NAME IS MORE CLOSELY associated with the Indy 500 than A.J. Foyt, Jr., the first four-time winner of the race. He's been a fixture at the Speedway since he first qualified in 1958. He's been a winner as a driver, an owner-driver-builder and as a car owner. He's won in a car and engine of his team's own design, the first and only time that has been accomplished. He drove in 35 consecutive Indy 500s, more than any other driver, and holds records for seven Indy car championships and 67 Indy car victories. Yet when someone suggested A.J. Foyt had made the Indy 500 famous, he shook his head no. "The race makes the drivers," he said. "The drivers don't make the race. The Indy 500 made A.J. Foyt."

***A.J. Foyt, Jr.** is the only driver to win the Indy 500, the 24 Hours of Le Mans and the Daytona 500. He was named Driver of the Century by the Associated Press.*

When I was a little kid working in my daddy's shop in Houston I would listen to the race on the radio. I'd think, 'Boy, I would really like to race up there some day.' Then I went up there a couple of years and watched it. Afterwards I thought, 'I'm not sure I really want to do this.'

I had a midget race car and they used to always have a race the night before the 500. I knew many of the drivers in the 500 because they'd come by my daddy's shop when they raced in Houston. I used to change tires and wash the cars for Johnny Parsons, Jimmy Reece and Bill Vukovich, and all of them when they came to town. So I knew them all.

The night before the Indy midget race, I'm working on my car and Jimmy Reece and a bunch of other drivers walked up. Jimmy asked me what I was doing and I told him I was jacking a little weight. He said, 'The only place you need to jack some weight is on the right side of the car, up in front of the steering gear.' I asked him what the heck he was talking about.

'That throttle foot,' he said, 'put a little more weight there.' I never forgot that.

My biggest thrill was when Dean Van Lines gave me a break. Jimmy Bryan had won the championship three times with them. I had won at Salem (Ind.) Speedway, and I guess because Salem was a high bank track and I was young and crazy, they thought I'd make a good Indy car driver. They gave me a break and I made the 500 in '58.

That's the biggest thrill in my life – just to say I raced at Indianapolis. It wasn't like it is today. You have a halfway decent car today and you're almost automatically in. You're lucky to have 35 cars today. Back then you might have 100 cars and you had to make the field.

Everybody had to put together their own motors. There were different chassis builders. The biggest thing when I started was just making the race and that was probably my happiest moment. Then of course, I was lucky enough to win a few.

I had a special relationship with Mr. Tony Hulman. His wife Mary and my wife Lucy hit it off and all of our kids were about the same age. We spent four or five Christmases together. They'd come down to Houston and we just got to be real close. It was just a good friendship. We weren't kin, but we were like kin.

I'm the only one he rode around with on the track, after I won it the fourth time, and it was a big honor for me. He was sick and had lost a lot of weight. That's something else I won't forget. Spent a lot of good years with the Hulmans – great years.

Lucy Foyt *has been married to A.J. Foyt, Jr. since 1956.*

A.J. had dreamed of qualifying for the 500 for years and when he finally did, he was so excited he said he had to win. I told him first he had to finish the race before he got all excited.

Back then you'd go for the whole month of May. It was a month out of our life every year that we really enjoyed. It was fun; we all had a good time. At the very beginning we lived in somebody's basement for the month. It only got better as it went along. For a long time we stayed with Mari and Elmer George. They were great friends of ours and we stayed at their house. Then they built the Speedway Motel and in its prime, that was a great place to be.

A.J. would get up and go to the track early in the morning, but I mostly had free time. At home I was always busy with kids, but this gave me a month to do what I wanted to do.

You never knew when you went to Indianapolis what the weather would be. When I packed for the month I took everything from a bathing suit to a fur coat. When it was pretty we'd sit around the pool. There were a bunch of us wives and we'd go shopping, just do what we wanted to do, because the guys were there working and practicing. It was good times.

For the race I would sit up in the tower with Mari and Elmer. Eventually we got a suite and I would watch from there. It was fun at first and very exciting. Going up in the tower and seeing everything that was happening.

It was nerve-wracking at times, but I never had that nervous feeling with A.J. With him I always had the feeling he knew what he was doing. I never saw him in an accident and that helped keep me from being nervous. All the accidents he had, I was never there. Not for one of them.

Now when my boys raced – I nearly went crazy.

All the winning races at Indy were special. They were all fun. But for the fourth win, they moved Victory Lane on me. I'd been to Victory Lane three times and I thought I knew exactly where I was going. But I got there after the fourth win and nobody was there. I had to go find the new Victory Lane. Thank God I was with my son on a golf cart so it didn't take long, but it was very confusing.

I never asked A.J. to hang it up. I knew he'd know when it was time. After his last accident I really didn't want him to race anymore because the doctors told him one more bad accident with your legs and you could lose them. I didn't feel like it was worth it. But he still had to do it one more time and that was good for him. That was his job, that's what he enjoyed doing. If your job can be something you enjoy, that's pretty good.

I haven't been back to the race for a few years now. When I sit home and watch on television, I know a heck of a lot more about what's going on than when I was up in the suite. Now I can see everything, where at the track I couldn't see anything. So I think that's a good excuse for me to stay home. I felt like I've done it a long, long, time.

***Larry Foyt** is the adopted son of A.J. Foyt, Jr. and president of AJ Foyt Racing. He competed in the Indy 500 from 2004 to 2006.*

Indianapolis left such a mark on me. I still get goose bumps driving up 16th Street. It was the only reason I wanted to get into racing or wanted to be a race car driver. A lot of it stems from being really young around there.

I think I've been to the race every year since I was born. I remember being a kid – back when you still had the Speedway Motel – and my favorite thing was waiting for my dad to go over to the track in the morning so I could walk with him. I don't really remember playing with the kids of other drivers. I would just wait for dad to be ready to go over to the track.

I always had A.J. race gear on. I can remember all the people hollering at him, yelling at him and saying, 'Good luck A.J.,' and 'Give'em hell A.J.' I loved hearing all the people cheer for him. It was just really cool.

It all left a huge impression on me and was a big part of me wanting to get into racing. But you really don't understand it or appreciate it as a kid. Dad didn't want any of the kids in racing, because he understood that not everybody could accomplish what he had accomplished. When you're young, you don't appreciate all he had done, but when you look back at his records, it just seems unbelievable. As you get older, you appreciate it even more. As a kid it was just cool, just awesome. My mom wasn't crazy about the kids racing either, but she went along with it.

We had our family box up in Turn 2. I love that view. When I first had a chance to drive at the Speedway, my first time on the track, I took a slow lap and looked up at the suite because I could remember him always waving up at us.

I always wanted to race Indy cars, but when Indy car racing split and I was young, I felt like I was losing that chance to race there. So I went and did the NASCAR thing. My first race at Indy was actually the Brickyard 400. That year I was a rookie in NASCAR and A.J. Foyt, IV was a rookie at Indy. So I flew up there and watched the start of the Indy 500 and got to see Anthony start the race, then jumped on a plane and ran Charlotte that night. That was fun, not missing the start of an Indy 500 and getting to see Anthony race.

Working with A.J. now, our relationship has been just awesome. It was a little more difficult when I was driving because we weren't having a lot of success. I wanted more out of the team and he wanted more out of me. It was tough, he was on the Indy car side and I was down in Charlotte doing the NASCAR thing. But since I came home and started working here and running the team, it's been really great.

He comes into the shop every day and we go over things. Such a wealth of knowledge to pull from, he's invaluable. It's been tough with him being sick. It's been a rough few years. But he's a fighter and through his whole career, whenever he's been hurt, what always helped him get healthy was getting back to Indianapolis, making sure he could make it to Indianapolis. No matter how tough it's been on him, I know he'll be at Indy.

***A.J. Foyt, IV** competed in five Indy 500s and is the grandson of A.J. Foyt, Jr.*

Going into my first qualifying day in 2003 I was 18 and trying to make the 500. It was just the worst day ever, cold, with 25 to 30 mph winds. It was a terrible day to be on the track. The type of a day you'd be in the garage if you were given a choice. But being qualifying day, you had no choice.

In my first attempt, coming off Turn 2, I got a gust of wind and it spun me around backwards. A.J. was watching on the big screen and he saw it happening.

I was going backward when I finally got the car under control. At that point I was just coasting, backwards, but under control, trying to catch my breath. I was wondering why or how I didn't hit anything. Good and bad. Bad that you spun, good that you didn't hit anything. I was thinking how thankful I was for that, just letting it coast.

Then A.J. comes on the radio and says, 'Press on the damn brakes.' He'd been watching me roll down the back straight and wanted it to be fully stopped before he could relax.

That's definitely a moment I'll never forget.

It was a rough day, but A.J. knows about being a rookie at Indy and we ended up getting into the race. He knew it wasn't going to be easy. He actually spun his rookie year as well. I probably spun a few more times than him. But he gave me the vote of confidence to get back out there and we got her qualified.

In any business, especially a family business, there are trials and it gets escalated with the amount of stress that comes with Indy car racing and racing in general. It was a lot of stress for my whole family. It *was* a family business. I was the driver, my grandfather the owner and my parents were there at every race.

With A.J., he's a professional and he demands all you've got. He was such a great driver and a winner. He doesn't like to lose. He's so competitive. So when you don't win, you hear about it. It definitely wasn't the smoothest with him as my car owner.

Looking back, I learned so much from him about being a man, not so much racing or driving-wise, but just in general. Growing up around him and getting to have those years with him, I'm just grateful for the amount of time we got to spend together. No matter if the racing didn't turn out how we wanted, that's all to the side now. It's just that bonding we got to have, doing it for so many years together, that I'll always remember.

***Jack Starne** is a longtime employee and current general manager of AJ Foyt Racing. He was born in Riverside, Calif., in 1939.*

When I was very, very young, back in the late '40s, I had a reel-to-reel tape player and I used to record the race off the radio. I probably still have some of those tapes. I just thought Indianapolis was the greatest thing.

The first time I ever went to the Speedway was in the winter of 1966. We drove in through the old entrance, up over the race track and into the garage area. It had just snowed and the whole race track was perfectly white, all the way around. It was really beautiful. I've seen it like that afterwards, but the first time will always stand out.

I'll also always remember my first day of qualifying. The whole place was jammed back then, just like on race day. I walked out through the garage area and the grandstands were completely packed with people. I looked down to Turn 1 and Turn 2 and I was like, 'Wow, this is really something.'

For the 1967 race I was working for a team put together by Jim Rathmann and two of the astronauts, Gordon Cooper and Gus Grissom. We didn't make the race. In those days you had 50-some cars trying to qualify and we didn't make it.

I had a regular job in California and was getting my stuff ready to go home to San Diego when A.J. came around the corner. I only knew him by name at this point. All his guys had quit after he'd won the 500 and he asked me if I wanted to go work for him. Here I was, a rookie, and the guy who just won the race wanted *me* to come work for *him*. Of course I did.

My first job was working on Joe Leonard's car. I got into fabrication and machinist work and then crew chief type stuff for A.J. I learned all that from A.J.'s daddy. A.J.'s daddy and his mother were like parents to me, and A.J. was like a brother.

We won a lot of races together. We'd run dirt, we'd run NASCAR stuff and we'd run the sports cars, midgets and sprint cars – all out of our race shop in Houston.

In '77 we built the 500 car ourselves in Houston. We did all our own engine work too. So it was really, *really* an honor to have the stuff we built win the Indianapolis 500. And it was A.J.'s fourth win. That one had a really big impression on me.

It's still very exciting, although I don't like the racing as much as I did back in the olden days. But times change and you have to change with them or you get left behind. I feel very fortunate to have made it to Indy when I did, with the people I was with, and the fact we had a little success there too.

***George Snider** started 22 Indy 500s, more than any driver who never won the race. Many of those starts came in A.J. Foyt, Jr.'s backup car. He still runs a sprint car team.*

Shoot, the best memory I have has got to be sitting on the front row of the Indianapolis 500 in my second start there (1966).

It was one of A.J.'s cars. A Lotus he had run the year before. It was a great car. Just had a little driver error. I spun in the race coming off Turn 2 and Chuck Hulse gathered me up. That was the end of that.

Driving for A.J. was a pretty big thrill too. I really didn't know him then and it turned into a long lasting relationship. We're still pretty close.

I had just finished testing at Indianapolis (in 1965) for Firestone and he came in to test for Goodyear. We kind of passed in the garage area. There was nothing really big about it when we met. I had run good in the test and I don't know, I guess he needed someone. You know how those deals go. He called me in January or somewhere around there. I flew down to L.A. and we got together.

After that we would usually wait until the last minute. Sometimes it was planned, but most of them weren't. We had to wait to make sure that he got in and he didn't have any problems during the next week. It just happened. I can't really explain why or how. But everything worked out pretty good.

That place has changed so much that I don't have much interest in the Speedway anymore. I hate to badmouth it – it's just not like it used to be. It was really a lot of fun when you could build your own motors and you could do this and that – build your own cars. Now it's like going down to Sears and Roebuck and buying a car. And I think all the older guys probably feel the same way.

There are no real mechanics back there anymore. You know, like A.J. Watson or A.J.'s dad. You've got to buy everything over the counter. And NASCAR is getting to be the same way. They're cookie cutter cars too. All the way through Formula One.

At least we got to live through the good times. I wouldn't trade that for nothing.

***Eddie Cheever** would eventually drive for AJ Foyt Racing.*

In my first year at Indy, about halfway through the month of May, I walked over to where (A.J.) Foyt was. I was stuck. Turn 1 was really difficult because the car I had – I didn't know it at the time – was very imbalanced aerodynamically and it was loose – the back end kept coming out. That isn't a problem when you're going 100 mph on an open road race, but if you're going around Indy at 230 mph, it is an issue.

So I went down there and I said, 'Hello, I'm Eddie Cheever,' and he just looked at me with great disdain. The disdain didn't bother me so I just sat there and said, 'Look, could you give me one good thought that I could use around here because I'm really stuck – I can't seem to go any quicker.' He paused and in that southern drawl of his, he said, 'Keep turning left.' I thought, OK, where's the punch line to the joke. He smiled at me and walked over and got in his car – and that was that.

Al Unser, Jr.

CHAPTER 3

Unser

WITH NINE INDY 500 VICTORIES and more than 70 starts between them, the Unsers are the most successful family in the history of the Speedway. Jerry Unser was the first family member to qualify for the race in 1958 but crashed in practice in '59 and later died from complications from his burns. Jerry's younger brothers Bobby and Al would later win the 500. All three would have sons that started the 500. Al, Jr. won twice, Robby (Bobby's son) would make two starts and Johnny (Jerry's son) would make five starts.

***Bobby Unser** is a three-time winner of the Indy 500 and one of only two drivers (Rick Mears is the other) to win the race in three different decades. He won two USAC series championships.*

The chance to drive Andy Granatelli's Novi at Indianapolis in 1963 was the best single thing that ever happened to my career.

Parnelli Jones had arranged a number of cars for me to test drive that year. I passed my rookie test in one, but it was too slow to make the race. I drove Andy's yellow Novi and went 150 mph. That was pretty fast. Parnelli also set up a test in the new Vita Fresh car, a very good car. But I figured a bird in hand was worth a whole bunch of them in the bush. Parnelli told me I should get $10,000 from Granatelli. I got $1,500.

I qualified fifth fastest, but it was on the third weekend, so I started further back. It immediately made me famous. Everyone loved the Novi. Suddenly I was on the front page of every newspaper and everyone knew my name. But in the race Andy had me so hyped up I crashed on the second lap. Completely my fault.

I drove the Novis two more years. Parnelli warned me they would never finish and they never did. But they were fast. They were smooth and they were loud. They fit Bobby Unser. Because of the Novi, people knew my name. People knew my phone number.

I had become good friends with Don Branson, who drove for the Leader Card team, pretty much the best team at Indy back then. We traveled together and stayed together.

He was talking about retiring because he didn't like the rear engine cars and recommended me to replace him. Then he was killed in a crash at Ascot Park (Calif.). I got the ride, but not the way I wanted.

I had signed on with Goodyear and was clawing my way to the top of their list of drivers. Not the top, but getting close. The tire companies were putting an unbelievable amount of money into the sport. More money than us drivers could have ever imagined.

Jud Phillips and I went to Akron to see the folks at Goodyear. They asked us what we wanted for the 500. Jud and I looked at each other and said we wanted a new Eagle. Done. Then we said we wanted one of the new turbo Offy engines. Done.

We were fast right from the start. I was the first to break 170 mph. Still have the tire and wheel in my house. That's when the Granatellis, Andy and Vince, cornered me on pit road and offered me a million bucks to drive a turbine. A couple of their drivers had been killed in crashes. But I had a deal with Goodyear and they were with Firestone. I turned them down. They started screaming and cussing at me, right there on pit road. But I had a contract with Goodyear.

In the race I led more than half the laps. But the transmission fell apart and I only had fourth gear. It was hard getting up to speed, but once I got the turbo lit, I was the fastest car out there. On the last restart Joe Leonard took the lead, but I figured I would catch him in a lap and a half from the finish. Then the Good Lord took care of him. I swear I could hear the crowd stomping and pounding their chairs. The decision to turn down a million dollars didn't look so bad after all.

It was really an Unser family win. I had been there when my brother Jerry died and my father had recently passed away. It would have been nice if they could have been there. But my mom and the rest of the family were there.

In later years I would drive for some of the very best teams and smartest people in racing, including Dan Gurney and Roger Penske. I was fortunate to win the 500 with both of them.

But it all started with Andy Granatelli and the Novi. If it hadn't been for them, I may never have had the other opportunities.

Al Unser, Sr. *is one of only three drivers to win the Indy 500 four times (1970, 1971, 1978 and 1987), registering his last win at age 47. He won one USAC championship (1970) and two CART titles (1983 and 1985).*

I'd say you always think of your last time at Indianapolis – or your best last time – and when I think of the Indy 500 the one I remember most is 1987, because of all the circumstances leading up to that race.

For the '87 race, I decided to go back to Indy even though I didn't have a ride. I had many offers, but I didn't think it was the right team or the right car to be able to win the race. So, I turned them all down because I'd rather sit and watch the race than run 10th or 12th or whatever. The team is very, very important to making any win come true, and you also have to have a lucky day.

Things went along and then the first weekend of qualifying was over and I was going to go home. I decided to stay in Indy to help my son, Al, Jr. He didn't qualify the first weekend and I thought maybe I could help him a little bit. It's always good to talk to somebody that you're close to – and not competing against – when you're having problems. I wasn't in the race so we could talk about it and I could try to help him.

All of the sudden, I get a phone call on the Tuesday before the second weekend of qualifying from Roger Penske, who I'd been with before for several years. That year was a funny one because I was supposed to run for Roger and then I didn't because, I guess you could say, a "money deal" came between us.

He said, 'Would you be interested in running my third car? It's an '86 March (chassis) and you'll have a new engine put in it. It's a car capable of winning the race.' I knew that because anything Roger Penske does is done the right way to try to win. That's what I was looking for. I said, 'Yes sir, I would.'

Things went along and they went and got the car out of Reading, Pa. – it was in a hotel on display. They got it to Indianapolis and I got in it and ran for a couple of days. We ran very quickly, but we only ran a few laps. We qualified Saturday and made the show.

If I had qualified the first weekend, I would have probably started eighth or ninth. But we qualified the second weekend so we started farther back – I think it was 20th. You're always worried starting that far back of having something go wrong the first few laps – a crash because some drivers are really just like that. If they're starting last they want to be first by about the third lap. It just doesn't happen. Sure enough we go down into Turn 1 on the very first lap and Josele Garza spins and almost takes me out. We even touched and I said, 'Oh man, today's going to be one of those days.'

I was taking it easy and trying to pick my way up through the field and all of the sudden about 25 or 30 laps into the race Mario Andretti goes by me and puts me a lap down. I said, 'What in the heck are you doing?' I'd never gotten lapped that soon unless I'd had problems, and I didn't have any problems that day. Everything was good. The car was good and things were going along good. Then I picked it up and Mario didn't come close to lapping me again. I passed him back later on, but he didn't care because I had been a lap down.

Things started happening and I got up to fifth-place and then to fourth-place and then I was third. Roberto Guerrero and I were going at each other. We were really kind of equal. He couldn't pass me and I couldn't pass him. Late in the race, Roger comes on the radio and says, 'We're going to put the pressure on Roberto Guerrero. We're going to come in and make our final stop early and then see what we can do to him.' Roger was running my pits at that time because both Danny Sullivan and Rick Mears had fallen out of the race. So, all of the sudden I got Roger on the radio and all the good people on the pit crew – which makes a difference. When Roger called me into the pits on the radio all he said was, 'Don't make a mistake. Don't make a mistake.'

I came in for my final stop and everything went fine. I went back out and then Roberto came in. He cooked his clutch and stalled the engine when he went to take off.

That did it and I ended up winning the race. It sank in right away when I saw the checkered flag. I'd already won the race three times. The first time you get the checkered flag you say, 'Did I really do it?' Thereafter, you kind of get used to it.

That race probably was the most rewarding because of going back there and not having a ride. Then all of a sudden I have a ride and end up winning the race. It's just unheard of. There was a lot of self-satisfaction because at that time they said I was too old and didn't have what it would take to win anymore. When you get older, people are looking at you in a different way. They say, 'He's got the smarts or he's got the talent, but he doesn't have the desire anymore.' I disagreed with that. I had as much desire the fourth time as I did the first time. It was very gratifying and a rewarding day.

Indianapolis means a lot to our family. It's "The Greatest Spectacle in Racing." It's one of those deals that when you're very young and think you want to become a race car driver – you always want to go to Indianapolis. It's got the most prestige, it paid the most money and it was the highest honor being able to make the race, finish the race – and then win the race. For our family to do as well as we've done there just shows that I guess all of us had the ability. We loved the place and it was an honor to win the Indy 500. We're glad to just be able to have three of us, Bobby and my son and myself, win that many.

Al Unser, Jr. *earned his first Indy 500 win in 1992 driving for Rick Galles and picked up his second victory in 1994 driving for Roger Penske. He won CART championships in 1990 and 1994.*

The first time I ever saw Indianapolis Motor Speedway was 1973. I was 11 and the only thing that I really remember that still stands out is how big the grandstands were – just coming down the front straightaway, all the way through turns 1 and 2. They were just huge. It was the biggest stadium that I'd ever seen in my life. My dad and Uncle Bobby were racing. My sisters and I – that was our first race. That's probably when I began having dreams about racing at Indy.

My first time racing at the Speedway was in 1983, my rookie year. I remember pulling out onto the race track for the very first time in an Indy car. It was just a dream come true. Pretty much that whole month of May was a dream come true. Every day was a new day – going through practice, qualifying and then making the race. Actually racing in the Indy 500 in '83 was another dream that came true. That first year running the 500 was all about dreams coming true.

If I had to pick out one Indy 500, it would be that one in '89 when Emerson Fittipaldi and I got together at the end of the race. I'm the one who crashed and Emerson went on to win. When he came around to get the checkered flag I was on the north end of the track and I gave him a thumbs up for a job well done. He was going on to win the 500.

I was leading the race the last few laps and we came up on lapped traffic on the back straightaway. That wrecked my momentum and it allowed Emerson to get on the inside of me – get beside me going down the back straightaway. We went into Turn 3 and touched wheels and I went into the wall. At that time, it was my best 500 of all the ones that I raced in. My team, Galles Racing, did a fantastic job that day. We operated as a team better than we ever had before and the pit stops were great. We just came up short at the end of the race.

I remember getting out of the car after hitting the wall and starting to walk out to the track. One of the safety crew got in front of me and asked where I was going. I said, 'I'm going out there – out to the track.' He said to me, 'Do you want to flip him off?' And I said, 'Yes I do.' He stepped aside and he said, 'Go right ahead.'

So, I took a few steps and was out there on the track. Everything came rushing at me all at once. You're at the Indy 500 and there are just people everywhere. It took Emerson a little while to get around – to come around the corner because of course the race was under yellow. There were a few seconds there that I honestly had a chance to reflect on the day. And the day was Emerson's. I didn't show how fast my car was until the end of the race and we just came up a little short.

So when Emerson came around, I gave him a thumbs up instead of flipping him off or shaking my fist or throwing something at him – which quite honestly was what I wanted to do. The only way to put into words what happened is that it was a moment of clarity. I knew Emerson as a person and knew that he was one of the safest drivers and he genuinely cared about his fellow drivers.

It was the last lap of the Indy 500 and both of us were going for the win. He came out of it and I didn't. There's a time in a race where the only thing that matters is winning. Emerson and I were both in that position. You're going to do whatever it takes to win. I couldn't fault Emerson.

Of course winning my first Indy 500 in '92 was very, very special, but I guess the one I'm remembered more for than anything else is that 1989 race.

Shelley Unser *is the former wife of Al Unser, Jr.*

When Al won in 1994, I had all three kids there, Al, Cody and Shannon. Cody was seven, Shannon five and Al was 11. Joey wasn't born yet. My parents were helping watch the kids and Al's mom Wanda was there too. That's when you were there all month. But I didn't worry about the kids, they were usually with one of their grandmothers and happy just to stay in the swimming pool.

Come race day, Cody was pretty quiet. My mom said she didn't feel good. But Cody had said that before and perked up when she got to go swimming.

Al ends up winning the race and if you look at some of the photos, she doesn't look happy. She's also a little nervous. Back then the winner's circle was pretty much like a mosh pit. I thought maybe she was nervous because it's kind of scary with that many people there all at once and with everything that's going on.

So we win the race and of course everyone is celebrating. We went back to the hospitality tent and Roger (Penske) always had a lot of corporate people there and everybody's waiting for you, so you stay there too long and then you continue to party at the hotel and you stay up too late – you don't get enough sleep.

The next morning you're up for interviews and the photos, so the kids went back with my parents and Wanda. Then you go to the banquet that night.

Back then the banquet was live on TV. We went to the tables for the winners and they have you sitting with your main sponsor, Marlboro, the Penskes and whoever from the team. My parents and the kids and Wanda, they're behind us at another table. At the very beginning of the dinner Cody – and Cody was never one to cause this kind of trouble – she wanted to come and sit on my lap and she was kind of whimpering.

Well it happened that one of the medical team was there and we took her out to the hallway – the dinner had already started, but the speeches hadn't started yet. They took her pulse and they said we've got to get her to the ER now, her pulse is really, really high – she's tender, we think it's her appendix. I was going to get a cab because Al had to give his victory speech, but the Marlboro people said, 'No, take the limo.' I will never forget how surreal it was. We pull up at Methodist ER in this limo and we're dressed to the hilt in our banquet gowns. They take Cody straight up to the pediatric department and they say she has to have emergency surgery.

Al is now sitting where they put the drivers before they make their speech. We're calling, giving him updates, and the pediatric surgeon is saying she's got to go into surgery. Al wants to see her first, but by the time they got to him, he was starting his speech. He could hardly say anything. It was the shortest victory speech in the history of the Indianapolis 500. He tried to thank everybody and then he said, 'Uh, my little girl is in the hospital and she's going to have her appendix removed and I got to go, so here's Roger.' Al took off and met us so she could get into surgery.

She had her appendix taken out that night. Years later we look back – it was just so bizarre because the timing of it. Just because you win the Indy 500, life still goes on and you drop everything for your kids.

***Cody Unser** is the daughter of Al Unser, Jr. and Shelley Unser.*

Right before we left for the hospital my mom wanted to see how serious I was, so she pulled me over to their table at the banquet. My dad was like, 'Tell me what's wrong' and 'Where does it hurt?' And I pointed to the right side and my dad looked at my mom and he's going yeah, that's appendicitis. But no one was telling me anything. It was kind of scary.

In the ER I got my first IV put into my arm, which was very traumatic. They didn't have a pediatric needle and they kept missing. So I was crying hysterically and my mom had to leave the room because she couldn't handle me crying. My grandma Wanda came in and they took turns because I was being stuck and I didn't want to be stuck.

But what scared me the most was what happened right before going into surgery. They had a TV in a corner where other nurses and staff were watching the banquet. My brother Al and sister Shannon were on stage with my dad as he was giving his acceptance speech. The look on the faces of my brother and sister were like they knew something bad was going to happen to me.

It felt like I was going to die because of the look on their faces. It was just bizarre, I was in so much pain but everyone else was focusing on the TV.

Tom Carnegie

CHAPTER 4

Voices

WHEN FANS RETURNED TO INDIANAPOLIS Motor Speedway in May 1946 for the first race following the end of World War II, they were greeted by the booming voice of Tom Carnegie. New track owner Tony Hulman had plucked Carnegie from the state's deep ranks of high school basketball announcers to handle the Speedway's public address system. In 1952 Carnegie was joined by Sid Collins, who spearheaded the first flag-to-flag radio coverage of the race. Together they became the first "voices" of the 500, as well-known as all but the most famous drivers of the day. While others assumed those roles over the years, their legacy lives on at the Speedway today and they remain the voices behind many memories.

***Tom Carnegie** was a well-known high school basketball announcer who called the famous "Hoosiers" game. He was the voice on the Speedway public address system from 1946 to 2006. He passed away in 2011 at 91. The following is from "Tom Carnegie, The Voice Remembered," on RTV6 ABC, Indianapolis.*

Nobody gave me any help (his first year) or anything like that. I just had names and numbers. Like calling a football game. I somehow got through it and satisfied Wilbur Shaw and Tony Hulman because they asked me to come back the next year.

It took me 10 or 15 years to have any confidence that what I was saying was right. And then you begin to realize this is theater. Speed theater. And growing up in the theater like I did, you begin to do those little things. Then when somebody said, 'Hey, I like that' about heeeeee's on it, then why not use it again?

I played to the audience. I got them excited. You get them excited and then you become excited.

My favorite day was when Tom Senva told me the night before on the radio and on television that he would do 200 miles an hour the next day. I said, 'What? You're kidding me.' He said, 'No you watch it, I will.' Sure enough, I was ready for him. On the very first lap he got over 200 miles an hour. What do you do? You get excited. It gave me a chance to say, 'It's a newwwwww track record.'

And then lap number two, 'Still faster. And you won't believe it, another new track record.' That's two track records in the first two laps. Third lap, still higher. Fourth lap, 'And it's a new all-time speed record.' I got more fun out of it than anybody. The crowd was really there for that occasion.

That's one I really remember. I was ready to quit, because that was the highlight of my day, my year, my life.

***Sid Collins** helped grow Indy 500 radio coverage from 26 stations in 1952 to more than 1,200 stations reaching millions around the world. Collins took his own life in May 1977 after being diagnosed with ALS (Lou Gehrig's disease). He was 54. The following is from the book "Stay Tuned For The Greatest Spectacle In Racing," by Sid Collins and Ron Dorson.*

The broadcast, for me, is a great challenge and responsibility. I realize any person involved in any form of media is only as good as his or her last show or performance. So we try to improve each year by adding more facts and giving better coverage technique. My job gives me a tremendous opportunity to promote the sport of auto racing because we can influence a lot of people – for good or bad. One wrong word can change a person's impression of what racing is all about.

As the broadcast hour approaches I take one last walk down the pit apron to soak up as much color and excitement as I can. I want to hear the shrill rattle of the pneumatic air guns as last minute adjustments are made on the race cars, to shake hands with drivers now retired from the sport, to have a few words with Tony Hulman to see how he's feeling and to exchange points of interest with friends who have come in from all over the world. I make this pre-race circuit so that I can share it with our listeners.

The Iron Duke Nalon, a legendary driver of the early fifties, is wearing a bright orange blazer and he still looks as physically fit and handsome as he always has. I make a mental note. I want his fans to know it. This is color radio! I want the other men on the broadcast to emboss and embellish everything they see. The car is never just red, it's candy apple red. It's never green, it's lime green. Let's see it! Let's smell it! Let's taste it!

My whole approach to any broadcasting, and particularly the format for the 500, is one of color and human beings, action and sensitivity.

The most prominent group of men noticeably absent from my pre-race circuits have always been the race drivers. Most of these men will be pacing back and forth inside their cramped team garages like caged animals, trapped by their fame, and unwilling at this one crucial moment only, to mix with their admirers and well-wishers. For them, it has to be a period of intense concentration – of last minute strategy discussions with the team manager and possibly a moment of prayer.

So with each tick of the clock, the visions expand, yet the parameters narrow. Because this one day, for these four and a half hours, there is nothing else for me. This is my world.

Reality now. In a magic instant we're on the air. It's 10:15 a.m. I gulp a deep breath – a sharp cue from Jack Morrow – and we are on the air.

'Good morning around the world from Indianapolis, the home of the world's greatest speed classic, the 500 mile race – which is bursting with color and tradition – a spectacle that has no equal anywhere. The competition displayed here by strong men and sleek, superlative racing machines, promise fame and glory for the winner – disappointment for many – and even heartbreak for some.'

***Walter McCarty** is from Plainfield, Ill. He has missed only one Indy 500 since 1956.*

Friday, May 30th, 1952. I was seven and just had my tonsils out the previous Wednesday. I was a whiny, pain-in-the-ass kid. My mother, who was from New Albany, Ind., set me up on the back porch with a radio and told me to be quiet and to listen to some auto race.

That's when I was introduced to Sid Collins. I was mesmerized. With Sid calling the race and all of his other cohorts painting pictures, I was hooked. I had never thought about auto racing as a sport. All that changed with Sid Collins and his descriptions.

All afternoon, I cheered for "The Mad Russian," Bill Vukovich. Even though he lost, he became my hero.

I listened again in '53. Sid described Vuky's terrific win! In '54 I was ecstatic with Vuky's second win! All along I felt like I was there, right at the track. All through Sid and the guys.

Then came '55, I was 10 by that time, and Sid's voice again transported me to "The Greatest Spectacle in Racing." When Vuky died, Sid was there to walk me through it.

I had never experienced death before, at least not so personally. But there was Sid.

By 1956 I talked my dad into taking me to the track for the race. For the first time, I was actually able to see the real 500, not just in my imagination. All the colors. The pageantry. Sid was right.

The 2016 race will be my 59th Indy 500. All because of that voice.

***Paul Page** was the hand-picked successor to Sid Collins and served as the radio voice of the Indy 500 from 1977 to 1987 following Collins' death. He moved to the television booth from 1988 to 1998 and 2002 to 2004. He returned to host the radio broadcast in 2014 and plans to retire after calling the opening laps of the 100th running of the race in 2016.*

Sid Collins was my friend and my mentor. He taught me so much. I go back and listen to some of the old tapes and remember why he did this, or why he did that.

I was working in radio in Indianapolis as a disc jockey for some tiny stations. Most of them were FM, and FM at the time was nowhere. I wanted to get in to a big station. I heard there was an opening at WIBC and I went and talked to the program producer. I thought it was to play music, but it was in the news department. That was fine too. I wanted to be in that building because Sid was the sports director there.

Eventually I had the evening shift and Sid, as the sports director, would come in and do a 15 minute sports show. I'd either go and see him, or he'd come over to see me in the newsroom and we'd just talk.

I remember one day when I had just done an interview with a girl who had won the Soap Box Derby. He came in and allowed that it was terrible. He said, 'Do you know that a 13-year-old saved you?' Then he started talking about the art of the interview.

Once he decided I was going to do the race, he started focusing on elements of the broadcast. The things you need to think of. How you need to order what you're talking about.

A very simple version is that with 50-some competitors, you're going to have the favorites. You have to start with the guys who are *not* going to make it. You have to have a story on each of them – and it has to be a human story. Give those guys a little credit early on and then you can tell stories about the favorites as you get closer to the finish. That's true of anything where you know that you're going to lose some throughout the competition.

I would certainly give that same advice. The guy who is 27th and is going to stay there, this is still the end of a hell of a long road. It's not just any event. It might be the only time he sits in a race car at the Indianapolis 500. So you have to have a story for him and everybody else in the field.

You must tell stories. That's my pet peeve with sports in general today. We have moved into a world where everything is about factoids or stats. You watch an ESPN show and it's all stats. I'm one of the old guys. It's more important for me to tell you a story. Put the stats on the screen. The announcer should be telling stories, having conversations with the analysts. They need to be honest-to-God conversations so you hit the comfort level of the audience.

Unfortunately, storytelling is all but gone in our business. I'm not saying what they're doing now is right or wrong, I'm just saying I would do it a different way.

And Sid taught me you have to do your homework. There are a good many people that don't prepare themselves for the event. It's even worse for a lot of the analysts who come in and think they're gonna live by their wits – and then something happens that they don't know anything about and now they're suddenly crap. None of these types exist within the Indy 500 network now, or ever have for that matter. I'm talking generally.

That homework can take any particular form. In racing, you have to have that fact tucked away and ready to go in your mind when something happens. You can't be shuffling between 20 documents to find something.

In my case I make notes. Mostly bullet points. Then I try to list them in descending order of importance. So I've written them a second time and the mere process of doing that puts enough of it in my head that I can react with it. That paper never sees the booth.

I've still got to look at that TV monitor. If I take my eyes off it, for even a microsecond, something could happen, and you look around and say, 'What the hell.' You have to be already fully prepared to do it, not sitting around with a book of statistics in your lap.

***Bob Jenkins** was the lead radio voice for the Indy 500 from 1990 to 1998 and on television from 1999 to 2001. He currently works on the Speedway's public address system.*

Probably my most outstanding memory was the first time I went to the 500, which was in 1960. I would have been 12. My family always went to Lafayette, Ind., during what we called Decoration Day. My mom's relatives were buried in the Lafayette area, so we went there.

My dad and I broke away from the rest of the family and traveled to Indianapolis for the race. We parked downtown and rode the train up to the Speedway. I remember walking to my seat and all the pre-race activities.

It was one of the best 500s in history and I remember so vividly standing up in my seat and looking toward the fourth turn in the second half of the race to see which driver, either Rodger Ward or Jim Rathmann, was leading that race. That was probably my fondest memory of the Indianapolis 500 as a spectator.

I went to every 500 after that except 1961 and 1965. I was on my senior trip in high school in '65 in Washington D.C. and I remember passing up a lot of the tours because I stayed in the bus and listened on my transistor radio to Sid Collins call the 500, wishing I was there.

I joined the Indianapolis Motor Speedway radio network in 1979 and of course it is a special memory when Paul Page asked for my help. The rookie worked the backstretch – there is no backstretch position now – but the cars were going a lot slower back in '79 so they needed a reporter there. I remember walking to my position that day. That was another a special moment.

The fondest memory of all, whether it be spectator or employee, was calling the 1992 finish on the radio network. That was the ultimate for me.

It was a terrible day, cold, windy. There were so many crashes during the race that we said to each other during a commercial break, 'Let's just get this miserable race over and get someplace where it's warm.' I was OK up in the tower, but my turn guys and the reporters on pit lane were just freezing.

Anyway, it came down to the closest finish in history when Al Unser, Jr. beat Scott Goodyear by just a few tenths of a second. When I'm asked what my most memorable moment was in all of my broadcasting career, that by far is the fondest.

They used the call of the finish on Valvoline commercials after that and those commercials aired on almost every sporting event, certainly on every race that was televised long after it happened. I kind of got tired of hearing it – 'Oh brother, here we go again,' but then the next (royalty) check would arrive and it wouldn't be so bad.

Since then I've joined the public address staff and that's what I do now – that's a very satisfying job. I really enjoy helping Dave Calabro and we of course live in the shadow of Tom Carnegie and try to carry on the incredible tradition and memories that he made at the Speedway.

That's a very satisfying and fun job for me. When people hear me on the public address they say, 'I thought you retired.' I tell them I retired from work – this is not work, this is fun. I would be here even if I didn't have a job. I'd be at the Speedway every day because it means that much to me and it's such a special place and I would be there as much as I possibly could – pay or no pay.

Ralph Sheheen *has served as track announcer at the Indianapolis Motor Speedway and broadcast motorsports events ranging from the World of Outlaws to Formula One. He is co-owner of National Speed Sport News.*

When I was a young boy I waited anxiously all day for the taped delay broadcast of the Indianapolis 500 on ABC. There was no social media or 30 different sports channels to ruin the outcome of the race back then. Just the challenge of waiting for the broadcast to finally start. That day always seemed to drag on forever.

When the show finally started, I was always greeted by the legendary Jim McKay, the even more legendary Jackie Stewart and the dean of American motorsports journalism, Chris Economaki. Three very distinct voices that helped to add even more color to what is already known as "The Greatest Spectacle in Racing."

As a kid I was immediately drawn to the speed of Indianapolis and the rocket ship looks of the Indy cars of the 1970s. The drivers were heroes to me. Andretti, Foyt, Unser, Rutherford, etc. Brave men who risked everything at incredible speeds to drink the milk. Of course they also would get their face on what I thought, and still believe, was the most beautiful trophy in all of sports, the Borg-Warner Trophy.

McKay would do a masterful job of setting the scene. Whether you were a diehard fan like me or a casual viewer, Jim would weave his words into a tapestry that made it easy for you to understand the challenge that lay ahead for the drivers. He also did a wonderful job of explaining the things that made Indy special. The pageantry, the history, the danger and the glory.

Jackie Stewart with his Scottish accent might have seemed out of place for a race broadcast from the Heartland of America, but his credentials as a World Champion proved he knew what he was talking about. Jackie was great at putting you in the cockpit and helping you to understand the difficulties of laps at over 200 mph around the daunting oval.

One of the things I found intriguing was the story of these rocket ship pilots. Who were these fearless crash helmet-wearing crazies? That's where Economaki came in. Arguably the most unique sounding voice of the three. He always had the inside story on where the personalities in the sport came from.

Of course he also had that little extra nugget that could make you a fan of a driver. A story about where they came from, a personal interest they had or a challenge they had overcome in their life to get to the Speedway.

Chris was excellent with his interviews as well. Simple yet probing questions. Some of them taking place when the driver had just crawled out of a smoldering car that had been vaporized by the unforgiving concrete walls. The last thing these racers wanted to do was talk to a guy in a suit with a microphone. However, Chris had earned their trust and respect and they always gave him an answer.

One day while watching another 500 broadcast I thought, if I can't be Mario, maybe I can be the guy interviewing him or the guy calling the race. All those years of watching and listening to Jim, Jackie and Chris had an impact I didn't see coming.

After years of pursuing my own broadcasting career I found myself standing in the announcer's booth high above the famed yard of bricks at the Indianapolis Motor Speedway.

It was May 2009 and I had been hired to announce my first Indy 500. The 93rd running of the event. I would help call the action with my good friend Dave Calabro. We would be working out of the same booth where Sid Collins and Tom Carnegie had called so many 500s over the years. More famous voices that were a part of the fabric of the 500.

Calling the race over the public address system is much different than television. You have different responsibilities and you're on the air all day. How you describe the action is also very different. The people sitting in Turn 3 can't see the action in Turn 1. They are hanging on every word of your description as the cars dive into the turn at warp speed.

I'll never forget peering out our window on race morning and seeing race fans packed into the massive grandstands. Down below us sat 33 glistening race cars with their drivers strapping in.

Everybody waiting for Jim Nabors to sing "Back Home Again in Indiana." Followed by the most famous words in all of auto racing, "Gentlemen start your engines!"

Shortly after the green flag, Marco Andretti hit the wall. I saw it happen and bellowed into the microphone, 'Marco Andretti into the wall!'

The collective groan of disappointment from the gigantic crowd to those five words was deafening. It drowned out the roar of the race engines and stunned me. You cannot believe the sensation of having so many people react the same way at the same time to something you say. It's incredible and I will never forget it.

Dave and I spent the rest of the day building the drama and calling the action as 33 drivers battled for a spot in Indy history. When the checkers finally flew, Helio Castroneves joined an exclusive club with his third win at the Brickyard. Later that day I rode in the Corvette convertible with Helio as he was driven around the track, as is customary, to salute the fans. Another amazing moment.

Helio, his family, the driver and me. Seven people crammed into a car built for two. Making one more lap around the Speedway. Helio waving to the massive crowd and me describing the scene live to those listening around the facility and asking Helio questions about the day along the way.

I never would have imagined that that little boy who sat there riveted to the broadcast of the Indianapolis 500 would have the chance to be a part of the history as it unfolded that day in May 2009.

I have worked the Indianapolis 500 many times in many different capacities as a member of the media. It truly is "The Greatest Spectacle in Racing" and Jim, Jackie and Chris did an outstanding job of capturing its magic and broadcasting it through my television.

***The eulogy of Eddie Sachs**, perhaps the finest moment in the broadcast history of the Indy 500, whether on radio, closed circuit, taped or live television – and a memory of tens of thousands – took place during the running of the tragic 1964 race. Eddie Sachs and Dave MacDonald were at the center of a fiery second lap crash and the race was stopped for the first time by an accident. Sachs was killed immediately, while MacDonald died several hours later at Methodist Hospital. Up until this time, racing fatalities were typically handled in a short, matter of fact statement. Track announcer Tom Carnegie followed form, saying: "It is with great regret that we make this announcement. Driver Eddie Sachs was fatally injured in the accident on the main straightaway." Sid Collins had long been unhappy with the procedure and prepared himself to say more in the event of a driver's death. With the race stopped and a hush over the Speedway, he saw the opportunity and felt the need to say more about his friend. He was acutely aware that many in the crowd were huddled around transistor radios, listening to what he would say. He turned to the astronauts he had interviewed earlier in the day for inspiration. He would receive more than 30,000 letters asking for a copy of the eulogy. Here, in its entirety, is Collins' eulogy for his friend.*

You heard the announcement from the public address system. There's not a sound. Men are taking off their hats. People are weeping. There are over 300,000 fans here not moving, disbelieving.

Some men try to conquer life in a number of ways. These days of outer space attempts, some men try to conquer life and death and they calculate their risk. And in our talking to them over the years, I think we know their inner thoughts in regards to racing. They take it as part of living.

No one is moving on the race track. They are standing silently.

A race driver, who leaves this earth mentally when he straps himself into the cockpit, to try for what to him is the biggest conquest he can make, is aware of the odds and Eddie Sachs played the odds. He was serious and frivolous. He was fun. He was a wonderful gentleman. He took much needling and gave much needling, just as the astronauts do, perhaps. These boys on the race track ask no quarter and they give none. If they succeed they're a hero, and if they fail, they tried.

And it was Eddie's desire, I'm sure, and his will to try with everything he had, which he always did. So the only healthy way, perhaps, we can approach the tragedy of a loss of a friend like Eddie Sachs, is to know that he would have wanted us to face it as he did, as it has happened, not as we wish it would have happened.

It was God's will, I am sure, and we must accept that. We are all speeding toward it at a rate of 60 minutes every hour. The only difference is that we do not know how to speed and Eddie Sachs did. And since death has a thousand more doors, Eddie Sachs exits this earth in a race car. Knowing Eddie, I assume that is the way he would have wanted it.

Byron said, 'Who the Gods love, die young.' Eddie was 37. To his widow, Nance, we extend our extreme sympathy and regret. This boy won the pole here in 1960 and 1961. He was a proud race driver.

Well, as we do at Indianapolis and in racing, as the World Champion Jimmy Clark I'm sure would agree, as he's raced all over the world, the race continues, unfortunately without Eddie Sachs.

And we'll be restarting it in just a few minutes.

Broadcast Interview

CHAPTER 5

Broadcast

THE FIRST FULL LENGTH BROADCAST of the Indy 500 took place in 1964. It was an early version of pay for view, shown on closed-circuit and in black-and-white at more than 100 movie theaters and convention centers across the country.

Color was added the following year and ABC's "Wide World of Sports" began airing an edited version of the race on a one-week delay. So began one of the longest running partnerships of a broadcast network and sporting event in history (exceeded only by the Masters golf tournament on CBS and the Little League World Series on ABC/ESPN). Commentary was added after the fact to match the edit. Coverage was eventually moved to same day status – but still delayed and edited.

A single production truck housed the crew in the early days and a producer had only a handful of camera shots to choose from. A lone pit reporter scrambled for updates.

It wasn't until 1986 that ABC undertook the first live broadcast of the 500. The Speedway, however, fearful live television would hurt attendance, insisted the Indianapolis area remain blacked out until the evening of the race. Despite the delayed broadcast, Indianapolis annually rates as the highest ranked city in terms of viewership.

Jim McKay, Jackie Stewart and Chris Economaki handled the early, tape-delayed broadcasts. In 1988, Paul Page, the radio voice of the 500, moved into the television booth, joining former drivers Bobby Unser and Sam Posey. Over the years a who's who of ABC's top sports leadership and broadcasters worked the 500, including Chris Schenkel, Keith Jackson, Brent Musburger, Al Michaels, Jim Lampley, Bob Jenkins, Jack Arute, Bill Flemming, Roone Arledge and Bob Goodrich, just to name a few.

Now about 100 cameras, including those mounted on race cars, are used in the broadcast. An army of ABC/ESPN personnel and support equipment beam the broadcast in high definition to an estimated 300 million people in more than 200 countries around the world.

Bob Goodrich, *an All-American football player, was involved in ABC Sports' coverage of the Indianapolis 500 from 1970 to 2003, including 16 years as producer. He earned two Emmys for his Indy work and also produced Super Bowls, the Olympics, baseball and much more.*

I did a lot of big events, but there's nothing bigger, in my opinion, than the Indianapolis 500. I started in 1970 as a gofer. I did a bunch of them and loved every one.

It's the single biggest one-day event in the world of sports. They don't give the crowd size, but it's in the hundreds of thousands of people. The television audience is enormous and there's so much excitement and tension.

I was fascinated by everything about it and everybody who was part of it. Every minute of the race there's something going on. Working my way up from being a gofer to being a producer was an absolute dream come true. I realize that's such a cliché, but it's true.

One of the difficult things about covering the Indianapolis 500 is that there is no place to put a camera where you can see the entire track. There's no other oval in the country like that. You might say, gosh, Daytona is the same size. But if you go up on the roof at Daytona, you can see around the track.

That makes it very difficult on the director to isolate on the leaders. You've got to keep an eye on the leaders when you go to a better battle back in the pack. You have to cut between at least two cameras, sometimes three, in order for it to look good, every single lap, and you're always forced to record the leader. Or when you're on the leader and recording a battle back in the pack, someone has to sit there and cut that. If you make a mistake it could be a critical mistake and if something happened we wouldn't have it. That was the most difficult thing about covering the race.

I take a lot of pride in the fact we won some Emmys for it, which was very unusual for auto racing to win an Emmy for best live program. Those kinds of things leave a good feeling with me. How much fun we had and how much we got to contribute to our viewers enjoying it. We had some great races and some tragic events, and all of the things that go along with auto racing.

I've never been back to the race as a spectator. I was afraid I wouldn't enjoy it sitting in the stands. I don't enjoy going to a football game because I miss everything we do in television to enhance the game. And the same is true of auto racing, I really enjoy sitting at home watching it. Watching how they do it with some of the new technology. I was there for the first in-car camera. It was as pedestrian as you could possibly get in the way we attached it to the car.

But I think I'm ready to go back and enjoy the race as a spectator. You can't go your whole life and not go to the Indy 500 as a spectator, especially after you worked it for nearly 20 years. I'm ready to go now.

***Paul Page** is a longtime radio and television broadcaster of the 500.*

When I started anchoring the Indy 500 it was on radio in 1977. Then I had Freddie Agabashian in the booth. He was pretty much a mainstay for most of that first 10 years of my career. Then the Indy 500 became a live television event and I was asked to broadcast that event for ABC Sports. They were trying to ramp up their coverage now that it was live.

It was a total revamp. So I've got Bobby Unser and I've got Sam Posey. Bobby and I had been friends forever. Sam, not nearly that length of time. But we were all really good and close friends.

I'm not really sure how the dynamics came to happen, I think it might have just been Bobby being Bobby, but he found the need to correct everything Sam would say. Sometimes those corrections started with, 'Well Sam that's not exactly right,' then he'd talk for a minute and talk himself around to exactly what Sam had said and we'd all laugh at it.

One year our pit reporter, Jack Arute, bought a referee shirt and brought it to a production meeting for me.

It was funny, the audience reaction. There was a segment of the audience that really hated it. One part would say Bobby's an idiot, can't even speak, why don't you just let Sam do it. The other half is asking why Sam is even there, Bobby's a three-time 500 winner. It was one of those can't lose situations. The important thing was it generated a buzz. And since we've all been gone, I can't tell you how many people have come up and said, 'Jeez, the best times were when you and Sam and Bobby were together.'

I was always trying to encourage Sam as a broadcaster. Sam is one of the best writers I've ever met. Sitting with him in the office, while we were each working on different features, watching the process he would use, and how many times he would cross things out and re-read and re-write, he was beautiful. But that was in some way his downfall on different occasions.

He'd come into the booth with 5x7 cards, and there might be 80 of them. Obviously he'd done a hell of a lot of homework; he had a card for everything. But the card became his primary focus. He wasn't into the race as much as he was into those cards.

So the second year he came into the booth and has his cards and I say let me see those. He hands them to me and I threw them to the other end of the booth, and they just went everywhere. Bobby enjoyed that.

Maybe the greatest aspect of how close those two were came on a flight to Australia for the race in Surfer's Paradise. The two were side-by-side in their seats. Now that's a 14-hour flight. And those two talked the entire 14 hours. They were great friends.

They brought a lot of humor, which hadn't been in the telecast before. Made it a little more lighthearted and achieved what I was looking for. I wanted us to be guys, sitting in the grandstands, watching the race. And that's what they gave us. I really enjoyed that relationship.

It's such an alien environment. You've got all this equipment around you, all these other people, the lighting guy, stage manager, somebody talking in your ear the whole time, telling everybody what do. The broadcast is in your other ear. The producer would say just relax and have fun and I'd ask how the hell do I do that?

Marty Reid *served as the lead announcer for the Indy 500 from 2006 to 2013.*

For me it's always been about two elements. First there are the viewers and how they respond to what you're doing. Hopefully at the end of the day they feel it was time well spent. Then there's the crew.

My first year Sam Hornish, Jr. did something no one had ever done before, making a pass on the last lap to win the race and beat Marco Andretti. It was the first year Rusty Wallace was working with us. He got so excited that he blurted out that Sam won. We still tease him about that. But what Sam pulled off – like I said – nobody had ever done it.

The 100th anniversary run, where J.R. Hildebrand hits the wall coming out of Turn 4 when he has the race won and here comes Dan Wheldon winning his second 500, that was another incredible moment. Obviously there was added significance in that we lost him later that year in Las Vegas.

But no matter what show or broadcast I was a part of throughout my 31 years, without all of those great people behind the scene, those of us fortunate enough to be in front of the camera – we're nothing.

Their talents don't get enough recognition. They're great people with great skills. Try panning a camera when a car is going 300 miles an hour down a drag strip. Trust me, I've tried it – I can't do it. They always made us look and sound better than we truly were.

When it came to the 500, the size of the crew swelled. Normally a race crew is around 60 or 70. We have almost 300 for the 500, counting runners and everybody. And no matter how small you think your job is, if you don't do it, it's a trickle-down effect.

The truth is, we're always a stroke away from a total disaster. The trick is to pull it off without the viewer at home realizing we were ever that close. There have been a number of times where power in the truck or one section of the track would be lost or a piece of valuable equipment comes down – like we lost scoring monitors one year in the booth. It's like you're blind. You're looking out the window and you're trying to figure out what the heck is going on based on the pylon. Those kinds of things happen from time to time. It's always a great feeling when you get to the next commercial break and everything is back to normal and you're looking at each other and going, 'Phew, we dodged a bullet and made it through.'

And that's why it was always so much fun when we got to the end of the race and we could look back and say, 'OK, we did good today. We crossed the t's and dotted the i's.'

***Allen Bestwick** is the current lead announcer for ABC/ESPN's coverage of the Indy 500.*

When I was a kid, one of the early things that captured me and fascinated me about the Indy 500 was the Johnny Lightning Special cars that won the '70 and '71 races. I had those little toy cars.

At the 2015 race, Al Unser, Sr. was driving that car around the Speedway as part of the ceremonial things they do. I was standing in the ABC booth getting ready for the broadcast and that car came by. It was a deeply personal moment for me.

It was this moment of tying childhood hopes and dreams into the adult realities of those dreams coming true. Having the privilege of standing there and doing what I enjoy doing so much, at that great place, at that great race. It was something that I had dreamed about and was fascinated by since I was a kid – illustrated by that car coming by. It was emotional and gratifying and something I'll never forget.

My dad had a race car when I was a kid and I grew up around short track racing. I've been a big fan of racing my whole life, but broadcasting was always my dream and the thing I wanted to pursue. I've been around the business now for a long time and it's worked out pretty well.

My career started on the NASCAR side of things and I've been involved there for a long time. As a result, most of my Memorial Days have been spent in Charlotte.

When I was assigned to the Indianapolis 500, I was obviously very gratified and very happy, but you put your nose down and you go to work. You're focused on what you're doing. Trying to deliver the race properly out of respect to the competitors and the fans and everyone involved.

You know you've got one shot to get it right and do the event justice. We all take that enormously seriously. I say that on behalf of the hundreds of people that work on this broadcast. Every one of them takes it seriously and is committed to doing it right. It's an honor and a huge responsibility.

That moment, watching the Johnny Lightning car come by, for whatever reason, brought it all together for me. Made me step back for a second and try to comprehend how this little kid from Rhode Island is standing in the broadcast booth at the Indianapolis Motor Speedway. It was just a little mind-boggling.

***Eddie Cheever** won the 1985 Indy 500 and joined the television broadcast team in 2008.*

In the beginning, I must admit, just like driving in the 500, I was very wary of the television broadcast. What happens if you make a mistake? What happens if you say something silly? It's just difficult to understand the sensation of having the attention of millions of people sitting there listening to what you're saying.

I was reluctant to do it because I didn't feel comfortable sitting in a room for three-and-a-half hours and not having a choice whether I wished to participate in the conversation or not. When you're part of that ongoing conversation – there are times when you'd just like to sit down and think for three minutes and you can't. You're always engaged and it took a long time for me to be comfortable with that.

There's a lot of pressure doing television and a lot of work and preparation goes into it, which is fine and that's very enjoyable. Working with ABC and ESPN is tremendous. So talented in what they do, I mean they just know sports inside and out.

I never really got to enjoy the Indianapolis 500 as a live event, because I was participating in it. So when you're sitting in a TV booth it is fantastic. You have an eagle's view of everything that goes on. You have all these feeds coming in from all these different TV cameras and you have some really bright people that you're talking with.

Scott Goodyear is one of the most knowledgeable people that has participated in Indy cars that I have ever known. And then you have these great broadcasters with us that find a way to guide the conversation. It's something that I've come to really look forward to. And my children like it, so that's good enough for me.

***Scott Goodyear** had three second-place finishes in the Indy 500 and has been part of the television broadcast team since 2002.*

My first year working television for ABC/ESPN was a real transition. Although I was ready to step out of the cockpit on a full-time basis, the process was accelerated when I was crashed out of the 2001 Indy 500 and broke my back for a second time.

Dr. Terry Trammell urged me to consider stepping away from Indy cars and continue competing in sports cars, which is what I did. He said running into a wall at Indy at 230 mph is different than going off the track at a road course and sliding into a tire barrier. He said if I broke my back a third time, I might not be so lucky.

That's all I needed to hear. My wife Leslie was in the hospital room with me, listening to Terry, and the decision was probably made there on the spot.

So after a week in the hospital, then spending four months in a torso clamshell brace recovering, I was no longer an Indy car driver. I knew it was the right choice, but it rips a part out of your soul. It's reality. I was still active in sports cars with Brumos Porsche, but I'd turned my last laps at Indianapolis in an Indy car. Later that fall, I was contacted about doing television.

I had raced in the 500 11 times, but in 2002 I was heading to Indianapolis for the first time in a long time and not racing in the event. I swear your body clock knows when it's the month of May and it's time to go 230 mph. But now I would be getting my adrenaline rush in a different way.

Paul Page, the play-by-play announcer, urged me to arrive on race day before 6 a.m. so I could take in all the activities that go on before the race. That sounded weird. I had been going there for years. But Paul was right. It was different from what I experienced as a driver – really different.

I arrived early so I could hear the bomb go off, signaling the opening of the track. As the sun comes up, the grounds come alive. The first few years our television booth was a small white hut perched on the roof of the grandstands above the start/finish line. I watched from our booth as the people, who were lined up at the gate all night, filed into the track. For the next couple of hours I sat on my stool in the booth and looked down on the front straight, marveling at how big an event the Indy 500 is, even before that race gets underway.

Every time something different came along the straight I'd say, 'Hey Paul, look at this, they have marching bands.' Of course Paul had seen it all before, he just wanted me to experience that side of the event.

Even today, after 14 years in the television booth, I get tingles up my spine when they sing the national anthem and when the cars come down to take the green flag.

I'm glad the first lap is covered by the play-by-play anchor. I'm not sure I could do that part as I'm busy feeling the rush of the cars coming down the front straight as if I was still driving.

***Tom Michaels** was 12 when he first listened to the Indy 500 on the radio in 1963. He has been calling races since 1985 on the CART Radio Network and IMS Radio Network.*

Two friends and I ordered tickets for Grandstand H for the 1968 Indy 500 without ever considering that three high school kids who had just gotten their licenses would not be allowed to drive from Dayton, Ohio, into that mass of humanity and machines on race day in Indy. Finally, my mom volunteered to drive us.

My friend Dan was in charge of the map and said he thought since there was just a two-inch distance on the map from downtown to the Speedway, we should park there. We parked near what would become Market Square Arena and set off on foot, leaving my mom and 12-year-old sister Vickie to fend for themselves.

We passed cab stands and shuttle buses as we walked in some vague direction towards the track carrying our coolers and cameras. Finally, a police officer stopped us, asked where we were going, and said we'd never make it in time because we were several miles away from the Speedway. The officer stepped out into traffic, stopped a cab and told the driver to take us to the track, even though he already had two passengers. Luckily, we barely had enough money for the cab.

When we got to the track, the three things that struck me were the size of the facility, how colorful the field was the first time by as I was used to seeing black-and-white pictures and film, and the noise of the field of 33 cars, even though three were turbines.

Meanwhile, mom and Vickie were trying to find something to do in a time when Memorial Day meant downtown was shut down. Two places were open, the police station and a book store. After some bored cop gave them a tour of the station they went to the book store. After a few minutes my mom figured out why they were they only women in there – it was an adult book store. They quickly vamoosed.

The next year my parents threw caution to the wind and let me drive to the race.

***Jim Murphy** joined the CART radio network in 1997 and was a pit reporter for the IMS Radio Network from 2002 to 2004.*

The first year I had the opportunity to work with the radio network was 2002 and as a lifelong fan of the sport, that in itself was very exciting. But when it got down to the end of the race, I had no idea what was in store for us.

Helio Castroneves was leading, but he was very tight on fuel. I was in his pit, keeping track of that story, when an accident occurred off Turn 2 which brought out a yellow. At the same time Paul Tracy made a pass on Helio that he thought put him into the lead with just a handful of laps left. In fact, race control determined that no, the pass did not occur, and Helio was reinstated as the race leader and winner.

My task on the radio broadcast was to do the next interview following the winner, which would be Paul Tracy. By the time I get down to Paul's pit, he's standing there with a scrum of reporters around him, watching Helio on the big screen along the front straight.

I will never forget the image of Paul sitting there looking up at Helio, who is laughing and cheering and pouring milk over his head on a forty foot tall screen. The look on Paul's face was like you were ripping his heart right out of his chest. They finish the interview in Victory Lane and came to me – it's my turn. I looked at Paul, he looked at me, and the only thing I could ask was, 'Paul Tracy, *who* won the Indy 500?'

Some of the commentary that he was sharing with people around him prior to putting a microphone in his face was exceptionally raw and frank. I wasn't sure what I was going to get. But I had to open the microphone up and let the man be the man, and he rose to the occasion.

I don't recall the exact answer he gave – but I recall it was heartfelt and it was professional. He wasn't going to embarrass himself or his team or his sponsors. I was incredibly impressed with how he handled himself. He had every opportunity to go full scale off the reservation – and he didn't.

It was clearly one of the toughest moments in his career and one of the fondest memories I have of the Indy 500.

***Rick DeBruhl** got Mark Donohue's autograph at the first race he attended, the inaugural California 500 in 1970. He's a pit reporter on ESPN/ABC's motorsports coverage.*

The very first year I did the Indy 500 was 2010. To finally get to work the Indy 500 was like the Holy Grail of racing.

I arrived on Wednesday night and was at the track on Thursday. I'm one of those people who tend to stay late, so Thursday night, everybody from the TV crew had pretty much gone home.

I went out to the front straightaway. It was one of those magical moments when everybody was gone. There was no one in the stands, no officials around, no people around. The light was starting to fade a little bit and I just sat there on the wall, at the yard of bricks, just looking up and down and thinking, 'Holy crap.'

I had wanted to do this race, to be at this race for any reason, since I was a kid. To think that I was actually going to work it. To think about ghosts of races past. Whether it was Ray Harroun or Ralph DePalma or Bill Vukovich or Wilbur Shaw or Mark Donohue. All the people who had come down this stretch. They had all crossed this yard of bricks. Yeah, the grandstands had changed and the Pagoda had changed, but this is still the place.

We used to do this thing called the Craftsman Pit Garage. It was a set off to the side. In 2011 they brought in a Marmon Wasp. They put it in the studio and they shot a bunch of features. I wasn't involved in the features, but then they left it there.

I came in to the little set and there was the Marmon Wasp. Just me and one other guy. I'm like, 'I'm sitting in the Marmon Wasp. I'm gonna sit where Ray Harroun sat. I'm gonna look in *the* rear view mirror.' You think about what those guys went through, and what those cars were like. To sit in the Marmon Wasp and think about Ray Harroun and the first Indy 500, what he had to survive just to make it to the finish line that day and rudimentary aspects of that car, it was just absolutely amazing.

Being alone with the car was like having the chance to meet Walt Disney or Henry Ford. It's truly larger than life and the machine that started a legacy. I swear it actually spoke to me!

If you ever get a chance to look at the Marmon Wasp, you'll have such respect for those guys. Those people, at 75 mph, were risking life and limb to prove that man could drive that fast. That cars could last that long. It was an incredible endeavor for them just to finish.

Look at the film back in those days. The dust that came off the track – I don't know how they saw. I don't know how they breathed. I don't know how they managed to survive. How long did it take to run the race? Six hours and fifty minutes or something like that? What an incredible feat of endurance.

I don't want to take anything away from the drivers today, because they're incredible athletes, the intensity of what they do and the speed at which they do it today. But look at what was happening to drivers back then. How often drivers were getting killed. For anybody to even think this was a semi-reasonable thing to do was insane. And yet they still did it.

Photographer Scrum

CHAPTER 6

Media

As befitting the world's largest one day sporting event, the Indy 500 attracts reporters from around the world. At one point virtually every major newspaper in America sent a reporter to cover the race. The media landscape has changed greatly in recent years and the number of reporters has declined along with the number of traditional news outlets. Yet it remains one of the most heavily covered sporting events of the year.

***Curt Cavin** has worked in the sports department of the Indianapolis Star since 1987 and has been covering the Indy 500 since 1988. He also covers college and professional sports.*

There were days in my Hoosier youth when I'd sit in my grandmother's home in Lebanon, Ind., and pore through her Indianapolis 500 scrapbooks. Newspaper clippings of Mario Andretti and Johnny Rutherford. Tickets of races she'd attended. Memories.

If only I could attend the 500, I thought.

One day, as a high school junior, I got the chance to visit Indianapolis Motor Speedway. I was sitting in Turn 4 that day in 1982 when Gordon Smiley lost his life in a crash. I'll never forget the curiosity I had over the incident. How did it happen? What safety measures could have helped him? How would the sport react?

As a Franklin College journalism major, I joined the *Indianapolis Star*'s sports department as an intern in 1985 and a full-time employee two years later. I covered my first 500 for the paper in '88, and I've never stopped wondering what makes these men and their machines tick.

The memories continue with each season, and it's more than just races and fantastic finishes, including those stirring final four laps in 2006 when Michael Andretti, Marco Andretti and Sam Hornish, Jr. each held the lead. It's spending time with A.J. Foyt at his

Texas ranch, visiting with Mario Andretti in his Nazareth, Pa., wine cellar, and having Rick Mears explain race strategy as succinctly as he drove those cars.

There was the spring day when Kevin Cogan sat on his patio overlooking the gorgeous Pacific Ocean and discussed how all the blame for the 1982 crash was shoved on him, and how Bobby Rahal got the best of him in the two-lap '86 shootout.

I've driven to Huron (Mich.) National Forest to sit at Gordon Johncock's kitchen table to talk racing, and I was able to connect Parnelli Jones with the young man who ran onto the track to fetch the cowboy hat Jones lost on his victory lap in '63.

There is so much else I've been privileged to experience, including being in Hollywood as Helio Castroneves danced his way into millions of homes, but it was even better when Castroneves took me to the Sao Paolo, Brazil karting facility where so many Indy car and Formula One drivers developed their craft.

Perhaps the best moment came a few months before my grandmother passed. Rutherford was her guy, so I handed him the phone so he could deliver a birthday wish. She would have put that in her scrapbook if she could have. I certainly put it in mine.

Tom Blattler *is a longtime sports publicist.*

Working the month of May in and around the Indianapolis Motor Speedway for more than two decades has been a privilege and one of the biggest thrills in my life. With family and friends on top of my most important life experience list, the start of the Indy 500 might be second or third.

Any person with a sporting interest has to put the Indy 500 on their bucket list to see live. I've worked Super Bowls, NBA games, MLB games, college sports and a variety of other motorsports activities, but the Indy 500 is still the biggest and best event to witness in person.

Identifying a single Indy 500 experience is a tough one. I was lucky enough to be in the winner's circle once with Buddy Rice and the Rahal Letterman team in 2004. I experienced the wild, thrilling rookie run of Danica Patrick in 2005 with the same team and the spectacular drives of Ed Carpenter to the 2013 and 2014 Indy 500 pole positions. However, one memorable day jumps out to me as the number one experience and it wasn't a good one.

It came on Bump Day with the Rahal Hogan Racing team and driver Bobby Rahal in 1993. Bobby was the defending CART series champion. After his 1992 title, the team decided to run the Don Halliday-designed Truesports chassis during the '93 campaign. Bobby had some reservations about the car, but the potential seemed to be there and a second-place finish at Long Beach kept the thinking alive. On the fast Indy oval, however, the car was a handful.

On the final weekend of qualifying, Bobby made the 33 car field on Saturday and things looked good entering Bump Day, as the weather forecast was not good. But the weather turned in favor of the slower cars in the afternoon and cooling "happy hour" track temperatures put Bobby on the bubble, knowing he could be the first defending series champion to miss the 500 since the 1930s.

The pressure on Bobby was incredible, with national television and radio, hundreds of photographers, media members and the crowd watching his every move. As the PR rep for the team, I was stunned that Bobby sat quietly waiting his final chance.

Once Eddie Cheever made the field, it was time for Rahal to jump into his backup car for one final attempt to get into the field. Team general manager Scott Roembke timed the car's movement through the qualifying line perfectly, with Bobby driving onto the track as the timing gun went off to close qualifications. Bobby would be the last to make a qualifying effort.

But the Truesports chassis just wasn't up for the fight that day and Rahal missed the race. It had to be the biggest racing disappointment of Bobby's career, but he calmly climbed from the cockpit and answered all of the media's crazy questions. It is still the most impressive performance by a driver out of the car that I have ever seen. I couldn't have been more proud of Bobby as a person and racer.

Bones Bourcier *is the author of many auto racing books including "As a Matter of Fact I am Parnelli Jones." His latest is "Foyt, Andretti, Petty – America's Racing Trinity."*

It's May 26, 1996. Like everyone in Indianapolis, I've spent the better part of three weeks dodging raindrops. The TV weather hairdos have been saying for days that it's the fifth-wettest May in Indiana history.

Why should race morning be any different? I'd driven to the track before dawn, arriving in a downpour. Now, with the rain easing a bit, I jog from my infield parking spot toward the press room adjacent to Gasoline Alley, but before I'm even halfway there the skies open again. I duck beneath the eaves of a concession stand, where I'm joined by an old man doing his best to avoid the puddles. And with good reason: his white shoes are part of an impeccable wardrobe that harkens back to those wonderful big event photos from the 1930s, when any respectable gentleman dressed like a dandy when showing up for, say, the Indianapolis 500 or the Kentucky Derby.

It's clear, just from the way this fellow carries himself, that he was *somebody* once. He's wearing one of those "500 Oldtimers Club" caps, the kind with the member's name embroidered on the side, but I don't want him to see me stealing a clumsy glance. We chat for a long while as daylight creeps over the soggy grounds, both of us optimistically circling back to this afternoon's more promising forecast.

When finally the rain slows again, we say our polite goodbyes and begin heading off in different directions. Now, at last, I catch a clean look at that cap, and the name stitched into it. Not only had this guy been somebody, but he still is, and he always will be. It's Duke Nalon.

I know his history all right. Born Dennis Nalon, racing out of Chicago, he was soon dubbed the "Iron Duke." He roared off the Midwest dirt tracks – he won big in midgets and was the AAA sprint car champion – and had an Indianapolis ride by 1938. Before and after World War II he ran the 500 in Millers, Offys, and Maseratis before landing, in 1948, in a Kurtis chassis powered by the brand of engine which with he'd be forever linked: the Novi. He finished third that year. He stuck another Novi on the pole in '49 and led the first 23 laps before exiting the 500 in a fiery crash. In 1951, still Novi-powered, he started from the pole again.

I watch him walk away, thinking, 'There goes Indianapolis royalty.'

Duke Nalon was 83 years old on that Sunday in 1996. He died in 2001, but I swear I still see him every May, in the darkness of race morning, walking the place in his white shoes, walking like the 500 prince that he was.

Jonathan Ingram *has been covering motorsports since 1976 and is the author of several books, including "The Art of Race Car Design" with Bob Riley, who designed the Coyote A.J. Foyt, Jr. drove to his fourth Indy 500 victory in 1977.*

There wasn't a better place for writers to watch a race than the old Indy press box located on a catwalk hanging beneath the upper deck opposite the pits. Just getting there – through a zigzag series of upwardly winding and then cascading stairs – was a story in itself.

The final passage was down a narrow walkway suspended from the formed concrete of the upper deck above and in full view of the thousands of fans seated in the grandstand below. A single row of seating was available along the catwalk with folding chairs set up behind a tabletop barely wide enough to hold a notepad.

Peering beyond the overhang of the deck above, on the opposite side of the track, you could see the front straight, the pits, the terrace grandstands behind the pits and just enough of the skyline if you held your head sideways a bit like a pigeon, to know where the back straight ran. A TV mounted at either end of the catwalk was the only view of turns 2, 3 and 4. If you craned your neck and hugged the tabletop, you could glimpse the entry to Turn 1.

There was enough of a view to follow the drama unfolding at incredible speeds as long as you knew the paint schemes. The scoring pylon was in full view. It sounded like Tom Carnegie was announcing the race right next to you as the loudspeakers in the cavernous grandstands boomed from below.

More importantly, you could feel the roar of the crowd, the whine of the engines, the wham-wham-wham of the speed and the smell of the grease, if not greasepaint. It was spectacular, high theater.

The only drawback concerned post-race interviews. They were held on the opposite side of the track. The eternal dilemma was deciding whether to leave before the end of the race to beat the crush of humanity headed for the exits that delayed getting to the post-race interviews.

Late in the 1991 race and with an *Atlanta Journal-Constitution* deadline looming, I waited for the last restart that would likely decide the outcome and watched Michael Andretti pass Rick Mears on the outside of Turn 1 as both were trying to get through lapped traffic. Andretti the Younger finally wins Indy! I got up to head for the interview room. But just in case, I paused at the narrow turn at the end of the catwalk for one more look with 12 laps remaining.

In talking with Mears years later, he said he never lifted for the entire lap after the restart and that it was the fastest of his race. The next time they came down the straight, it was Mears who passed on the outside at full song as Andretti feinted and then protected the inside line.

Mears made the boldest pass for victory that we will likely ever see. I was crouching, nearly on one knee, peering beneath the overhang, scanning for a distant move at breakneck speed, just glimpsing Mears and his Marlboro machine entering the corner on the outside – a split-second sliver of color, speed, guts and history.

***Kevin Kennedy** is the longtime communications director of Ford Racing and executive vice president of Campbell Marketing & Communications.*

My favorite memory of the Indianapolis 500, not surprisingly, involves a victory.

Sure, there are great personal memories, like the first time watching a race start down in the grassy area of Turn 1, or going around in a Mustang Cobra pace car at top speed with the likes of Parnelli Jones and A.J. Foyt. There's even great memories of the old infield media center, where you always knew where everyone was going to be sitting when you went in the first week of May. After all, tradition did not only occur on the track.

In my case, my favorite memory was the victory by Jacques Villeneuve in 1995, which many called the last "real" Indy 500 before the split with the IRL.

After Ford, with Cosworth, returned in 1992, we thought we had it won the first year until the crushing late engine failure with 11 laps to go by Michael Andretti. I wanted to sink through the media center floor. In 1993's Nigel-Mania, we thought we had it until the late restart misstep by Mansell cost him what would have been a massive victory. And, of course, it's hard to forget the agony of the 1994 race where everyone was running for second behind the one-off Mercedes-Penske motor, unless it blew up.

So, it seemed 1995 was going to be our year. And there was certainly an urgency to win with the pending CART-IRL split looming over the sport.

To have Jacques go two laps down on an early penalty and then see him battle back to win after 505 miles for him, well, let's just say there was a great sense of accomplishment afterward.

We had a lot of good cars that day (10 of the top 12 finishers), but Jacques and his team were at the top of their championship game right then. The controversy over the late start by Scott Goodyear notwithstanding, Jacques and his team were the best car that day, so to come back and win was very memorable, especially when it appeared to be slipping away again.

The funny thing was, I don't remember our Ford or Cosworth people going crazy afterwards in terms of screaming or jumping up and down. But I do remember there were a lot of hugs, a toast of champagne, and smiles that went on for a long time.

Our people – like so many before them - knew how hard it was to win at Indy. They knew it was more than planning, and preparation and hard work. They knew it was all those things, but that you needed a little luck thrown in for good measure.

Thirty years after Jim Clark brought Ford its first win in the Indianapolis 500, we were back. And it was so satisfying.

***Michael Knight** worked the Indy 500 as a reporter, public relations rep and as head of public relations for CART.*

God willing, as they say, 2016 will be my 38th Indianapolis 500. All but the first three have had me on-site in a working capacity, as a journalist or publicist. I've often thought Indy could fill a never-ending series of books because there is always another new, memorable experience.

Back in 1975, I was on-site covering for the *Philadelphia Daily News*. A.J. Foyt was on the pole and in quest of a record-breaking fourth victory. In those days there were no organized press conferences. The practice was for reporters to stand outside a driver's garage and hope to get a few minutes. Getting an interview with Foyt was a must for any writer seriously trying to do the job.

I was one of about eight who gathered in front of Foyt's garage late morning Wednesday of race week. The doors were open and A.J. knew we were out there. Finally, after about a half-hour, he waved us in. This was one of those years when Gasoline Alley rumor had it that Foyt was cheating on horsepower. Those of us with some experience figured we'd ask him about that, but not until after we had gotten enough quotes to write a proper story. Unfortunately, just a couple of minutes into our session, some guy – I think he was a Chicago columnist – blurted out a question on cheating. Sure enough, A.J. blew up and told us all to, 'Get the hell out of here.'

A few evenings before the Daytona 500, somehow I had been seated next to Indianapolis Motor Speedway owner Tony Hulman at a corporate dinner. It was a very pleasant experience. And that connection was about to pay off big time for me.

Our media group exited Foyt's garage and scattered in different directions. As I went around the corner toward the main Gasoline Alley entrance, who happened to be coming toward me but Mr. Hulman. He smiled and we shook hands and he said, 'Welcome back to Indianapolis.' Mr. Hulman asked me how I was and I told him what just had happened. 'Come with me,' he said, and we walked back toward Foyt's car. When we got in front of the garage, Mr. H said to me, 'Wait here a minute.' He went inside and I watched as he had a few words with A.J. Just that quickly Tony came back out and said, 'Go on in!' and I looked up to see Foyt waving me in. Thanks to Mr. Hulman, I got an exclusive. That was a huge moment early in my sports writing career in a large market with three competing daily newspapers.

***Michael Levitt** is a photographer with LAT USA, which specializes in automotive and motorsports photography.*

With a lap to go in 2011, I was ready to shoot J.R. Hildebrand crossing the bricks, victorious. I had been rehearsing the shot for about 20 laps from the top of the Pagoda, panning with the "winning" car as it raced out of Turn 4 and over the finish line. Dan Wheldon was far enough behind that there was no pressure on J.R. and no chance that Dan would pass him.

When J.R. hit the wall exiting the last turn, I kept following him, and when he passed over the bricks, dragging pieces of his car and trailing a stream of sparks, I thought I had the shot of the race. So when I looked up at the scoring pylon, I was shocked to see the 98 of Wheldon on top. My happiness at the realization of Dan's win mingled with my disappointment with shooting the wrong car passing the bricks.

I raced down the 15 flights of stairs with my cameras and managed to beat Dan to Victory Lane. I waited for the celebration, grabbed the memory cards from my other shooters, then went back to the media center to take a look at my photos. Unbeknownst to me, I had captured the moment of Dan's pass of J.R. while I was following his car, and still managed to end up with the shot of the race. Just blind luck.

As Indy has proved many times, sometimes you are just better off being lucky than smart, fast, or brave. Dan and I were both pretty lucky that day.

T.E. McHale *was a sports reporter for the Mansfield News Journal and worked in CART public relations prior to joining Honda in 2003, where he is currently the manger of motorsports communications.*

Motorsports makes strange bedfellows, and it would be difficult to find a better example of that than the 2004 Indianapolis 500.

My first year at Honda, 2003, coincided with the company's first year in what was then known as the Indy Racing League. Honda brought 65 race victories, 65 pole positions, six drivers' championships and four manufacturers' championships to the IRL from its nine-year tenure (1994-2002) in CART competition.

Despite that impressive resume, however, it was not an immediately successful transition. Honda won only two of 16 races during that inaugural IRL season, and insult was added to injury when Gil de Ferran, who had won Honda's final two CART driving championships for Penske Racing in 2000 and 2001, won the 2003 Indianapolis 500 in a Toyota-powered car.

So, from a purely provincial point of view, it was an utterly forgettable first IRL campaign. But that had been true during Honda's initial foray into CART competition, as well. Honda had struggled mightily during its first season in 1994, to the point where its lone partner team, Rahal Hogan Racing, turned to Ilmor engines to power its two Indianapolis 500 entries after it became apparent the RHR Hondas weren't going to be fast enough to make the field.

A year later, Honda had rebounded to earn its first CART pole position with Parker Johnstone at Michigan, followed by its first race victory by Andre Ribeiro at New Hampshire. And it likely would have won the 1995 Indianapolis 500, but for an incident in which then-leading Scott Goodyear passed the pace car during a caution period on the race track with only 10 laps remaining.

Those successes set the stage for a run which resulted in six straight drivers' championships and four manufacturers' crowns between 1996 and 2001. So, despite its initial IRL disappointments, there was reason for the Honda camp to be hopeful as the 2004 season dawned.

Sam Hornish, Jr. drove a Toyota to victory in the '04 season opener at Homestead, but Tony Kanaan of Andretti Green Racing followed that by repeating his 2003 victory at Phoenix in a Honda. Kanaan's teammate, Dan Wheldon, then became the first Honda-powered driver – after six extraordinarily frustrating attempts – to win the company's home race, at the Twin Ring Motegi motorsports complex in Japan.

The 500 was next. A decade after forsaking Honda power in the 1994 500 – amidst considerable acrimony, it must be mentioned – the team co-owned by three-time CART driving champion Bobby Rahal and his new partner, late-night television host David Letterman, dominated the month of May. Driver Buddy Rice captured the pole position for the 500 at 222.024 mph, then led 91 of the rain-shortened 180-lap event – nearly three times as many as anyone else in the field – to bring both Honda and the Rahal team their first Indianapolis 500 victory.

'I don't think that irony was lost on anybody,' Rahal said afterward, with uncharacteristic understatement.

Overall, Honda took the top seven finishing positions in that 500 and it launched a run of nine consecutive victories in "The Greatest Spectacle in Racing." By the time the 2004 IRL season concluded, Honda-powered drivers had won 14 of the year's 16 races, and Kanaan, who claimed his first series driving championship, had completed every lap of every race. Following upon the struggles of 2003, it brought an extraordinary sense of accomplishment to everyone associated with the Honda Racing program.

***Robin Miller** was a former motorsports writer for the Indianapolis Star and currently works for Racer Magazine.*

I was sitting in Turn 1 with my dad at the Indianapolis Motor Speedway on the final day of qualifying in 1960 when my life changed abruptly. A rookie driving a beautiful purple roadster had me, the crowd and announcer Tom Carnegie, standing and screaming.

Jim Hurtubise came within an eyelash of running the first-ever lap of 150 mph. We didn't know he was sliding the car through the corners to go three mph faster than the pole-sitter, but we damn sure knew it was exciting.

From that moment on I was hooked on Hercules (his nickname) and race cars. I started stalking him at Terre Haute, Indianapolis Raceway Park and the Indiana State Fairgrounds. I heard he liked beer, so I would steal some from coolers in the pits and take them to him after the races – praying he might remember me some day.

In 1968 I was a senior in high school and May featured three weeks of practice for the Indianapolis 500. So I cut school opening day and snuck into Gasoline Alley to hopefully see Herk.

It turned out to be the greatest day of my young life because Jim's regular crew wasn't coming for another week and he needed some help, so he asked me and a college kid named Skip to give him a hand. You had to be 21 to get into the pits and I looked all of 12, but Herk gave me a Goodyear jacket, an STP hat and a Mechanics Laundry rag and told me to keep my head down and push the car when we were going back-and-forth between the garage and pits.

My other duties were taping his goggles onto his helmet, showing him the pit board and fastening the bodywork. Helping push my hero's Mallard roadster down the pits at Indy pretty much topped anything and everything I'd ever done.

But, as it turned out, my mechanical ineptitude would come back to haunt me.

Jim had forgotten his helmet so he borrowed one from Joe Leonard but it was too big for his head so I had to stuff a few rags inside it to make sure it didn't wobble around on his head going down the straightaways. Then I would tape his goggles onto his open-face helmet. Except one day we were running late, the track was about to close, and Herk wanted to run the engine he'd just replaced.

As he barked at Skip and I to hurry up, I panicked and taped a shock of his hair onto his helmet along with his goggles. He blew up, literally, on the first lap. Then he blew up, figuratively, when he tore off his goggles *and* a clump of hair.

That was strike one. Strike two was failing to recognize the box of paper things I threw on the garage floor were, in fact, the gaskets Jim had asked me to bring him.

The last straw came when his new sponsor, Pepsi/Frito Lay, painted the bodywork and I lost control of the dzus wrench and ruined the paint job with a nasty streak down the middle.

That was it. Even though I was free help, Herk fired me. I was devastated. I had failed my hero.

When qualifying was extended to Monday because of weather, I skipped school and headed to the Speedway to watch Herk become the last driver to ever qualify a roadster for the Indy 500. I stood by the fence cheering for him and he spotted me and gave me the wave, so I hopped over the fence and tried to make the qualifying photo.

I think I got cropped out, but it didn't matter. Herk was in the show and he knew my name. My life was complete.

***Doug Stokes** is a motorsports public relations professional.*

I was sitting at a table in the middle of the old coffee shop just outside Gasoline Alley in 1982 when Jim Hurtubise walked in the door. I didn't know him, but certainly recognized him, and smiled. He caught my smile and walked directly to my table, saying, 'Hey man, good to see you. How's it going?'

I was a little stunned, but able to put my hand out and say, 'Fine.' He just said 'Thanks' and went to take a seat.

This was early in race week and just about everyone in the coffee shop was either crew or track personnel. Yet no one else had even looked, or maybe they had done so quickly and just as quickly turned away.

It took me a few minutes to realize that Hurtubise must still be considered something of a pariah by the rank and file for his Bump Day shenanigans years before. I was the sole smile of recognition in the whole damn place. Herk was never very successful at Indy, but his exploits on dirt in the big cars, while running with all the big names of the day, are an indelible part of a lot of fans' best memories of motorsports.

***Dick Mittman** spent 50 years covering sports for all three major Indianapolis newspapers. He is a member of the Indiana Sportswriters & Sportscasters Association's Hall of Fame.*

A.J. Foyt was having some problems with his car back in the late 1970s. He pulled into the pits after a run, climbed out and headed for Gasoline Alley and his garage. Waiting for him was a swarm of media at the gate exit. I worked for the afternoon *Indianapolis News*, which at that time was the sister paper of the morning *Indianapolis Star*.

A.J. told us he would talk to us back in the front of his garage – the old wooden ones – and we all knew not to question him until we got there. Well, that is, all but one young rookie radio guy from out of town.

We hadn't walked 15 yards when the newcomer's mike was shoved in front of A.J.'s face. Foyt shouted at him, 'I told you I'd talk in front of the garage.' In another 30 yards or so the mike reappeared in Foyt's face. This time A.J. told him exactly what he would do with that mike if it happened again.

By now we had reached Foyt's garage. The front of the garage has a tape barrier around it, like at a crime scene. Foyt steps inside of it and I do the same. Now he turns around to talk to us. Guess what was in front of his face. A.J. explodes. He grabs the mike with one hand and jerks it and the stunned holder toward him. Foyt's other hand is a fist and an arm about to swing it.

I grabbed Foyt around his stomach and jerked him backwards to prevent him from hitting this young radio reporter who didn't know what the word "wait" meant. He would have had a big story if A.J.'s fist had reached its target.

That is, once he got up off the pavement.

Well, things settled down. Since nothing actually happened it became a non-story to me. I didn't know any photographers had been around.

The next morning my wife opens *The Star* and there on the front page was a two-column photo of an enraged Foyt shouting and pointing with his right hand at the determined reporter. And I was holding A.J.'s left hand at the end of jerking him backwards.

Later in the morning I got a call from my mother who lived in San Francisco at the time. That same photo was on the front page of *The Chronicle*.

Since then I've wondered how many newspapers published that picture.

And I've wondered whether that young radio guy ever returned to the Speedway. And if he tried to interview Foyt again.

***Jeremy Shaw** is a longtime motorsports journalist who since 1990 has run the Team USA Scholarship program to assist talented young American drivers.*

In 2011 my better half, Tamy, was looking after PR for Bryan Herta Autosport (BHA) and I was just a hanger-on with no specific duties. I don't think I even bothered to obtain a proper credential. I watched the race from the BHA garage in Gasoline Alley, which meant I couldn't see anything other than the live scoring and TV feed. But that was enough to keep my usual lap chart, so I was well aware of strategies and how the race was unfolding.

As the race reached its conclusion, I realized that J.R. Hildebrand was in a position to win. In 2005, J.R. had won a Team USA Scholarship and since then had gradually worked his way up the ladder. Suddenly, here he was, leading the Indianapolis 500 – and seeking to emulate the feat of another Team USA driver, Buddy Rice, in 2004.

I have a real soft spot for J.R. because he is such a fine young man, in and out of the car, so I was quite emotional as he sped into the final lap. He had been quick for most of the month, although few people considered him as a potential winner.

Then, of course, going into Turn 4 with a quarter-mile to go, J.R., who seemed to be cruising toward the win, came up behind Charlie Kimball, ironically, another past Team USA Scholarship winner. Kimball was running out of gas and slowing dramatically. J.R. had no option but to lift abruptly off the throttle, which meant his car lost downforce, which sent it up into the gray and heavily into the wall. It was heartbreaking.

However, I was well aware that Dan Wheldon was in second place, albeit some distance behind. Dan had become a good friend, not a close friend perhaps, but someone whose company I had enjoyed since 1999 when he first arrived in the U.S. to race in USF2000. Plus he was driving for Herta, with whom I had been close ever since he started his own racing career in 1991. And Tamy was responsible for the team's PR.

An instant later, as J.R. kept his foot on the gas in the vain hope of coaxing his demolished car to the finish line before anyone else could catch up, Dan caught and passed him just a few hundred yards from the finish. I was distraught for J.R., but deliriously happy for Dan, Bryan and indeed Tamy, all of whom had worked so hard. It was surreal. The final few seconds of the race had brought a truly bizarre roller-coaster of emotions, the likes of which I cannot envision ever happening again.

That evening, after all the usual celebrations and fanfare, Dan and Bryan finally left the track for a proper victory dinner. Tamy and I remained at the Speedway to complete her follow-up duties. Our celebration consisted of a meal from McDonald's which I had brought back to the garage, where we sat, gazing at the race car that had just won the most famous race in the world. Another surreal moment.

The following morning, well before the sun had risen, Tamy and I met Dan back in the garage to begin his victory tour, which consisted of countless interviews with members of the media from around the world. He was bright-eyed and bushy-tailed, despite a very late night. Dan treated every single interview as if it was the first, with equal joy and passion. It was a sight to behold. I was *extremely* impressed. So was Tamy.

Both J.R. Hildebrand, who handled his crushing disappointment with true grace, and Dan Wheldon, are class acts.

***Steve Shunck** is the former head of IndyCar public relations and continues to work in motorsports PR.*

I've had many memorable moments since I attended my first Indianapolis 500 in 1973. One day a year I look forward to and enjoy getting up and arriving at the track before 4 a.m. Sometimes I arrive at 3:30 just for fun.

I've been lucky enough to attend the 500 as a spectator, working for ABC Sports, as a team member, working for IndyCar and for a sponsor. Each has given me a different perspective of the race and the events surrounding it.

Before my father passed away in 1995, it was always special to share Indy memories with him – from sitting in the Turn 2 stands during rain delays that first year to putting him behind the wheel of the Ford Mustang pace car in 1994 – they are memories I will always cherish.

My mom never attended the race. 'You should have memorized your spelling list, not the Indy 500 starting lineup,' she would say. 'How will that ever help you?' But each year Santa knew that a Hungness Yearbook under the Christmas tree would be the best gift of all. Thanks mom, I mean Santa.

Cuing Mari Fendrich Hulman to give the command "Gentlemen Start Your Engines" for six years when I worked as pit producer for ABC Sports was a thrill. From 1990 through 1995 I'd meet up with David Cassidy from the Speedway who, as one of his many duties, handled the schedule on race morning. It reminded me of the scene in Animal House. I had a digital running watch set to the exact second, matching the time in the TV truck in the infield and the master control room in New York City. David had a 1970's Timex with a sweep second hand that was about a minute and 38 seconds fast. But we were a great team – the bright-eyed, eager young pit producer and the old guard from the Speedway that had an office in a bunker under Turn 4.

I worked with David to cue the beginning of the invocation, then a few minutes later "Back Home Again in Indiana" with Jim Nabors. During that song we'd take a golf cart driven by the most senior and trusted Yellow Shirt from the start/finish line to the front of the field. When we arrived, the Yellow Shirts parted the massive crowd of fans and photographers around Mari. Then David and I would kneel directly across from Mari with a slew of TV cameras and still photographers shooting over our shoulder.

Jim Phillippe would intro Mari and David would ask, 'Is ABC Sports good?' I'd pause for a second, knowing that since the start of "Back Home Again in Indiana" ABC never went to commercial so of course we were good. But I'd wait about two or three seconds to build even more anticipation for the most famous words in racing.

I'd then tell David we were 'Good' and he'd signal Mari to give the command. David never figured out my happy little moment when I paused, took a deep breath, enjoyed the moment and then said, 'Good,' knowing it could have happened without my approval and still be televised to millions around the world.

Les Unger *spent 30 years in Toyota Motorsports before retiring in 2014.*

Without a doubt, my most significant Indy 500 memory occurred in 2003. Gil de Ferran and Helio Castroneves captured first and second place for Marlboro/Team Penske – powered by engines designed and built by Toyota Racing Development, in Costa Mesa, Calif.

It was like a dream come true. Thinking back to where we started and the problems and challenges we faced, it was just an incredible journey in terms of designing and developing an engine that would last. You're talking about the biggest race in the world. To win it was unbelievable.

We'd won championships before – in off-road with Cal Wells and IMSA with Dan Gurney, and those were unbelievably exciting. But having to go through what we went through as a company, from being on top of the pinnacle in IMSA, then segueing into Indy and the problems and the challenges Toyota faced, it just made winning the 500 that much more meaningful.

By the early '90s we knew we couldn't continue in IMSA. We had dominated two years in a row and were blowing away the competition. So we looked at open wheel racing because of the Indy 500. We made several trips back to Indianapolis with some high-ranking Toyota Motor Corporation engineering folks to talk about what it would take to get Toyota involved. But about that time the Indy Racing League was established, which threw a big monkey wrench into everything. Because Toyota was CART focused, that blew us out of the water in terms of participating in the Indy 500. So from 1995 to 2002 we were shut out of racing in the 500.

It may have been just as well. Our first three years in CART were an absolute disaster. The engines were the primary problem. As someone said back then, the engines had three shortcomings: horsepower, durability and fuel economy.

It wasn't until TRD in the United States took on more of the engine development responsibilities that Toyota's Indy car fortunes slowly began to change.

In late '99 and early 2000 we had hooked up with Chip Ganassi and Carl Haas and some other CART teams and then we began to rock 'n' roll.

After four or five years of drama, we won the CART manufacturer and driver championships in 2002 with Cristiano da Matta and Newman/Haas Racing. It was then decided TRD could develop an IRL spec engine that would enable us to run at Indianapolis.

So even though we'd won the Indy car championship the year before, watching Helio and Gil battle for the lead was very exciting and everyone was ecstatic when we crossed the finish line one-two. Not only that, Toyotas finished in seven of the top 10 positions. It was the end of a long, long, *long* journey.

I had the good fortune to be present on the Monday following Sunday's race for the live interview with Gil on ABC's *Good Morning America* at the Speedway's start/finish line. As an unexpected bonus, I was included in several team and driver photos that Gil inscribed for me with personalized messages.

***Bill York** was the manager of the IMS media center for 35 years. After graduating from Purdue in 1957, he began working with the Stark & Wetzel Rookie of the Year program. The 100th running of the 500 will be his 60th race.*

The one thing that happened at the Speedway that really stands out in my mind was the pace car incident back in 1971, when Eldon Palmer misjudged stopping the pace car and ran into the photo stand in the South end of the pits.

That day I had gotten a late start. One of my responsibilities was that photo stand and who was on it and who was not supposed to be on it. I got there a little bit late and was still on the steps of the photo stand at the start of the race. All of the sudden, I see something fly up in the air. I later found out that it was one of the Yellow Shirts and Eldon had knocked him, I'm going to guess, eight or nine feet in the air. The next thing I saw was the car coming straight for the photo stand.

At that point, I remembered something that race starter Pat Vidan had once told a group of us. He said, 'Race cars and speeding cars do funny things. Make sure that your last move is your best move.' Well, I saw the car coming straight for the photo stand and as it got closer and closer, I remember jumping – using my legs and hands or something – over the hood of the car as it came in contact with the stand. It crashed into the stand and injured photographers Ray Mann and Dr. Alvarez. They were the two most seriously injured photographers. Both of the gentlemen lived and there were no life-threatening injuries or anything.

I ran over to the pace car – Elmer George and myself were the first two people to the car. I reached down and pulled TV announcer Chris Schenkel out of the car and Elmer George pulled Mr. (Tony) Hulman out. They had all slipped down below the seats and we pulled them up and got them out. Fortunately none of them were hurt. One of the astronauts, I think it was John Glenn, was in the front seat with Mr. Palmer. Those were the four people in the car and Elmer and I both pulled them all out of the pace car. It was quite an ordeal to start the race.

Over the 59 years that I've been at the Speedway there are so many good things that have happened, including being named media center manager and moving to the current media center, which is one of the best in the world. However, the pace car incident certainly stands out as one of the major remembrances of my involvement with the Indianapolis 500.

***Mike Zizzo** is a longtime motorsports PR professional, currently at Texas Motor Speedway.*

I was the CART vice president of competition media relations at the time of the split from the Indy Racing League, so the most significant Indianapolis 500 for me was Juan Pablo Montoya's victory in 2000. It was the first time a CART team had opted to break the picket line and compete in the Indy 500, as Chip Ganassi entered cars for Montoya, the reigning CART champion, and former CART champ Jimmy Vasser.

In the first four years of the split, we held the U.S. 500 at Michigan International Speedway, but I personally missed the prestige and history of our series competing in the Indy 500. So in 2000, we put together a select media dinner at St. Elmo's in Indianapolis during the month of May with Juan Pablo and Jimmy and took advantage of the opportunity by flying key media to our CART race in Nazareth the day prior and back to Indy for the 500 the next day.

CART had touted since the split that we had the best drivers compared to the IRL and this was our chance to prove it in their equipment and rules. I'll never forget the ill-advised idea of starting three-wide like Indy at the inaugural U.S. 500 in 1996. A good portion of the field wrecked on the opening lap, giving the series a black eye, especially as the race tagline was, "The Real Stars, The Real Cars." This was a chance to redeem ourselves in front of the world and Ganassi brought along a pair of extremely talented drivers to give CART a legitimate chance to win over the IRL field.

It was a significant storyline with the media and we took advantage of it whenever possible to make CART part of the Indy 500 discussion. My colleague Steve Shunck and I were present for race weekend and watched a tremendous day unfold for CART loyalists. Montoya dominated, leading 167 laps en route to the victory, while Vasser finished 7th.

I remember being in the back of the media center at IMS with some of our closest media friends, trying to temper our excitement that a CART driver was going to win the Indy 500. It turned out to be a monumental decision by Ganassi, and CART adapted its schedule to allow its teams to compete in the Indy 500 the following year.

Other teams, including Penske and Team Green, followed his lead. It provided true representation of the series in the Indy 500. That year CART's Helio Castroneves won the Indy 500 for Penske as CART teams took the first six spots, including NASCAR's Tony Stewart, running for Ganassi. More importantly, I thought the situation was ideal for long-suffering fans to finally see *all* of the best Indy car drivers in the world competing together again in the world's most prestigious race.

Fans

CHAPTER 7

Fans

BECAUSE THE INDIANAPOLIS MOTOR SPEEDWAY is privately owned, there's never been an official crowd size released for the Indy 500. But in its heyday, police estimates put the number of fans pouring into the Speedway at close to 400,000. Pole Day qualifying easily topped 200,000 and a regular practice session on a sunny spring weekday would attract 25,000 people as children and grownups alike played hooky in order to visit the track. Total attendance during the month might easily top one million visitors, more than all but the most successful baseball teams drew during the course of an entire season.

While attendance at many of the events during May at the Speedway has drastically declined in recent years, race day still draws more than 200,000 fans, making it the largest one-day spectator sporting event in the world.

***Steve Barrick** is from Flemington, N.J. He has attended 33 Indy 500s and counting.*

My parents brought my brother and me to the Indianapolis 500 for the first time in 1964. I still meet my brother there every year, our parents having recently died. Over the years, I have come to the 500 with my best friend from high school, two college roommates, an ex-girlfriend's brother, my wife, son and daughter, an 'unofficially adopted' son and my best friend in racing.

My fondest wish is to be able to take my year-and-a-half-old grandson to the race in a few years.

What first captivated me and what keeps me coming back is being part of a crowd that reveres the race, respects its traditions, and worships its drivers. I know I am not alone when a tear comes to my eye during the singing of "Back Home Again in Indiana" – the "through the fields I used to roam" line always gets me.

The most memorable Indianapolis 500 moments for me have been times of being wholly in sync with the mood of the crowd as history is being made, right in front of our eyes. Here are three that stand out.

The horror, confusion, mourning and resignation of 1964 – The gasp of sadness when Eddie Sachs' death was announced, the quiet sobs from every row of seats, the rustling intrusion of wind-blown paper breaking the silence. Then the race went on, each pass greeted with the murmur of heightened anxiety.

The inhaling, holding of breath and exhaling of awe, twice, of 1991 – A late race pit stop under caution put Rick Mears ahead of a dominant Michael Andretti with fifteen laps left. On the restart, Michael swept around Mears heading into Turn 1 with a bold, risky pass. In a split second, anticipation became fear, became shock, became awe. On the next lap, Mears swept around Michael as they screamed into Turn 1 at full throttle. Magnified anticipation, heightened fear, shock of disbelief. This was mortal combat on wheels.

The roar of roars when Danica Patrick passed Dan Wheldon for the lead late in the 2005 race – Danica had been flirting with destiny all month. On a late restart, through clever Team Rahal strategy, she had her chance. As the green flag fell, she passed Wheldon for the lead. It unleashed a torrent of cheering – a sound wave that rolled along the home-stretch grandstands, building in intensity. That moment shook the Speedway and everyone in it. It was watching history being made. That she didn't win didn't matter. One pass and one deafening roar, of a magnitude unlikely to ever to be duplicated.

Brian Cotterell *is from Fort Wayne, Ind., and has been to 30 Indy 500s.*

I grew up near the Speedway at 30th and Moller and I've been going to the track since I was six. I'm 37 now. Back then the whole town would roll out the red carpet for the month of May. My grandfather was a big fan and he would take the entire family to the race. My grandmother always worried and warned us not to turn our backs on the cars.

My grandfather passed away in 1984, the day after Rick Mears won. Before my mom passed away, her last wish was to be cremated and to have some of her ashes scattered at the Speedway. She got her wish. Now every year I go out to the track and have a beer with mom and tell her how my life has been going. I have the Speedway's "Wheel and Wing" logo tattooed on my back, along with "In Memory of Mom."

I've always been an Andretti fan, which means there's been a lot of heartache at the track. The worst was probably Sam Hornish passing Marco just before the finish line.

In recent years I've done crazy things with my hair for the race in hopes of getting my photo in the program. One year I had checkered flags cut and dyed into my hair. Another time I dyed my hair blue with a red stripe down the middle, like Marco's helmet when he drove the Snapple car.

Many of the traditions are gone now, but the Speedway is still a magical place for me. You go under the tunnel and come out the other side and it's like you're home. There's nothing like watching the 11 rows of three go by in one blur of color. I still get chills. The colors, the smells and the energy from the crowd.

***Mark Endicott** attended 32 Indy 500s races in a row before suffering a stroke in 2002.*

I grew up in the shadow of the Turn 4 grandstand, on the other side of the Coke field. We listened to the race on the radio with my uncles and cousins while we barbequed as TV was still blacked out back then.

A.J. Foyt was my favorite. He always seemed to be at the front or clawing his way to the front. I liked him because he respected the Speedway. I thought Mario Andretti disrespected the Speedway when he went to Formula One and sometimes missed qualifying so he could race in Europe. I always wondered if that wasn't one of the reasons for the Andretti Indy curse. But I came to like and respect Mario in later years.

I worked awhile on the construction crew at the Speedway and took the opportunity to try out all the seats. I thought the best seats were in either the first or third turns. You can see the cars coming out of the turn and all the way down the straight. That's plenty of time to identify them because you can see their colors and paint job. If you're in the second or fourth turn, all you see is the back of the cars.

I sat in the Turn 3's NE Vista for 32 years before I had a stroke and wasn't able to attend anymore. My uncle would buy an entire section of seats and I would buy about 30 from him and sell them to my friends. There were times I could have scalped them for double the face value, but I never did. They were for my friends and real race fans. When they attended they were guaranteed a ticket for the following year if they wanted to go.

I would get goose bumps as big as mountains when they said "Gentlemen Start Your Engines" and I loved the parade lap, when the cars were still cold and came by snorting and stumbling, like thoroughbred race horses getting ready for the start. On the pace lap the cars were accelerating right in front of you and the back of the field was already at speed when they came by.

I was 11 when I went to my first race in 1967. That's the year Foyt beat "Silent Sam" (Parnelli Jones' turbine-powered car). But his victory in '77 was probably my favorite because it was his fourth win. I felt sorry for Gordon Johncock because he dominated the race and probably should have won. Johncock beating Rick Mears in '82 was probably the most exciting. You could see Mears gaining on Gordon every lap on the back straight until he was chomping on Johncock's tailpipes.

Johncock just stuffed it into Turn 3 on the last lap. You could even hear the tires squealing. A great finish.

Randy Groves *is from St. Peter's, Missouri and the 100th running of the Indianapolis 500 will mark the 35th time he has attended the race.*

My story begins in 1978 when my brother's neighbor, a longtime Indy 500 fan, invited us to go to the time trials. I was 27 and living in St. Peter's when we made the drive to Indianapolis for the first time.

Back then the track workers wore pith helmets and there were still really large crowds. It was the first time I heard the Gordon Pipers. I saw all the famous drivers of the time – A.J. Foyt, Mario Andretti, Johnny Rutherford, the Unsers and Janet Guthrie, just to name a few. After only attending the time trials for four years, my friend invited us to go to the race in 1982.

The first time I attended the race, I was amazed at the size of the crowd. I heard the singing of "Back Home Again in Indiana," saw the release of the balloons and the eleven rows of three race cars abreast on the pace laps. That was the year of the famous duel between Gordon Johncock and Rick Mears, where Johncock earned his second 500 victory. I was so impressed with the Indy 500 after attending my first race, I decided to apply for my own nine tickets to ensure I would always be able to see "The Greatest Spectacle in Racing."

In 1983, my first year as a new ticket-holder, I went to the race with a group of family and friends. We sat on the inside of Turn 1, in the bleachers near the creek. I was excited because Al Unser, Jr. was racing against his dad. It was the first time a father and son raced against each other at the Indy 500. Al Unser, Sr. and Tom Sneva were battling it out for the win and Sneva finally prevailed, after coming in second so many times before.

After the race, I happened to be in the right place at the right time. In those days, they opened the track after the race to allow spectators to get to the other side. While crossing the track, Sneva pulled up right in front of me and my family and friends. It was near the entrance to pit road – and Sneva was in the back of the tan Buick Riviera pace car. He was wearing the victory wreath around his neck – and a big smile on his face. As he exited the car and walked by us, I said, 'God bless you Tom,' and he reached out and shook my hand.

***Scott Groves** has been making an annual pilgrimage to the Indy 500 since 1980. He has attended the race 25 times, both as a fan and working for teams and sponsors in the sport.*

My first visit to Indianapolis Motor Speedway was in 1980, when I was six and attended the first weekend of qualifying. I accompanied my father and my Uncle Randy on the four hour drive from our home in St. Louis on the Friday before time trials.

On that first visit I was in awe of the size of the track and such iconic items as the Pagoda and the scoring pylon on the front straightaway. I quickly learned the names of the star drivers – Johnny Rutherford, A.J. Foyt, Mario Andretti and the Unser brothers – Al and Bobby.

I remember sitting behind the pits in the metal grandstand seats and watching the drivers and cars line up to make their qualifying attempts for the race and the coveted pole position. I paid attention to the car colors and their numbers, so I knew who was on the race track and where they were listed on the pylon that signaled the current qualifying order for the race. I studied the official program and learned the past winners of the race and could recite them going back many years.

After that first visit in 1980, I continued to attend qualifying weekend with my family. A favorite memory was sitting in the upper rows of the Paddock Grandstand seats, charting the one- and four-lap average speeds for all of the cars attempting to qualify for the race. The highlight of those Saturdays would be when a driver broke the existing speed record and longtime track PA announcer Tom Carnegie would call out, 'It's a new track record!' and the large crowd gathered that day would cheer and applaud.

In 1985, when I was a little bit older, I attended my first Indianapolis 500. The reason I did not go earlier was because of the revelry and partying that took place outside the track on Georgetown Road the weekend of the race. We always camped outside the track, in the open fields that were directly across from the front straightaway. I quickly realized the sights and sounds of the colorful characters camped out for race weekend were dramatically different from that of the time trials weekend.

But the greatest sights and sounds were reserved for race day. The pre-race festivities and traditions held prior to the start of the Indianapolis 500 became my favorite part of the race. Then there was the first time I witnessed the starting field of 33 cars pass by me from my seat in the SW Vista Grandstand, which only heightened the amazing experience. After each race I attended, I would return back to school wearing the official T-shirt from the race, to celebrate the race-winner and show everyone that I attended the race.

I have attended 25 of the 99 Indianapolis 500s that have taken place to date. The first races I attended were as a fan, sitting in the grandstands, watching the best drivers in the world compete on the most famous race track in the world. Later in life, I was able to work in the motorsports industry, including jobs for teams and sponsors participating in the 500. My career in the motorsports industry can be directly traced back to those first visits to the Speedway when I was just a kid from St. Louis. It's then that I first fell in love with the "The Greatest Spectacle in Racing" and became a fan of the Indianapolis 500.

Wayne Kepner *lives in Greentown, Indiana.*

I was living in the Indiana Children's Christian Home in Ladoga in 1973. At age 13 I was already a racing nut because my Uncle Ray raced sprint cars at Warsaw and Kokomo.

I wasn't doing my school work, just enough to scrape by. My house parents, as a last resort, contacted Mel Kenyon, after hearing that he was not only a professional race car driver, but also a Christian. Mel agreed to become my pen pal and he and his late wife, Marieanne, began writing to me.

Mel took the time to explain to me that I needed my English so that I would be able to talk to people and sponsors. He explained that I needed spelling so that I would be able to write letters. He also explained that I needed math, my worst subject, in order to figure out gear ratios, cam lift and duration, tire stagger and many other things that go into building and setting up a race car. It worked a bit and my grades improved somewhat.

I first met Mel in 1974. I was in the Soap Box Derby in Fort Wayne that year and one of the perks was a free trip to the Speedway for qualifying. As soon as that bus stopped, I was off like a shot to the garage area.

I found Mel's garage and stood outside the fence, waiting for the doors to open. When they did, I got the attention of someone in the garage and Mel had that person bring me a Hero Card. I handed that person a newsletter from the children's home I lived in and asked him to give it to Mel and to show him my picture. The man said, 'I don't have time to get you an autograph, kid.' I told him I didn't want one, I just wanted Mel to see the newsletter because he would know who I was.

The man took the newsletter to Mel and pointed out my picture. Mel turned and looked at me, held up one finger as if to say, 'one minute' and finished talking to a mechanic. Then he walked out to the chain link fence that surrounded the garage area and talked with me for about fifteen minutes. He was trying his best to devote his attention to me, but his presence at the fence was drawing a crowd. He finally told me that he had to get back to work before there were too many people at the fence and he couldn't get away. I understood completely.

Mel walked back to his garage and I just stood and watched them work on the car, still in awe that I had met my racing hero. Now, 41 years later, Mel and I are still friends. I visit as often as I can and even though Mel is retired, he and his brother Don still go to the race track each weekend with their own series, the USSA Mel Kenyon Midget Series, a kind of starter series for young drivers. He may not be driving, but he is still influencing racing through his knowledge and love of the sport.

***Serge Krauss** is originally from Elkhart, Ind., and now lives in Cleveland Heights, Ohio. He first attended in the Indy 500 in 1947.*

Since my first 500 at age two years and a day on May 30, 1947, I've acquired myriad track memories, the most powerful coming from my first 20 years, when it was truly "The Greatest Spectacle in Racing."

Some of the more vivid memories concern on-track triumphs, disappointments, and tragedies. Like Duke Nalon's smoldering Novi in 1949, newspaper "Extras" announcing the Bill Vukovich tragedy of 1955, wins by my boyhood heroes Jimmy Bryan and Rodger Ward, the 1960 Ward-Rathmann duel, Eddie Sachs' 1961 loss to A.J. Foyt and 1964's bomb-like sounds followed by silence, billowing black smoke and Sid Collins' eloquent eulogy.

Deeper memories concern the aura and excitement of race day. Driving down from Elkhart, we passed fascinating layered rocks and derelict airplanes outside Wabash and many "Indianapolis 500 or Bust" signs taped in car windows, especially in heavier race traffic along the last 50 miles.

After our early morning wait on 16th Street, we parked in the infield, spread our picnic blanket, and had fried chicken, potato salad, New Era potato chips and pop, as the Goodyear blimp and a beehive of aircraft trailing signs circled overhead. Tall, home-built scaffolds and license plates from every state abounded.

With its grassy, hay-like smells, the Speedway was a world unto itself in which this kid reveled. At first mom and dad took me to vantage points, and sometimes my attractive mom got us into the privileged parking places up by the first fence on the north end. Soon I romped around looking at sights and finding my own varied places along the fences. Later, I ran across the infield from my *own* car, hurdling low wire "fences" in the early morning, to buy one of the last south-end bleacher seats at the office/museum off the SW turn. For years after that, they were already sold out by race day.

The spectacle of the race is what I love most. My earliest memories are of the beautiful, multi-colored cars with wire wheels, transparent in their rotation. I learned later that the metallic blue ones were the Blue Crowns of Mauri Rose and Bill Holland, and the red flames identified J.C. Agajanian's cars. I especially remember the drivers' arms working their steering wheels, wind rippling their sleeves.

I came to love the multi-colored balloon release, the color and crackling of engines on the pace lap in rising tension and excitement, leading to the roaring start, cars diving into the first turn and exiting onto the short chute. Late in the race I was fascinated by the soot on the tails of those beautiful uprights and roadsters. The greatest sounds were the Novis and I'll always remember that sound, with its supercharger's whine, echoing off the back stretch and the grove of trees, as Jim Hurtubise charged toward the lead for the last time in 1963. No one ever forgot the Novis.

The race was my greatest birthday present, and the ride home was already my time to think of next year.

***Greg McConnell** is originally from Scipio, Ind., and now lives in Fountain Hills, Ariz. He will attend his 56th consecutive Indy 500 in 2016.*

My love for the Indianapolis 500 and Indy car racing started at an early age and was completely home grown. My great uncle, C. B. McConnell, was the president of the Hamilton Harris Cigar Company in Indianapolis and that company sponsored cars in the Indy 500 from 1935 to 1939, with a best finish of second in 1937 with Ralph Hepburn driving. His son, Robert McConnell, was the 500 Festival president in 1966.

In addition to the family connection, my hometown of North Vernon, Ind. was home to racing legend Pat O'Connor, who was killed in the first lap crash in the 1958 race. O'Connor and three-time 500 winner Wilbur Shaw are buried in our county's cemetery in Vernon.

My great uncle sent our family 10 tickets to the race every year until his death. Our seats were in Grandstand A, across from the entrance to Gasoline Alley. Every year it was kind of a lottery to see who would get to go that year. I finally won the lottery, at age six in 1961, and haven't missed a race since.

Even before getting to the Speedway on race day in 1961 I had already been told who my favorite driver would be – A.J. Foyt, Jr. I learned that an older couple sitting next to us was from Houston and were friends with A.J., Sr. and the Foyt family. It was a no brainer that I would be a member of the A.J. fan club that day and I have remained an A.J. fan ever since. I remember thinking that I was the lucky charm that A.J. needed to win his first 500 that day. My most vivid memory of the race was watching as Jack Turner flipped end over end on the straightaway, coming to a rest within view of our seats.

I've been so lucky to have seen most of the greatest drivers in Indy 500 history in my 55 years including Foyt, Parnelli, Ward, Sachs, Hurtubise, Gurney, Clark, the Unsers, Mears, the Andrettis, Rutherford, Johncock, Luyendyk, Castroneves, Wheldon, Franchitti, Dixon, Kanaan, Montoya and so many more.

The race has meant so much to our family over the years and our family has been represented at every 500 since before 1935. I've been fortunate to have been to the race with my grandparents, parents, aunts, uncles, cousins, sisters, wife, sons, nephews, nieces and many, many friends. I am now in charge of our Tower Terrace tickets and am proud to say we have a record number of 38 for this year's historic race.

I can't wait until the command to start engines for the 100th running of the Indianapolis 500 and once again enjoy it with family and friends. Sometimes people ask what it would take for me to miss the Indianapolis 500 and I tell them a death in the family – mine.

***Steve Noffke** is a longtime Indy 500 fan and builder of a Ronnie Duman 1964 Indy tribute Watson Roadster.*

Watching Gordon Johncock and Rick Mears duel in 1982 was the most thrilling thing I have ever seen in sports – 250,000 people cheering and screaming so loud you could hardly hear the cars. And Tom Carnegie's booming voice calling it, 'Will he?... Will he?... *No*! Johncock wins it.'

But my personal story dates to the 1980s when I had garage and pit passes and liked to go on the fourth day of qualifying or Bump Day. It was a nice Sunday afternoon in

1988 as I walked to the north end of the pits to see what teams were trying to put a car in the field and follow them for an hour or two.

In the early afternoon, I walked to the far north end of the pits and there was a white car with no lettering or sponsorship, obviously a back-up car. They were trying to fit a driver into the cockpit and he was struggling to get comfortable. There were five of us total, with me as the only one behind the pit wall. I soon realized three of them were Bill Vukovich, Jr., his son Billy Vukovich III, and the struggling driver was Gary Bettenhausen. This should be interesting, I thought.

Gary was struggling to get the belts fastened, hampered by his paralyzed left arm, the result of a dirt car crash in the 1970s.

Billy Vukovich III, who was considerably shorter than his father, was safely qualified and rather cockily strutting around, twirling a stop watch around his hand and offering Gary "advice" on how to qualify. Suddenly the long arm of Bill, Jr. came out, grabbed his son by the collar, pulled him to the pit wall and sat him down.

'He knows how to do it and when to do it and he doesn't need any advice from you,' Bill, Jr. said sternly. From that point on BV3 sat on the pit wall with a stunned look on his face. I felt uncomfortable and thought they wanted to be alone, so I left. As I looked back after a time, BV3 was still sitting on the pit wall not moving.

Gary didn't make the race, while BV3 went on to be the 1988 Indy Rookie of the Year. I don't know if any of the "advice" helped.

***Gregg Stevenson** is from Avon, Ind.*

I was a member of a group they called the Alley Cats. Every day we would hang out along the fence and talk to the drivers and crews as they moved from Gasoline Alley out to pit road and back. We would get liquored up drinking capful shots of Jim Beam. By day's end we were pretty toasted, mostly in a good way. But we could be abrasive to a few we didn't like, including Tony Stewart and Paul Tracy.

Most of the people were very good to us. Tony and Mari Hulman took a liking to us, which helped with the Yellow Shirts. One year the Bell Helmets guys made up honorary Alley Cats hats and presented our group with them. Someone got a hat to A.J. Foyt and he stood in the middle of the group for a picture.

We were all wearing our hats backwards except A.J. and we finally got him to turn his hat around for a photo. A.J. was very strict with his crew about wearing their uniforms and hats correctly, including not wearing their hats backwards and the crew bugged him when he went back to the garage. A crewman later told me Foyt said, 'You go around the corner and talk with them sons of bitches and see how you'd act.' The crewman said it really loosened Foyt up. Of course that was the year Kenny Brack won for them.

In '96 Ron Hemelgarn and his driver, Buddy Lazier, would always stop and talk. When we made up some Alley Cats stickers, they put one on Buddy's car. Of course it won the race. Years later I saw the car at the Indianapolis airport and it still had the sticker on the nose.

On the day before the race we would rent a spot in one of the yards close to the track, waiting for the "Back 40" to open, the parking lot off 30th Street. We always had a junker vehicle because it was going to get banged up. When the lot finally opened, it was mass pandemonium. We called it qualifying. Everyone trying to get as close to the front as possible. And that was just to get in the parking lot.

When the bomb went off to open the track, not even the Yellow Shirts would get in the way. You had five lanes that narrowed down to three for the tunnel under the track. The wreckers would lead us in like pace cars with lights flashing. Cars were bumping and crashing into each other. Once inside the track, everyone raced for their favorite spot.

In 1977, after Foyt took the checkered flag to win his fourth 500, my brother and I snuck through a hole in the fence and ran onto the track. There were still cars going by at speed. Just a couple of young, drunk and stupid guys. Later Foyt and Tony Hulman came by in the pace car, the only time Hulman did that, and Foyt slapped hands with my brother. Hulman would die later that year.

We're older now. I'm 57, but we still go the race. Only now our kids go in the night before and save our spot.

***Art Tidesco** is from London, England.*

I was living in London when I received an invitation from two Canadian friends to attend their wedding on May 27, 1988 in Toronto, their hometown.

The first thing I did was to check for races in the U.S. around the wedding date. The NASCAR race was to be run at Charlotte on May 29, as was the Indy 500. Indianapolis seemed a lot closer to Toronto than Charlotte, so I decided to visit Indy. It's something I had wanted to do since reading a book by Tommaso Tommasi called *From Brands Hatch to Indianapolis,* in which a precise description of driving the track is given by Peter Revson.

Early on the morning after the wedding I headed towards the U.S. border in Detroit and then Indianapolis. The only difficulty I had was keeping to the 55 to 60 mph speed limits which seemed excruciatingly slow compared to the 70 mph I was used to in the UK.

Eleven hours after I set out I arrived at the Lafayette Shopping Center parking lot, having picked up a ticket for the bleachers from a vendor at face value of $15. I felt very much at home as some lads were having a kick about with a proper round football. Turned out they were telephone engineers from Manchester, England.

I spent the night in the car. The weather was more than warm enough to feel comfortable sleeping on the back seat wearing a t-shirt and shorts.

On race day I woke up with the dawn, had a round of salami sandwiches I packed in advance and my customary breakfast apple, then headed off to the track. Before I knew it I was standing on the hallowed pavement of the Indianapolis pit lane. I was as inspired by the Indy timing tower as I had been by any tourist sight I had ever seen including Big Ben, the Eiffel Tower, even the Pyramids. Shortly thereafter I was pinching myself, standing before the gates of Gasoline Alley. I felt a little like I was standing before the gates of heaven itself as the sun came up.

I took a walk around the infield while the hullabaloo that starts the day's proceedings got underway, including a look at the infamous and hard partying Snake Pit. I saw "Supersonic" Chuck Yeager prepare himself for duties in the pace car and took my seat in the bleachers.

The race was dominated by Rick Mears on pole with front row mates Danny Sullivan and Al Unser, Sr. All three were driving Penske PC 17s designed by new boy Nigel Bennett and would be three of the only four drivers to lead a lap.

For eight laps I was beside myself with excitement as Scottish born Brit Jim Crawford became the only non-Penske team member to lead the race. Jim, who just two months earlier had been unable to walk as a result of injuries received at Indy in 1987, became a father the following week.

Two weeks later I was back at one of my other favorite tracks for the 24 Hours of Le Mans, but that's a story for another day.

***Dan Zukowski** resides in Portland, Maine and formerly worked in the automotive business.*

A.J. Foyt. Andy Granatelli. Dan Gurney. Mario Andretti. Those were the names I learned in the late 1960s as a young boy interested in cars and racing. Growing up in the

Bronx, my family didn't even own a car. I learned to ride the subway before I learned to ride a bike. It was the *Popular Science* and *Popular Mechanics* magazines that my father subscribed to that got me hooked on automobiles.

There wasn't much in the way of motorsports on TV back then. The Indy 500 would be shown in a highly edited version on ABC's "Wide World of Sports," as was the Daytona 500. I remember having lots of model cars that would vroom around the living room floor while the races were on the black-and-white television.

I got my first car in 1973 and by the late 1970s I was working in the auto industry as a sales representative at a BMW/Alfa Romeo dealership in New York. That gave me inroads to IMSA sports car racing and Formula One, as Alfa fielded a F1 team beginning in 1979. That led to an invitation to the Watkins Glen Grand Prix and dinner with Bruno Giacomelli and Patrick Depailler the night before the race. Patrick would die the following year in testing at Hockenheim. Bruno went to sports car racing and limited appearances in CART from 1984 to 1985. He tried and failed to qualify for the 1984 Indy 500.

As BMW was fielding the M1 in IMSA, and Lime Rock was just a couple of hours north of New York City, I began making the annual Memorial Day weekend trek to Connecticut. By that time, ABC was showing the same-day tape delayed version of the Indy 500 in prime time. My weekend would start with Saturday practice and qualifying at Lime Rock. Sunday was a quiet day at Lime Rock due to the local noise restrictions, but the World 600 from Charlotte was on cable and the Indy 500 was on ABC and both were shown in the hotel bar. The IMSA race ran on Memorial Day and after that I'd drive home.

I followed the tradition through most of the 1980s, by which time I was working as an automotive journalist and I often recruited my young cousin to join me so that I could corrupt his morals and turn him into a car guy as well. I succeeded. In 1989 I left for California and a PR job in the industry. That career took me to many areas of racing, from Indy car to NASCAR, along with AMA Supercross and Superbike, Baja off-road, Trans-Am, Pro Rally, and probably a few others I've forgotten.

But it was those early days in front of the black-and-white console television in my parents' living room, watching the Indy 500, that fired up my love of the sport.

Sam Hornish, Jr. and Family

CHAPTER 8

Family

Family is a recurring theme throughout the Indy 500 memories of many. Fans remembered traditions passed down from generation to generation including Memorial Day picnics and trips to the race, eating at the same restaurants and staying at the same motels every year. Wives talked of being relegated to the grandstands while competitors recalled the sacrifices made by parents so they could pursue their dream of someday competing in "The Greatest Spectacle in Racing."

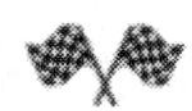

Sam Hornish, Jr. *grew up in Ohio and won the 2006 Indy 500 driving for Roger Penske. He won the IndyCar championship that year, a title he also won in 2001 and 2002 driving for Panther Racing.*

For me, my best memory of the Indianapolis 500 is the 2006 race. Being able to win the way that we did, on a last lap pass. I feel like if I'd been leading that race for the last four or five laps – instead of chasing the leader – I probably would have been so shaken up by the time that I got to Victory Lane I wouldn't have been able to talk.

What makes that day so special for me is what it means to me and my family. I had been married for about two years, but it really goes back to my dad, who had been attending the Indianapolis 500 for some time.

He was allowed to start going to the race when he was 10. They would drive down to the Speedway in my grandfather's Studebaker pickup truck. They would wait for the bomb to go off and then drive into the infield and set up their scaffolding to watch the race. That was one of his favorite things to do each year – have that special trip to the Indianapolis 500 with his dad.

As time goes by, my mom and dad met and one of their first dates was at an Indy car race at the Milwaukee Mile. It really led to them having a relationship where one of their favorite pastimes was motorsports. Not necessarily taking part in it, but more as a family thing. My mom was eight months pregnant with me at her first Indianapolis 500 in 1979 when Rick Mears won.

I was a young kid the first time I remember going to Indy and having that experience. My parents owned a business. There was a lot going on and a lot of working late nights. To be able to have that little trip to Indianapolis with them, where we got to go and do something fun that didn't really have anything to do with work, was quite welcome. It was enjoyable sitting in Turn 1, getting to eat some cold fried chicken and watching the race. I probably got to see as many races from the grandstands as I did from the race car.

To have the opportunity to start racing and to go to Indianapolis and qualify for the 500 – that was my only goal. We never would have had that lofty of a goal until I started winning races and championships in karting. Then it seemed like maybe something could happen with this racing thing, and wouldn't it be awesome to qualify for the Indianapolis 500. I remember the day after qualifying for my first 500 thinking, 'Man, I'm 20 years old and I've achieved my lifelong dream. What's next?' I felt really proud just qualifying for the race.

To win the Indianapolis 500 and to ride around the track with the winner's wreath on – with my wife and parents – that meant so much. It probably meant as much to me to have them there as anything else. So many things had to happen just to be able to get to that point, and then to share it with them was special. Just thinking about what they sacrificed, whether it was time or money, or time with each other, or time with my brother or my sisters. It gets me emotional thinking about.

John Andretti *made 12 Indy 500 starts between 1988 and 2011 driving for teams fielded by A.J. Foyt, Jr., Vince Granatelli, Jim Hall and Richard Petty. He is the son of Aldo Andretti and nephew of Mario Andretti.*

One of my most memorable moments in motorsports was my rookie year in 1988 when I qualified for the 500.

We had some issues with the race car and I was on my third qualifying attempt. It was my last attempt because the car had broken, believe it or not, in both previous qualifying attempts. We were plenty quick enough; we just didn't get to complete the runs.

In my last run, I really wanted to be the quickest on the day. We were now into the second weekend of qualifying and I knew that we could be the quickest for that day. But the car picked up a push when we went out and it slowed us down a little bit from where we had practiced. We weren't the quickest.

Back then, you had to fight your way into the race and I was really frustrated. It was really upsetting because I didn't run as fast as we should have. I wasn't thinking about the big picture or how difficult it is to make the race – and I had just made my first 500. Everything was about the fact that we just didn't run as fast as I thought we should have, even though we were easily in the race.

As I came down pit road – they stop you and take your photo with the race car. Which is cool, because where else does that happen? And when I stopped for the photo, my father was the first one there. For my dad, as good as racing is to some, racing didn't always shine on him. But, he was right there and he was smiling. He was happy and here I was upset because we weren't as fast as I hoped. At that point, I just realized that I got to do something he never got to do.

There's a photo of us shaking hands. At that point in time, everything sort of fell into place. The realization set in that I had just done something special and something that he should have gotten the opportunity to do. Yet, I got to do it. Not that he was trying to live through me, but in a way I felt like I got to do it for both of us.

That is what's special about the Indianapolis 500. It really wouldn't be that special anywhere else but Indy. It's one of the things I talk about the most, because it's one of the things that meant the most to me.

If you look at the photo you just see – everybody who knows my dad thinks of him smiling – and of course he's got this big grin on his face. I'm kind of looking at him and you could see I'm smiling in the photo and all the way there I wasn't. We never said a word. I guess it didn't take words. He didn't say congratulations, he didn't say anything, he just smiled and looked at me and shook my hand.

Jeffrey Boles *started working for the Speedway and USAC in the mid-1950s and is an observer on the flag stand during the Indy 500. He served as a Circuit Court Judge in Indiana for 36 years. His son is Speedway president Doug Boles.*

Our whole family has grown up with the Indy 500. It gets in your blood and won't let go. From my mom and dad, to my wife Sue and I, our kids and grandkids, it's a generational thing.

The rule in our family was you had to be 10 years old before you could go to the race. My wife Sue and I talked about it and decided all the fighting and drinking and raising hell that went on along 16th St. wasn't for a seven- or eight-year-old. Now people look at Sue and I when they hear about the rule and think we were crazy.

My dad took me to my first race in '46. I was four. I just remember being in an old wooden grandstand and it was *loud.* Looking back, it was a big deal because it was the first race after the war.

My first job at the Speedway was in '55, sweeping the track. We'd ride our bikes every day from the school to the track. My dad worked at Allison and they were all racing nuts in that company. My mom was one of Mr. Thomas Binford's secretaries at D-A Lubricant. He helped get me a job at USAC in 1959 or '60. I would get the race results from around the country and write them down on cards. Then I went off to college and law school in the mid-1960s.

The very best memory was in 1977. We had gone to all the Hoosier 100s and my oldest son Doug was a huge A.J. Foyt fan. He had turned 10 and that was his first Indy 500. We had some great tickets a friend had given us. A.J. won and he rode around the track in the pace car with Tony Hulman. It just made the day for all of us.

A.J. was always a winner. When I was keeping the statistics for USAC, the points and everything, that's when he was running the sprints and midgets and big cars. I would collect the stats from tracks around the country and we would publish them in our USAC newsletter a week or so later.

If I made a mistake, the first I would know of it was when I would get a phone call from A.J. He'd say, 'You're the boy that's keeping the statistics, right? Well you got me down for 220 points in sprint cars and I've got 227.' I'd go back and figure the numbers again and he was always right. He always knew exactly where he was in the points and the standings.

Most of all he was – and is – a very, very gracious, giving kind of person. He's a winner. He was our hero and still is.

The Indy 500 is all about winners and losers. It's the colors, the excitement, the music and the traditions. You've got 33 people that are coming down to the starting line and they're gonna take their car and just wring its neck. How many people in the whole world can do that?

You're seeing great competition, there's nothing more to it than that. It's not filtered by any political deal, not filtered by any media deal. It's just here they are and it's happening right in front of you.

***Joie Chitwood** is president of the Daytona International Speedway. Previously he served as president and chief operating officer of the Indianapolis Motor Speedway. His grandfather, George "Joie" Chitwood, raced in the Indy 500 seven times from 1940 to 1950, and later founded the "Joie Chitwood Thrill Show."*

One of my earliest memories is going to the Speedway with my dad and grandfather when I was 15 or 16 – a sophomore in high school. I believe it was my first time at the Speedway and the first time I really got introduced to the things that are special about it. That year my grandfather was being honored along with all the other living members from the 1946 Indy 500.

When I think back to that visit, I remember sitting in the Old Timer's Club, which was underneath the old Tower Terrace Grandstands before they tore them out for the new Gasoline Alley suites. It was a Saturday afternoon and I was sitting there with my grandfather and Duke Nalon, Emil Andres and Cowboy O'Rourke. I just remember the camaraderie and the needling that would go back and forth. Whether it was the lifelong friendships, or what they achieved together in terms of racing in the 500 – there was this credibility among them for what they had accomplished. Seeing them interact and listening to what they would say to each other just showed me that the Speedway was a special place. To see my grandfather interact with those other legends of the sport was pretty special for me.

Race morning I recall taking a lap around the track with my grandfather in the Oldsmobile pace car. People were yelling at him, 'Hey Chitwood, put it up on two wheels.' For me, my grandfather was a stuntman. That's what I knew about him. Going to Indianapolis and realizing it was something different – that was new. I was like, 'Wait a second. He raced here in 1946 and these are the guys he raced against.' It opened my eyes a little bit about my grandfather and what he did. It was me being initiated into that special Indianapolis tradition. It was pretty cool realizing that my grandfather was more than a stuntman – he was a race car driver first, this was his world and his standing in that world was pretty significant.

Years later, in the early 2000s during the pre-race ceremonies, they were going to run the winning cars from different decades from the Speedway's history. Well, my grandfather drove the Noc Out Hose Clamp Special in the 1946 500 and finished fifth. That car won the 500 in 1941, but it was his race car in '46. So when the Speedway asked if I wanted to drive my grandfather's car around the track in the pre-race ceremonies I absolutely, unequivocally, said yes.

What was really cool about that day is while I'm driving his car around the track, I had Tom Sneva driving next to me and Vince Granatelli behind me in a turbine. Words can't describe that opportunity. To think I got the chance to drive my grandfather's race car around Indy 50 or 60 years after he drove it in the race – I don't know if anything could ever surpass that unique experience. I felt a special personal connection with my grandfather. It was truly surreal.

I count myself very, very lucky to have a chance to do something like that. It's like hitting the lottery. It was unbelievable.

Peppy Dallenbach *married Wally Dallenbach in 1960. Their first date was on Halloween and he picked her up driving a hearse, which doubled as the tow vehicle for his race car.*

We had three young children when Wally first started racing in Indianapolis. We were young and tried to do everything we could together. I went to most of the races, but of course I didn't go to all of them. Some of them were great. Some of them were not so good.

Women were not allowed in the pits at Indy then, so we had to sit in the stands. It wasn't easy because when something did happen, we were stuck. Nobody came up and said, 'This is what happened' or 'Wally is fine' – nothing. So that always bothered me.

I was very, very nervous at every race. I never took my eyes off of his car. And yet, when my children started racing, I couldn't watch them. It was completely different. But I always respected what they wanted to do and just went from there.

Prayer had a lot to with it. Believe me, I prayed a lot.

I supported him as much as I could. We've been married 55 years now, so it works. A lot of the younger drivers' wives would come over to me and ask, 'Why do you let him do this?' or 'Why do you let him do that?' You know, blah, blah, blah. I felt differently. I felt that was Wally's dream and always felt that he should follow his dream.

We had wonderful years in racing and we had some not so wonderful years. But all in all, I have to say that racing was good to us. One of the things Wally did as chief steward was start a church service for the drivers. That was a big plus in the eyes of the drivers and their wives and something I'm very proud of.

Evi Gurney *is the wife of Dan Gurney. They met while he was racing in Europe and she was working at Porsche.*

It was 1970, my second time at the race. Dan and I were staying at the Holiday Inn in Speedway and leading a decidedly unglamorous life. We got up at 7 a.m. and had breakfast in our room with a view of the fenced swimming pool without water, state regulations not allowing it to be filled until later in the month. Soon Dan jumps on his motorcycle and rides off to Gasoline Alley to join his team in the All American Racers garage.

He usually works there all day. On rare occasions we meet for lunch in one of the fast food places along 16th Street. He comes back for dinner and afterwards often heads back to the track until late at night. I spend my days reading up on the history of the race and the city. I make occasional excursions to downtown Indy in my rental car which is a mixed pleasure, as I often get lost on my way back.

On many days I go to the track and sit in the "rattlesnake" grandstand reserved for wives, ex-wives, girlfriends, parents, relatives, observers, spies and sponsor reps. It is located behind the pits on the right side coming out of Gasoline Alley. From there one has a very good view of the cars being pushed out from the garages to the track, an action which is accompanied by a booming voice emanating from the loudspeakers and occasional applause from the spectators, especially when the name (Jim) Hurtubise is announced. I don't know why.

Dan and I have only been married a year and I don't know many of the women I am surrounded by, but a certain camaraderie bonds us together. I get to know Betty Rutherford, Judy Jones, Wanda Unser, Mom Unser, Alice Mosley, Linda Vaughn, Pat Donohue, Sandy Grant, Peppy Dallenbach, Dee Ann Andretti, Dolly Granatelli, and many others during the long hours spent together.

All of us are nervous when our man is in the car circling the track and we exhale a bit when he appears out of Turn 4 racing down the straightaway and soon passing in front of us. After every lap our eyes go to the white letters on the black scoring pylon displaying his lap time. How did he do? Did his time improve? How much? Is he a contender for the pole? Will he make the first weekend of qualifying? Will he make the race? Opinions vary and the gossip never stops.

Around lunchtime the grandstands empty. We are now trying to make contact with our husbands and also look for a bite to eat somewhere. Both these things pose major difficulties as ladies are not allowed in Gasoline Alley and cell phones are not even imagined yet.

So we wait outside the fence surrounding the compound, shouting hellos at our men while they pass by to go eat lunch at the only restaurant on the premises. No women allowed. Everybody around me accepts this situation as normal. But I'm fresh from

Europe and wonder, 'How did this happen? Some months ago I was on a yacht in Monaco and now I am a fence-hanger in Indianapolis. A fence-hanger married to a major racing star.' Half an hour later, Dan comes out of the restaurant and hands me a hamburger in a brown bag and says, 'Sorry, no time.'

One evening after dinner downtown, he needs to go back to the track to check on a modification of the Eagle's suspension. He is too tired to drop me off at the hotel and suggests I make myself into a pretzel, put an old driving suit over my body and hide in the backseat of our Mustang. I can hardly suppress a giggle when we are stopped by the guard at the entrance to Gasoline Alley. It feels like Checkpoint Charlie in Berlin. I hear him say, 'Hello Mr. Gurney, late night?' and waves us in. Under the cloak of darkness I unwrap myself and for the first time in my life, my feet touch the sacred ground of Gasoline Alley. After an hour we go out the way we came in, proud of ourselves.

A year later, in 1971, two women journalists who were denied access to Gasoline Alley, went to court and won! The Speedway changed its rules. The smuggling of women was over. Lunch was now served for all!

Oh, how I miss the good old days.

***Dan Hoff** is a former track announcer and regularly travels from his home in Hawaii to attend the Indy 500.*

When I was about 5 years old in the mid-1950s, we lived in Grants Pass, Oregon. Bob Christie, who had just begun a string of 500 starts, lived around the corner from us. Thus began my love of the 500.

In August of 1992, my family and I visited the Speedway for the first time. Having lived my entire life on the West Coast, it was my dream to see Indy, even though it was in late summer when no cars were running.

While staying in the fabled Speedway Motel, we were fortunate to see Al Unser, Sr. and A.J. Foyt on the premises. They were apparently in town on business. The track was being modified for the eventual arrival of stock cars. Workers and machines toiled away on the retaining walls. My family and I decided it would be fun to walk out on the track through a construction opening just past the Turn 2 suites. A worker immediately waved us off.

Later, after dark, my younger son and I decided to try to sneak out on the track through the same opening. We succeeded and eventually walked around the entire track, stopping to climb up on the flag stand in the darkness. Only a couple of feeble security lights were on throughout the entire facility. No one around. Virtual silence.

To this day, Darren and I claim to be the only father/son team to have been at the track when there was absolutely no one else there. The story is true, although the claim may be disputed!

***Art Knepper** is the son of race car driver Arnie Knepper.*

Qualifying in 1968 was plagued by rain, and it was well after 6 p.m. on Monday (yes Monday) when my dad, Arnie Knepper, finally qualified Rolla Vollstedt's car. It was an evil handling car, but he put it in the race in the 32nd spot. There was hardly a soul in the place at the time, except officials and crew members. When they interviewed dad after his run he said, 'I'm tired, I'm hungry and I'm broke, and I have to go to the bathroom.'

***Troy Lephart** is from Columbus, Ohio.*

It all began in 1915 when a Maxwell auto dealer in Greenville, Ohio decided to run the Midwest dirt tracks. That man was James Lephart, my great grandfather. Thus began a tradition that has survived the generations as our family made the annual pilgrimage to the Speedway as my grandfather and father carried on the tradition.

I was named after Troy Ruttman. My first appearance was as a toddler in 1962 and my first vague memories were from 1964. We were seated in the backstretch bleachers with a family from Chicago. Our families had sat together for years, since before I was born. The father thought I was a cute little boy and bought me one of the souvenir toy roadsters. Then one year the father wasn't there. He had passed.

As I entered my teens I realized how much the race meant to my father and I. We continued our yearly trek, even though, as a typical teenager, I couldn't stand him and he felt likewise. But every year until his death we came together as one during the month of May. In 1988 I met a girl three days before the 500. The 500 was our first real date. First time at Indy without dad. I'm sure he was hurt, but I married the girl and we are still together, 27 years later.

Vivid race memories include 1973, with Dick Simon pushing a stray tire back to the pits after the first lap accident. I had found another hero. In 1975 I'll never forget

Tom Sneva sailing through the air in Turn 2 and later the chaos when the skies suddenly opened up and flooded the track.

The most memorable year was 1977. Being a fan of A.J. Foyt, I was dejected as Gordon Johncock looked unbeatable. With just laps to go I was snapping photos with a cheap Instamatic camera when Johncock's Wildcat let loose with a huge plume of smoke. Of course A.J. captured number four and I snapped a photo as he approached the bricks and another as he entered the pits to waves from crews.

Now each year on race day I arrive at the cemetery at 6 a.m., to have a talk with my dad. I play a recording of "Back Home Again in Indiana." Funny how dad and I both would tear up at that song, but pretended not to notice.

Then it's off to the race.

I commute now between home in Columbus, Ohio and work in Chicago and as I drive through Indianapolis, joy and sadness mix as I remember dad and the gift he gave.

***Tom Malloy** is a businessman, race car collector and vintage racer who lives in Villa Park, Calif.*

I grew up with racing. My dad was Emmett J. Malloy, who built the Carrell Speedway dirt track in Gardena, Calif. Later he ran the famous Malloy Black Deuce sprint car for drivers including Troy Ruttman and Bill Vukovich.

In 1953 my dad decided to enter a car at Indianapolis, but it failed to qualify. The next year Jimmy Reece was the first to go on the track in qualifying, which was a big deal back then. He qualified seventh and I've never seen my dad happier than in those photos of him with the team. It was the pinnacle of racing to have a car in the Indianapolis 500.

I made my first trip to the Speedway the week before the race. Back then Gasoline Alley was a sanctuary for men only. No women and no one under 21 allowed. But Rocky Phillips, the crew chief, pushed one of those Bear Alignment pith helmets down on my head. We drove up to the garage in the car hauler like we owned the place and they waved us in. This 15-year-old, zit-faced kid, was in.

I had to stay in the garage, but I helped get things ready for the race. That went on for about three days before they stopped us at the gate and made me get out. I spent the day walking around the track. I couldn't believe how flat the track was. My dad's track was dirt, but it had more banking than the Speedway.

Being at the Speedway was magical. It was a special place. You see pictures of places like the Eiffel Tower and wonder if you'll ever get there. I wondered if I would ever see the Speedway and now here I was. My seat was across from the start/finish line and I was so proud to see dad on pit road, talking with Tony Hulman and Wilbur Shaw. Somehow I expected we would win. But the car was slowed by overheating problems and finished 17th. Reece qualified again in '55, but he blew an engine and finished last. After that dad sold the car.

I helped sponsor Rocky Moran when he ran one of A.J. Foyt's cars in 1988. Foyt had so many cars in the race we started it with only three air guns for pit stops. But at one point near the end Rocky was the top running rookie and the media began gathering around our pits. Then he came down the front straight smoking and the media disappeared. Fame is fleeting at Indy. We were totally elated one minute and absolutely crushed the next.

I've been fortunate to acquire several Indy cars over the years, including Rocky's car. Favorites include Bobby Unser's winning car from 1981, the Watson McNamara Special Dick Rathmann drove in 1958 and '59 and one of A.J. Watson's rear engine cars.

But the one car I would really like to have is my dad's Indy champ car. I've looked for it for years and hired people to find it without any luck. That's the one I want most of all.

***Dutch Mandel** is the publisher at the Autoweek Media Group and has written for Car and Driver, Motor Trend and Sports Car Graphic magazines, among others.*

The Indianapolis 500 has always been a North Star in my life. I was born May 30, 1958 – the original Indy 500 race day. With my father in the car magazine business, he would often spend a good portion of that month at the Speedway. One year when he stayed home in California, he took me to the Cow Palace in South San Francisco to watch "The Greatest Spectacle in Racing" on closed-circuit television. That was 1964, and the scene remains vivid in my mind's eye: *Black Noon.*

Maybe because of my natural exposure to cars and racing, I did not have stick-and-ball heroes growing up; my idols donned Nomex and wore the smell of Castrol.

This was never more evident than in 1972, following Pole Day, when I received a Western Union telegram from Peter Revson. See, my father was writing a book, *Speed With Style* with Peter and had spent that month with him. Revson qualified second on the grid, and still Peter knew what it meant for a boy to have his dad gone on his birthday.

The telegram, which I kept with me in my wallet for the longest time, read:

DEAR DUTCH:

I WANT YOU TO KNOW THAT WHEN I WIN THE INDIANAPOLIS 500 I WILL APOLOGIZE IN FRONT OF 100 MILLION AMERICANS FOR KEEPING YOUR FATHER AWAY FROM YOU ON YOUR BIRTHDAY.

SINCERELY,
PETER REVSON

Many more memories are etched with 16th Street and Georgetown as their boundaries – learning that we were pregnant with our first son while at the Speedway, an extraordinary post-win celebration in an infield suite, or getting to drive a Corvette pace car for a pre-race lap with my three sons in attendance to watch as dad stalled on the grid! All these memories are great and wonderful, like the institution itself.

Steven Manning *is from Plainfield, Ind.*

In 1956 my dad worked with a member of the Dean Van Lines pit crew. I was five and a half years old when someone put me on the lap of driver Jimmy Bryan. He was smoking that big cigar. The next thing I know the car started and we went down pit lane about 100 feet or so. I rode on the lap of Jimmy Bryan. JIMMY BRYAN! He has always been my hero!

Angela Savage *is the daughter of Swede Savage. Her radio show, "Good News with Angela Savage," is available on the Las Vegas Radio Network.*

I was 40 on my first trip to Indy in 2014. Maybe that was meant to be, since 40 was the car number my father last raced with.

My father is Swede Savage. I was born just three months after he died from injuries suffered in the 1973 Indy 500. I never knew him and I grew up struggling with the fact that he lost his life in such a horrific way in front of fans that included young boys and girls. I just never knew how to process that. I felt abandoned. Adults who knew who my father was would get tears in their eyes in my presence. That can really affect a young child!

I struggled to assimilate into my stepfamily. My stepfather developed a drug addiction and became abusive to my mother, sister and I. In such a toxic environment I developed chronic depression, which spiraled into drug abuse and alcoholism. My older sister, Shelly, died of leukemia in the mid-1990s and shortly after that my stepbrother decided to change his last name to Savage and began telling people he was the son of Swede! It was more than I could handle at the time.

Several years later, when my oldest son was born, I was determined to get my life back on track. I was approached by a Facebook friend about the possibility of coming to Indy for the first time. My initial reaction was, 'No way!' But I began thinking that I could use the trip as a way of finally reconciling my feelings toward my father by better understanding the life he pursued. The trip turned out to be a life-changing experience.

I never knew that there were so many people out there who still admired and remembered Swede. They all reached out to tell me their stories about him and express their love to me. I was blown away…and I still am. A small group put together a beautiful reception for me and Bruce Savage, Swede's brother, at the Indianapolis Museum of Art, which was the best night of my life. I'll never be the same.

After the race, the Speedway arranged some quiet time for me at Turn 4 where my father crashed. I wanted to stare at that wall and overcome the demons I had been running from my whole life. My healing was set in motion.

I now have a radio show called *Good News with Angela Savage.* In addition to talking with interesting people in racing I also use the show to talk openly about alcoholism, drug abuse, depression and PTSD and to help remove the negative stigma that has been associated with those and other mental health issues.

I'm trading the ashes for beauty. I feel that for the first time in my life I'm in the right place at the right time doing the right thing. God has answered my prayers and I now look at my father in a completely different light than I did the first forty years of my life. I know that he and Shelly are proud of me.

***Barry Wanser** is the team manager of competition for Chip Ganassi Racing's Indy car program. He joined the team in 1997 and resides with his family in Zionsville, Ind.*

I guess my favorite is a win. Fortunately it's been four Indy 500 wins during my time at Chip Ganassi Racing. But my favorite has to be our 2012 win with Dario Franchitti.

On the first pit stop we were turned in pit lane. We basically had to straighten the car out and then finish the pit stop. We came out last and I had to tell Dario on the radio,

'Hey, don't worry about that. It happened early. We got the rest of the race to recover.' Of course, he probably thought I was nuts and it was over.

I was on the timing stand in the pit box during the race. Chip and I shared the duties of communicating with Dario that day. I would say I provided the information and Chip provided the motivation. We're very fortunate to have great drivers, great teams and great guys on the pit stops. We go into every race thinking we can win it, even when we have a setback.

It wasn't just psychological for me to tell Dario, 'Don't worry about it, it's early. We're going to get it back.' It was for everybody on the team to hear, including myself, because we have the confidence to be able to do that.

Certainly what makes that race special is that Dario dedicated the win to Dan Wheldon, a great friend of many of us on the team, and also to my late son Michael, who passed away that same year. Dario said, 'I just want to dedicate this to two of Indianapolis' finest, Dan Wheldon and Michael Wanser.'

I was right there when he said it – and it was really pretty special. Obviously more so for the racing world and the racing community for Dan. But Dario and a lot of the guys on the team were very close with me and my family and were there for my son Michael.

Michael was diagnosed with AML (acute myelogenous leukemia) just after Thanksgiving in 2010. The most common leukemia has about a 95% cure rate, where AML is not very good. As with the way I go into racing, my wife and I said, 'We're going to do what we need to do and battle it. Our goal is to win and that's what we're going to do.' So, we battled with our son. He received three rounds of chemotherapy. We pretty much lived in the hospital. My wife took care of Michael in the hospital. I took care of my job, our house and our younger son Robert, who was four at the time.

We knew down the road, if we could get him in remission, we would need a bone marrow stem cell transplant. Our son Robert was tested and even though there was only a 25 percent chance of him being a match – he ended up being a match. In April of 2011, we were able to get Michael into remission to have a bone marrow transplant. The transplant worked – it was great and Michael was recovering.

One of the difficult things about this type of leukemia is that even though they can test you to determine if you're in remission, AML cells like to hide in the body. Michael had a relapse. At that point, there's no cure for an AML relapse. We went to St. Jude's Children's Research Hospital in Memphis. St. Jude's has been a part of Chip Ganassi Racing since the very first race because of Target's association with St. Jude's through the

Target House. I never thought we would need them. We went there for an experimental treatment and couldn't get Michael in remission. We brought Michael back home to Indianapolis, and Dan Wheldon visited before leaving for the Las Vegas race.

Michael died on Oct. 23, 2011, just one week after Dan died in an accident during the Las Vegas race.

People were thinking of Dan and Michael after Dario's Indy 500 win in 2012 and it's great that they remembered. We never want to forget great people.

Holly Wheldon *is the sister of Dan Wheldon and lives in England. Her brother won the Indy 500 in 2005 and 2011.*

There's something about Indy, the adrenaline you get just walking through Gasoline Alley and the history of it. It's a weird feeling to describe and something you have to experience.

I did Indy from 2003 to 2008. I think I missed 2009 and '10 because I had school and then college. Then I went back for 2011 to 2015. So I have been to quite a few. I didn't take full advantage of the early years – I was young then and I would go, 'Oh it's just another race Dan's in.'

But now I love going to Indy, it's one of my favorite places in the U.S. Anytime I'm in Indy I try to head to the track. Last summer I went and checked out the museum to see his car. I hadn't seen it since '12 when Bryan (Herta) drove it around the track. But I went and saw the car in the museum and that was really cool. Emotional, but very cool to see.

What obviously stands out for me are Dan's wins in 2005 and 2011.

Certainly '05 is one of my favorite memories, but in 2011 I got to spend the whole month with Dan and experience it from his side. They were so different. In '05 he wasn't married; he was this crazy young kid; this party animal and '11 was very different. He got married and he had matured.

It was really cool just to spend every day with him and experience what he did from a driver's side. I know he was desperate to win. He wanted to win another Borg-Warner Trophy and a pace car for his other little boy, Oliver. He wanted one for each of his boys. And he wanted to win for our mum, too.

It was a proud moment to see him come onto a new team, to qualify sixth and then prove everyone wrong. For me it was just being that proud sister and seeing what he achieved – it was a moment I'll never forget. And it was very nice seeing how happy he was. I have to say that milk tasted really sweet.

I enjoy the 500 more now because I'm a lot older and I've experienced it and obviously had some great times. Dario (Franchitti) winning in '12, that was a crazy one. Then Tony (Kanaan) and Ryan (Hunter-Reay). It's just been exciting. I love going and hope to go to many more in the future.

Linda Vaughn

CHAPTER 9

Personalities

The Indy 500 has always attracted more than its share of interesting personalities, drawn by the glamour, speed and danger that is uniquely Indianapolis. From race queens to celebrities, military heroes, astronauts, sports stars, musicians and politicians, they have long flocked to the Speedway each May. Hollywood has tried to capture this fascination and actors including James Cagney, Jimmy Stewart, Mickey Rooney, Clark Gable, Barbara Stanwyck, Paul Newman, Joanne Woodward and Robert Wagner have all starred in movies trying to capture the mystic of the 500, with varying degrees of success. One thing for certain, Indianapolis has never lacked for personalities.

Linda Vaughn *is the "First Lady of Auto Racing" and is as well-known as many of today's drivers. She first appeared at the Speedway as Miss Pure Oil Firebird in the early '60s and still drives her Hurst Oldsmobile Pace Car*

In 1972 I was working for Hurst Industries and Jack Duffy and I went in Mr. (George) Hurst's office and told him we wanted to do a pace car program. The year before the pace car had crashed into the photographer's stand and almost got someone killed. So we decided we were going to go to Mr. (Tony) Hulman and offer him a professional service. We built the first of the Hurst Oldsmobile pace cars.

Then we went to Hollywood and contracted with Mr. James Garner to drive the pace car. He was having trouble with the studios at the time and I said this was the biggest and best publicity that you could possibly have. We worked very hard to put all that together, to get the cars built and to hire James Garner.

It was a beautiful promotion. And we had every one of those cars sold before we left the race track. They're among the most valuable pace cars ever. People still belong to the Hurst Oldsmobile club and I get to go to the meetings occasionally.

Of course Mark Donahue won the race, and Roger Penske still has the pace car in his showroom in Phoenix. It's part of history. I did a couple other pace car programs, including one with the late, great, Marty Robbins.

I'm very proud of those pace car programs.

I'm fix'n to go out and drive one of the pace cars right now. I have a great love affair with those cars. A lot of people have kids, I've got my cars. I call them my babies and my children. But I figure the Foyts, the Andrettis, the Unsers, those kids are my kids because they all grew up around me.

In our racing community, we're a family. To be accepted as a model and a spokeswoman and to stay there for the 50 long years that I've been a part of the Indy 500, I'm very proud of that connection. It's something I look forward to every year. There's nothing like the Indy 500. Nothing else in the whole world is like the Indy 500.

A.J. and I have always had this thing for each other. He's cantankerous as hell. He walked up to me at the starting line one year, one year when I was really skinny, and he said, 'Wow, Linda, you have a case of no ass.' I said, 'Yeah A.J., and you found it. It's on your belly.' After that he said, 'I'm gonna leave you alone. I know better.' But he's a great man.

So many great, great friends. If I had it to all over again, I'd do it just like I did. You've got your health and all the love and passion. The Speedway means passion to me. I love all the guys and I've grown very close to a lot of the women at the Speedway. We've gone through a lot together, looking out for each other.

And I've always tried to do things to make the racing community proud.

Paul Blevin *first threw the green flag to start the Indy 500 in 1999 and has been the flagman ever since.*

We call the flag stand the pirate ship because it's like the lookout on a ship.

My first year, when I walked down Gasoline Alley and made that right turn, it was like, 'Holy crap, where did all these people come from?' The hair on my arms and the back of my neck stood up.

Everything happens in split seconds. The year J.R. Hildebrand crashed coming to the finish line, we never saw the accident. The way the flag stand is positioned, the way the fence line is situated and the way cars come out of Turn 4, we actually lose sight of them for a split second. We saw it on the Jumbotron.

The night before the race I don't sleep very well and once it starts, it takes me about 15 or 20 laps to get into the game mode. By then we're usually done with the guest starters, they're down on the ground and out of harm's way. I can concentrate on my task at hand, which is to keep track of 33 cars along with my observer and my backup. Hopefully we stand around and do nothing except watch the race like everybody else. But every year is a new experience.

We've had a lot of neat people serve as guest starter. All types of dignitaries, CEOs, actors and politicians. One year we had Reggie Miller, the basketball player. He was scared to death. The crowd was chanting, 'Reggie, Reggie, Reggie' and that made it worse. And they're all afraid of dropping the flag. I tell them I've dropped it, so don't worry about it. That seems to help.

The year Jack Nicholson was the guest starter in 2010 stands out. When I heard it was going to be Mr. Nicholson, I asked if anyone told him the stand is 38 feet in the air and you have to climb up on a steel I-beam ladder to get to it.

I wondered if there was a Plan B if Mr. Nicholson didn't want to go up the ladder. Yes and no. There would be an area below where he could wave a flag if necessary. But no one would tell him that. So on race day we go over to the stand and he starts up. I get up there pretty fast, but as soon as I started, he was already at the top. No Plan B needed.

Usually the guest starter watches a few laps and heads down. They have things to do. So after a few laps, one of his handlers says in my ear, 'Tell Jack it's time to leave.' I looked at him and said I wasn't going to tell Jack that, if he wants to stay, he can stay.

We had a yellow flag right away and I asked Mr. Nicholson if he wanted to throw the flag for the restart and he said sure. Then there was another incident and he wanted to restart that one too. He stayed for about 50 laps and then all of sudden he turned to me and said, 'OK, I'm leaving.'

Then he was gone.

***Doug Boles** is president of the Indianapolis Motor Speedway. He also is a former Indy 500 car owner and the stepfather of Indy driver Conor Daly.*

I can't remember a time in my life that I didn't think about the Speedway and the 500. It's always been my favorite sporting event and at some level, the only event I cared about. My first 500 was in 1977. The rule in our house was you had to be 10 before you could go to the race. We went to practice all the time, but in order to go to the race, you had to be 10.

I grew up worshiping A.J. Foyt, so that year turned out fantastic for me because it was Foyt's fourth victory. To this day, I don't know if I've had a 500 that has meant as much, or impacted me as much, as that first one. We sat in the Paddock Penthouse seats and even in the days when I went to practice, I'd never been in those seats before, so that was brand new way to see the Speedway for me.

I haven't missed a race since. So that was the most important one.

I can think of other memories that are pretty powerful as well. The race in 2013 is probably my favorite modern-day event and it's because TK (Tony Kanaan) won it. TK was, at that time, the Lloyd Ruby of the day. The guy everybody wanted to win.

To have him win – and to know how passionate the fans were about him – that really was one of those powerful memories. Our security at Victory Lane completely failed – but in a good way that day – because everybody in the entire pit lane was so excited for TK. He'd driven for different owners in the past and he was with a multicar team, so everybody wanted to be in Victory Lane and it just became chaos. But it's Victory Lane, at some level you want it to feel like somebody has just won the most important sporting event in the world. And it really felt that way with TK because there were so many people and such excitement. That's a real favorite memory for me as well.

I also was part-owner of a car for ten races in a row at the Speedway starting in 1998, and in 2001 Sam Hornish drove for us. Unfortunately Sam had an incident and we had to take the car back to get it fixed during the race. But to watch him come back out and see the intensity and focus of a driver who knew he didn't have a chance to win, but laid everything on the line to show his guys his way of apologizing for having an incident was remarkable. I think he got two laps back and had the fastest lap of the race. That's one of those races to me - it's like the box score – you don't have an assist, it's not a point, it's not a steal, but it was a spectacular performance. It's one that sticks out for me as well.

My favorite 30 minutes of the year, like almost everybody in the venue, are those 30 minutes that lead up to "Gentlemen Start Your Engines" and the green flag. At some level when the green flag drops – I compare it to Christmas Day. It's like the presents are all open, it's really cool and you can enjoy the rest of the day. But the anticipation and the excitement – it has sort of rubbed off and at some level, I can't wait until next year when we get to do that all over again.

***Kim Coates** was one of the stars of the hit television series "Sons of Anarchy" and has appeared in more than 100 films and television shows. He also participated in the Toyota Pro/Celebrity race at the Long Beach Grand Prix.*

There's no more fun event to be at than the Indy 500. To experience it, to smell it, to see all the people, the noise, there really isn't anything quite like it.

I've been on the back of a pace car with actor Billy Fitchner, waving to the crowd while we went around the entire track. We've been in the parade and we've been to parties. We put on tuxedos and we drank more liquor then I want to tell you about. But it's about the people. And the people we've met there, I'll never forget. Their love for the sport and the party atmosphere. Everyone works so hard in that town to pull it off.

My story is called "The Look." I'd met Alex Tagliani a couple of times, he's Canadian like me. Every time I'd meet him he'd go kooky with me. He knows all my work. He loves *Waterworld* and *Sons of Anarchy*. He was just all over my movies. He's a big fan and I was right back a big fan of him. Every time I saw him, whether it was in the pits, or at the starting line at Long Beach, whether he was starting sixth or eighth or fourth, he was just cool, always happy to see you.

But I'll never forget the year he had the pole at the Indianapolis 500. He was sitting there in the number one position and I go out to see him and it was different. He had a look on his face that was different. He was so ready to go. He was pumped, but he was calm too. I'm sure he was nervous, there has to be incredible butterflies that every racer must have. But he had the look like no other.

I'd never seen that in him before, it was just different. And shaking his hand – not a lot of conversation – it was a different feeling. I was so excited for him. He didn't win that year, but he had the pole and he had that look that I bet you every pole-sitter has when they're starting off that race. It's the race of all races.

I remember being right by the first turn for the start. Right where those cars fly by. I'll never forget the feeling and the sound and being so close. Those guys and those girls who do what they do is something we as fans can only relish, dream of and support in wonder. I'm in wonder of them. To see Tags with that look on his face just before the race started – I'll just never forget it – ever.

Donald Davidson *is the Indianapolis Motor Speedway historian. He grew up in England where he became enamored with the Indy 500, memorizing the finishing order of races and other facts before ever visiting the track. He is a member of the Auto Racing Hall of Fame.*

Singling out one memory is just about impossible. But worthy of consideration among a considerable number of personal "pinch me" Speedway moments would be the afternoon before the first day of qualifications in 1964, when I finally arrived at the magical IMS grounds for the very first time. I entered the bustling garage area and witnessed, up close, all the legends I had been reading about for years.

Another would be two days later when, during a lull in qualifications, I was interviewed over the public address system by Jim Phillippe and Fred Agabashian, something fans still come up to me and recall all these years later. And then, during the race itself, when I made my debut on the IMS Radio Network and was interviewed by Sid Collins, my mentor to whom I owe so much gratitude.

Much more recently, there was a never-to-be-forgotten photograph taken just before the drivers' meeting on the morning before the 2011 500. A longtime fantasy of mine was finally realized by posing, in one shot, as many Indianapolis 500 drivers as we could possibly assemble. Months of planning boiled down to just a few precious minutes when the current 33 drivers would be available to line up in the Plaza Area with as many of the others as we could get.

Of the total number of 275 who were living at the time, we had, along with members of the Hulman-George family, an amazing 161 drivers. Just before the shot was taken, it was decided that I should make a quick check to ensure that there were no interlopers. I shuffled along sideways from right to left, scanning the four rows which included 20 winners and several veterans from the 1950s and 1960s. It was positively surreal as they were all looking back at me, many grinning, making faces and calling out various and sundry comments.

Other than for a handful of the more current drivers, I realized that I knew almost every single one of them. In many cases I had interacted with them during my days at the United States Auto Club and had taken part in radio interviews, ghost-written for them, visited their homes, had been befriended by their families and had travelled with them to give talks.

That "pass" took about 20 seconds, and it was an overwhelming experience.

On race morning, I realized another longtime wish, when it was arranged for a number of 500 winners to be given a lap of honor around the track in pace cars. Rather than piling three or four into a vehicle, it was, as we had hoped, one winner per car, with each of the 15 who took part sitting up on the back seat. As the cars rolled out, the roar from the grandstands confirmed our longtime belief that the fans would love this.

Then, quite unexpectedly, several people motioned for me to get into one of the other pace cars which were there for standby use. I politely declined, but the smiling faces and assuring nodding heads caused me to reconsider.

My personal ride around the track that morning, with groups of fans in the grandstands yelling and calling out my name, is something I will never forget.

William Fitchner *is a lifelong race fan who attended drag races as a kid in Buffalo, N.Y. He became an actor, starring in more than 40 films including "Black Hawk Down," "Crash" and "Armageddon."*

I'd been to Indy three years in a row, and then missed a few years because I was working, when I got a call about doing an intro to kick off the television coverage for the 100th anniversary of the 500.

I guess they were tossing around names to do the intro and someone said you need somebody that absolutely loves being there and gets the sport, so, long story short – I get this call about going to Indy to do the intro in 2011.

Even though I'd been to the track a few times, I'd been down in the pits. So now I was alone on the track with a film crew. We had one day to do it because it was going to rain. We had one shot to film the entire thing. But I'll never forget that day. We took our time as we moved around the track from the front straight to Turn 1, to Turn 2, to Turn 3 and to Turn 4.

It was just so quiet that day. You could feel the size and the spirits of the place. It was absolutely magnificent. Even with a handful of people and a film crew, we were like a needle in a haystack.

I'll always remember how proud and honored I was just to walk that track and talk about it. It was really something special.

The other little story I have is when they asked if I would like to do one of the ride-alongs. I'd been in the two-seater on the streets of Long Beach, which is exciting and fun, but it's not Indy. So I get there and lo and behold, I know one of the guys that is setting up the cars. There were two cars there that day and I said to him, 'Can you work it out where you put me in the car that has the faster driver, because I just really want to go as fast as I can possibly go.' He said, 'Yeah, no problem, just get suited up and I'll make sure you're in the right car.'

I get the suit on and I come back and I'm supposed to stand by one of the cars. The guy says, 'Here comes your driver now,' and I'm looking around and I'm thinking, 'I don't see anybody, what the heck is he talking about?'

Then here comes this guy with gray hair and I swear he can't be more than 5' tall and I'm looking at him and I'm thinking, 'That's my driver?' Then the light bulb goes off. 'Holy shit, it's Mario Andretti.'

So Mario comes walking up to the car and I'm like, 'Morning Mr. Andretti' and he just gives a little nod and climbs in the car. I'm thinking to myself, 'Can he drive this car?' I mean, I know it's *Mario Andretti*, but he's getting up there in the years.

I climb in the car and get strapped in. Now they're letting the cars go out – they kind of stagger them. So one car goes out, then we go out second. It's like Indy qualifying – you go out there for four laps. By the time we got on the fourth lap you could see up ahead that he was catching up – he almost caught up with the car in front of us. He was just flying down the backstretch.

It was so exhilarating. I thanked him and everything and I looked over at my buddy and I asked him, 'How fast were we going there?' He asked one of the tech guys and he said, 'He topped 200 on the backstretch on the last lap.' I don't know how fast those ride-alongs normally go, but I'm not sure if they all go 200.

I've got several automotive thrills in my life, but that is certainly in my top three – no doubt about it.

***Scott Gallett** is vice president of marketing, public relations and government affairs at BorgWarner. He joined the company in 1991 and has been going to the Indy 500 ever since.*

The Borg-Warner Trophy is given as an emblem of victory to the winning driver of the Indianapolis 500. Its history goes back to 1935 when we first established the trophy. We had 3D images of all the past winning drivers engraved on the trophy and it captures the entire history of the race.

The trophy stands for innovation, excellence and performance, things we value as a company even today. Our employees are proud to be associated with the company that owns the trophy and feel pretty special that we're good caretakers of its legacy.

My strongest personal memory is probably the first time I ever got to be in Victory Lane. It was the year Tony Kanaan won the race, 2013. You know, fan favorite, hadn't won, and the place went crazy. It's difficult in Victory Lane because you can't see the end of the race. But I could tell who won by the way the fans reacted.

When Tony came out of the car and he's in Victory Lane, with all the emotion that's going on, he still had presence of mind to say, 'Hey, I'm finally going to get my ugly face on that trophy.' It was pretty special to know that, in all the emotion and chaos, he's thinking about getting his face put on the trophy.

Being responsible for the Borg-Warner Trophy is the best part of my job. It's just one small part of my responsibilities, but it's probably the thing I'll remember the most. Long after I'm retired and sitting in my rocking chair, the trophy will still be out there and I'll think, you know, I was responsible for that, for one little piece of its history.

Mike Harris *covered motorsports for more than 40 years for the Associated Press.*

Actor James Garner was a regular at Indy over the years and I got to know him fairly well. A real gentleman and true fan, he liked to come into the AP's little office in the old media center or hang out at the Champion hospitality room under the grandstand and talk racing.

On a practice day sometime in the late '70s, Garner was walking past the door of our office when longtime *Indianapolis News* writer Dick Mittman and I walked out, heading for the grassy area in Turn 1, a great observation area between the track and the old Snake Pit, the infield area where you never knew what you would see or hear.

We asked Jim if he would like to join us and he did. We were chattering away, mostly oblivious to our surroundings, as we strolled past the security fence and onto the grass next to the parked fire trucks at the south end of the main grandstand.

Suddenly, we heard a shrill woman's voice calling out, 'Jimmy! Jimmy! Jimmy!'

She was obviously trying to get Garner's attention and we all looked her way as this very buxom young lady pulled up her blouse and flashed our famous movie actor friend.

He kept walking, but looked her way and hollered, 'Very nice honey.'

But that wasn't enough for her. She began again yelling, 'Jimmy! Jimmy! Jimmy!'

Again, Garner looked over at her and nodded as she flashed him again with a huge smile on her face. And, as he kept walking, she again began the Jimmy chant.

Finally, Garner stopped, turned toward her and shouted, 'Honey, I've seen better.'

With that, he turned back toward the track and resumed our conversation as the cars roared past, diving into Turn 1.

Richard Lugar *is a former senator from Indiana.*

From the time my brother Tom and I were elementary school students, we enjoyed every opportunity to visit the Indianapolis Motor Speedway, usually with the assistance of our parents, who were equally enthusiastic, or friends of the family.

By the time that I was elected Mayor of Indianapolis in 1967, we counted race day as one of the most important family events of our year and we attended eight consecutive 500s in seats in the balcony along the main straightaway.

These exciting days followed the annual 500 Festival Parade in downtown Indianapolis in which we occupied an open car and waved to an estimated 200,000 citizens of Indianapolis and distinguished visitors. Frequently, our four sons had opportunities to visit with race car drivers before the parade.

In the years that followed, I gained the support of Tony Hulman in establishing an annual military ceremony to be held on the first Saturday of qualifications each year. Approximately 30 young men and women, who had volunteered their services to the armed forces of our country, assembled near the starting line. Frequently, aircraft flew over the track and on several occasions, parachutists came out of those planes, landing as close as possible to the track. As a United States Senator, I would swear in these young volunteers into the armed services of the United States and they made plans to proceed to their duty stations. The combination of patriotism and the 500 was always very strong.

During the past quarter century, I enjoyed an additional opportunity on the first Saturday of qualifications in a breakfast meeting with those planning the 500 Festival in Indianapolis and members of the Hulman family. I was grateful that on almost every occasion, Mari Hulman George was present for breakfast and Tony George joined us on many occasions. We celebrated the growing historical significance of the 500 and tried to envision ways that the historical impact could be enlarged in the future.

I must add one footnote which indicated how unexpected events sometimes garner attention. After travels to Europe, I invited all of the mayors of the world to come to Indianapolis to help celebrate Indianapolis as an international city. Over 50 accepted the invitation and I invited at least a dozen to come with me to the Speedway for the race. We occupied seats just behind pit row and were enjoying the day when suddenly the pace car, driven by the owner of an Indianapolis car dealership, came roaring off the track and was obviously going to find it very difficult to slow down. The car was stopped by a press tower. The collision threw one or two photographers off the higher reaches. No one was badly injured, but our foreign visitors carried away an unexpectedly exciting Speedway experience.

I join all Hoosiers and all Americans in celebrating the 100th running of the 500. Indianapolis is known all over the world for hosting such a spectacular event whose longevity has enriched the lives of millions all over the world. It is an honor for each one of us to have enjoyed and even been a small part of that glorious history.

***Jim Nabors** first sang "Back Home Again in Indiana" prior to the Indy 500 in 1972 and performed it 34 times before his final performance in 2014. The following is from an IMS tribute video.*

Mr. (Tony) Hulman came over in the stands to say hello to Mr. Bill Harrah (of Harrah's Casinos) and he recognized me. He'd seen my show in Lake Tahoe. He said, 'Hey, do you want to sing a song?' And I said, 'OK.'

So I got up and I thought it was the Star-Spangled Banner. And I went down on the track with him and I asked the band, 'What key do you do this in? They said, 'We only got one key.' I said, 'Oh no, the Star Spangled Banner has two keys.' And they said, 'Well you're not signing that.' And I said, 'Oh, what am I signing?' 'Back Home Again in Indiana,' was the reply. I said, 'I'm from Alabama, you still want me to do it?' He (Hulman) said, 'Well do you know it?' I said, 'I know the melody, but I don't know the words.'

Just to be sure, I didn't get a rehearsal, or anything, I wrote the lyrics on my hand so I wouldn't forget them.

***Joie Chitwood** is president of the Daytona International Speedway. He previously served as president and chief operating officer of the Indianapolis Motor Speedway and was part of his family's entertainment business, the "Joie Chitwood Thrill Show," founded by his grandfather.*

An interesting story that was really special to me happened when I was running the Speedway. The pre-race ceremonies were always a big deal. I understood the importance of the pre-race activities at the Indy 500 – the build-up and Mari (Hulman George) delivering the words and all those things. So, I'm at the victory podium, which was built when the new Pagoda was built. I would hover around there in the back and the marketing team would run pre-race. I would check-in with people and talk to Mari.

This was probably around 2007 or 2008. I'm standing off to the side at the podium and Jim Nabors calls me over. Now this was only five or six minutes before he was going to sing "Back Home Again in Indiana." Jim says, 'Hey Joie, come here.' I say, 'Jim, what's up, what can I do for you?' I'm nervous, does he need something? He goes, 'Listen, I've got to tell you this story.'

And Jim starts telling me this story.

'It's in the early '50s and I'm playing the Wisconsin State Fair,' he says. 'It's me and Doc Severinsen – we're out on the road. We're touring and we're going to perform, but we're going after your grandfather's stunt show, The Joie Chitwood Thrill Show. Doc and I are both pissed. The stands are full and your grandfather is wowing the fans by jumping cars and wrecking cars.

'Both Doc and I know that the minute that stunt show is over, everyone is going to leave and we're going to have to play to an empty house. Doc and I are arguing about who's going to stay and do the show. Finally, I got so mad I just told Doc I was leaving.'

So Jim left and Doc had to play to empty grandstands after the Joie Chitwood Thrill Show at the Wisconsin State Fair.

What really blew me away is that Jim is telling me this story and we're literally minutes away from him going out to perform "Back Home Again in Indiana." For me though, it's an appreciation of my grandfather and his legacy. I'm running the Indianapolis Motor Speedway and Jim Nabors wants to tell *me* a story about my grandfather right before he gets on the biggest stage. It was surreal. Is this really happening? It was so cool that it was happening right at that moment – that Jim Nabors is telling me a story about my grandfather right before he goes out to perform before the Indy 500.

I thought if I tell people this story, I'm not sure if they'd believe it. But that's how the best stories happen, because you can't believe it occurred.

***Dr. Terry Trammell** is a noted Indianapolis-based doctor/safety expert who has served as a medical director and consultant for Indy car racing.*

Race day 1992, was a very cold day. So cold that urban legend is that all the outerwear in the place was sold out by the time the green flag fell.

It was my custom to watch the race from the safety station in the short chute between Turn 1 and Turn 2. If there was a crash, I would walk back to the infield hospital to assist the medical staff with the assessment of the driver and to provide care for any orthopedic injury. If the injuries required surgical care, I would head to Methodist Hospital to provide that care.

My memory is a little foggy on the order of events that day. But I do remember I was probably the only person in the place that was dripping wet with sweat, because after lending a hand in the infield care center, I would jog back to the safety station in time for the restart, only to have to turn around and run back to the care center.

Eventually I ended up in the ambulance with Rick Mears, Mario Andretti, Emerson Fittipaldi and I think Jim Crawford, all of whom had foot or leg injuries. Mario and Emerson were engaged in animated and heated conversation that somehow I was in the middle of. Not sure what it was all about since Emerson frequently defaulted to Portuguese.

Eventually, in the ER at Methodist, the four drivers ended up in one of the community minor trauma bays together, which was curtained off from the rest of the ER. I couldn't help but notice a little boy – probably about six – in a fresh long arm plaster cast crying uncontrollably. I was concerned that his cast was too tight or something wasn't right, so I approached him to see why he was crying.

In between sobs he cried that he was missing the race. Once I was sure that was the only problem I tried unsuccessfully to console him. All he did was to keep sobbing that he missed the race. At this point I pulled the curtain back and pushed him into the bay where the drivers were, between the carts with Mario and Rick, and said loudly to the drivers that this little boy was missing the race and needed their attention and would they please sign his cast! I don't remember who was more aghast, the drivers or the little boy. I do remember that the drivers all stepped up and made that kid's day. Those guys were a real class act given their circumstance.

Shortly thereafter I had to do one of the hardest things I have done in my motorsports career. That was to tell Mario that I was delaying his surgery because Jeff Andretti was en route from the track with severe injuries to his legs and feet and what else I didn't know, only that it was serious.

I'm Italian, and Italian men communicate as much by what they don't say as what they do. Mario could see the concern in my eyes. Nelson Piquet was already in the hospital with incredible injuries to his legs and feet that more than tested my surgical mettle. The word from the track was that Jeff's were even worse. The rest is history. In all, nine drivers were taken to Methodist from the track that day and I was still operating 24 plus hours later, along with at least one of my partners.

HONDA
ShopHonda.com
HONDA
KURT
BUSCH
SOL REP
SIEMENS
Firestone
SUR
SURETON
Firestone

Kurt Busch

CHAPTER 10

NASCAR

WHILE INDY CAR RACING TRACES its roots to the first Indianapolis 500 in 1911, NASCAR was established in the years following World War II as a series for production-based automobiles. Although A.J. Foyt derisively referred to the stock cars as "taxi cabs," Indy drivers often competed in the upstart NASCAR events during the 1960s and 1970s, with both Mario Andretti and Foyt winning the Daytona 500. Some NASCAR drivers also gave Indy a try, Bobby Allison among them. But with more foreign drivers and sponsorship dollars moving into Indy car racing in recent years, young American drivers including Jeff Gordon, Tony Stewart, Danica Patrick, and Kyle Larson, have increasingly shifted their focus from Indy cars to the growing purses and popularity of NASCAR. The occasional NASCAR driver still attempts "The Double," running in both the Indy 500 and Charlotte 600 on the same day, including Kurt Busch in 2014.

***Kurt Busch** finished sixth in the 2014 Indianapolis 500 driving for Andretti Autosport and was named Rookie of the Year. A veteran stock car driver, he won the 2004 NASCAR championship.*

I've always been drawn to the allure of the Indianapolis 500. When I think of Memorial Day weekend, that's when motorsports takes center stage. Formula One is in Monaco and NASCAR is in Charlotte, and Indianapolis is center stage.

Growing up in Las Vegas, sporting events always came on early. On Memorial Day weekend, we were usually back late that Saturday night from wherever we were racing with my dad. As soon as I was waking up on Sunday morning, I remember hearing "Back Home Again in Indiana" and the Indy 500 would be on TV. I would watch the race with my dad at home.

Some of my favorite Indy 500 memories as a kid were watching Al Unser, Jr. That Valvoline car he drove just seemed to be electric, no matter which race he was in. The year (1992) he beat Scott Goodyear to the finish line at Indy was a big memory.

Right around that time Emerson Fittipaldi also won the Indy 500 (1993). As a kid your parents are always telling you to drink your milk. When Emmo won the 500, he drank some orange juice instead because he had orange farms in Brazil. I remember thinking orange juice would taste a lot better than milk and if I ever won it, I'm going to choose orange juice. My dad laughed because he knew I knew nothing about what the heck was going on.

I got the bug to do the 500 when I signed on to drive stock cars for Roger Penske in the mid-2000s. Roger brought the Indy cars down from Pennsylvania and put them in the race shop in North Carolina. That's when my juices really started going because I could see the Indy cars in the race shop and talk to the engineers and team members about the cars.

It just seemed like we never could turn the Indy 500 dream into a reality. There was one year I got to go to Indianapolis and hang out with Roger on race day. That was like walking around with the Pope – when you go to Indy and have full access and you're standing there with Roger Penske. It was 2006, when Sam Hornish, Jr. won the race with a last lap pass of Marco Andretti. That's where my infatuation with Indy turned from just being a kid with a dream into being an adult with ambition. It just didn't quite materialize when I raced for Roger.

Then I had the chance to do the Indy 500 with Andretti Autosport in 2014. I jumped in – or more like swan-dived straight on in – and thoroughly enjoyed it. I was treated really well at Indy and was blown away by the hospitality for the new guy coming in from the stock car world. It was neat to be treated as an equal, but it also felt like being a rookie all over again. I enjoyed my time being a student and learning about Indy cars. It was also great to share stories with Mario Andretti while I was there, and with Michael and Marco (Andretti). It felt like I was with the first family of Indy car.

The couple of weeks I was in Indy were a thrill. Having practice sessions lead into qualifying runs and then back into practice sessions for the race with the dirty air and the draft out on the track. There was no comparison to the Sunday of race morning though – the feel of the grandstands being full and the place abuzz with energy. It was intimidating, even for a guy like me that has been in sold-out NASCAR races for decades and has raced in the Daytona 500 many times. It was just me being a rookie heading into the morning of the Indy 500.

Then there was the responsibility of the three-wide start. That was the first time I'd ever done something like that, where you have the responsibility of the pageantry of the three-wide parade and when they drop the green – that's the first time I'd really been in all of that dirty air. That was probably the most intense moment of the whole month. Everybody was telling me how insane it is once the green flag drops. Then there was also the responsibility – with guys like Scott Dixon and (Juan Pablo) Montoya on my inside. It was just like, 'Whoa. Here we are and it's real. It's race time and here we go.'

It was an amazing race the way it unfolded. I ran the first half as conservative as I could, but also to get an education. Once the team told me we were halfway, I said to myself, 'We're halfway through and we're done learning. Now we have to apply everything we've learned. It's time to go. This is as best prepared as I'm ever going to be.'

That's when we started working our way back up. I think I'd fallen down to 18th or so, and it was just a matter of applying everything I learned and being slightly on the aggressive side to try to find positions out on the track. I was surprised to work my way into the top 10. Then we took advantage of a couple of guys having some misfortune. I do remember a moment of trying to run for fifth place. I was trying to grab that spot away from Montoya on one of the restarts. That's the moment it hit me that I didn't have enough experience with the car and the Indy car draft to know how to maneuver around some of those top guys. It was amazing to be in a group racing with guys like Sebastien Bourdais and Will Power.

I felt like I accomplished everything I could have possibly accomplished on that day with that preparation. Immediately after the race, I felt my own internal satisfaction from the day. There was that moment of celebration. It was a great finish, but I also said, 'Wait a minute. I still need to go run 600 miles.' That was probably the hardest part of doing the full 1,100 miles that day. It was an accomplishment in my first ever race in an Indy car to finish sixth. It was a reason to celebrate, but I had to quickly focus back to the stock car world and running a full 600 miles. That was the toughest part of the weekend.

It really sunk in the week after the race when we had our team meeting at Stewart-Haas Racing. Tony Stewart gave me a hug and said that I did a great job. He told me that I might not realize it right now, but it was a significant accomplishment to go out there and perform at the race like I did. Stewart helped make it all settle in the right way.

***Ray Evernham** teamed with Jeff Gordon to win three NASCAR championships at Hendrick Motorsports (1995, 1997 and 1998). He now restores and collects vintage race cars and serves as a racing analyst.*

I can't ever remember not being a fan of race cars. It was my dream, my desire, to race at Indy. I would do everything I could to try and follow what was happening there. Whether it was listening on the radio or watching on "Wide World of Sports" or going to the closed circuit television broadcast.

I started going to watch midget races when I was six or seven years old, with my father and a gentleman named Frank Stoddard. He hadn't missed an Indy race since 1947 and I would later work at his Texaco station. I loved listening to their stories. Being from New Jersey, Mario Andretti and Wally Dallenbach were right up the road. They used to come to Trenton and Langhorne every year. They came into my backyard. It was about Andretti and Foyt and the Unsers. That era was, and still is, really exciting to me.

My graduation present from my mom and dad was a trip to the Indianapolis Motor Speedway for the 1975 race. Bobby Unser won in Dan Gurney's Eagle. Rain-shortened, but it was still a great event. I will never forget the feeling of walking into that stadium. I just knew that someday I was going to be racing there.

Of course, I thought I was going to be driving and it was going to be an Indy car. Little did I know it was going to be a stock car with that Gordon kid driving. Back then there really wasn't a lot of opportunity to get involved or pay attention to NASCAR racing. Everything was about Indy cars.

To me, walking into Indianapolis is like walking into a cathedral or a church. You feel like the ghosts, the spirits of all these great people who have walked there before you, are staring over your shoulder. You have a responsibility to them to act as a racer, to appreciate the grounds that you're walking on.

I get the same feeling every time I walk through the gates of the Speedway. For as much success as I've had in racing and all the things that I've done, it's still a very humbling experience. After all those years, 2015 was the first year that I was back there for the 500. That's 40 years later and an amazing turn of events when you think about everything that's happened. To walk the grid before the start was one of those moments where you don't want to talk to anybody because you think that if I talk too much, I'm gonna start balling.

To win at the Brickyard was a very emotional experience and a surreal day. I was so focused as a crew chief, I didn't pay a lot of attention to things going on around me. But I remember when we pushed the car out onto the race track. I turned around to walk back to the garage area to change into my race uniform and it hit me. We were at Indianapolis. We were lined up with people on both sides of us. The pylon. Our name written on the pit wall just the way they had done it for so many years, in simple block lettering. I had to reel it back in. I had a race to run and had to get myself focused.

If you look at some of the pictures of Victory Lane after we won that race, everything just kind of hit me. People say those are the blankest stares that they've ever seen from me, but when that much emotion hits you at the same time, it's like getting hit with a bolt of electricity, you just go numb.

I make my living with stock cars and wouldn't trade it for anything in the world, but my passion is still when you take those fenders off.

***Bobby Allison** made two Indy 500 starts driving for Roger Penske in 1973 and 1975. He is a member of the NASCAR Hall of Fame with 84 wins, including three Daytona 500s.*

When you look at the whole picture, my Indy 500 experiences were really disappointing and pretty bad.

I'd never been to Indy before I went there to race in 1973. I had watched the race a time or two as they began to televise it, and had also listened to it on the radio – and had some interest. Of course my brother Donnie went to the Indy 500 in '70 and '71. He had an incredibly good run there and finished fourth in 1970. It was his first time there and he was the Rookie of the Year. Then he went back and got a sixth the following year. I paid attention to that and knew some of the Indy drivers because a few of them showed up at a NASCAR race once in a while.

When Roger Penske asked me to go there in 1973, it started out because I had driven a Can-Am car at Riverside, Calif. I went really, really fast in that car and then got pushed out by one of the team members. Although I didn't get to race the car, I did some very fast laps.

Roger saw that and said he wanted me to go test the Indy car over at Ontario Speedway. I did, but with not a friendly reception from the McLaren group that was conducting the test. I got put off for most of the day. Finally, I got to run laps and ran the second fastest speed of the day.

My first time at Indy I qualified up front and the engine blew up on the pace lap – which was heartbreaking. That was the year that Swede Savage was killed and Art Pollard was killed at the very beginning of a practice session. It was a month that I spent dedicated to the event and the engine blew up on the pace lap – which was a real disappointment.

That second time there, I went through all kinds of difficulties trying to get organized and get the car where I could drive the thing like I wanted it. I finally did qualify and the car was really, really good. I came from the rear and I guess it was during a pit stop sequence, but I still led a lap in the 1975 Indy 500. There are not a lot of guys that can say that, so I'm able to enjoy that moment and that's probably the highlight of my whole Indy career

Kyle Larson, *from Elk Grove, Calif., won features in midgets, sprint cars and Silver Crown cars before moving to NASCAR with Chip Ganassi Racing, where he earned Rookie of the Year honors in 2014.*

Growing up, there were many times when I wasn't able to watch the Indy 500 because I was off doing my own racing. I do remember driving down the road listening to the race on the radio and to this day I still try to follow it as much as I can.

The first – and only time – I actually went to the race was in 2013. Early that Sunday morning I flew to Indianapolis, the day after my NASCAR race in Charlotte.

It was really cool being able to go to the Indy 500. I got to talk to some drivers before the race and see how important the race was going to be to them. I don't really remember all the conversations, but I do remember their attitude. I talked to Scott Dixon and Charlie Kimball and was surprised that they were both just really calm. It's hard to think about if I was in that situation how calm I'd be.

Something I'll never forget from that day is walking down Gasoline Alley with Scott Dixon's team before the race. We were walking through there and people were screaming at Scott and Chip. Some fans even noticed me and were yelling my name! When we got to the grid, I remember all the pre-race ceremonies – there's really nothing like it. As a race fan, I think that's the only time I've gotten emotional before a race. You kind of get a little choked up.

Everything about the Indy 500 leading up to the green flag is prestigious and you can just feel all the history behind the event. Then once the racing starts – it's really, really good racing too. I watched from a suite in Turn 1, on the infield side, where you could see the cars coming from the exit of Turn 4 down into Turn 1, and then a little bit through Turn 1.

We had to leave the Speedway in a hurry after the race to beat traffic, and then get on the plane for Charlotte and that night's NASCAR race. I wish I could have taken in more of the post-race activities. If I were able to go to the Indy 500 again – although now that I'm Cup racing I'm not sure if that will ever happen – I'd love to experience those post-race activities.

When I was young, my dad was a big Indy car fan and that's originally kind of what I wanted to do. Then once I started racing more and more, NASCAR was where I wanted to end up. But, I still would love to run the Indy 500 someday. It's just a really cool event. There's always lots of passing and exciting finishes, and I think it's definitely the greatest race in world.

Darrell Waltrip *is a member of the NASCAR Hall of Fame and a three-time series champion. He registered 84 wins during his stock car career, including the 1989 Daytona 500.*

I've never been to the Indy 500, although I'm a huge fan. I grew up in Owensboro, Ky., which is on the south side of the Ohio River. My friend Ray Skillman and I used to go to a lot of the sprint car races. We'd go to dirt tracks in places like Du Quoin, Ill. and Terre Haute and Springfield (Ind.). I was a huge open wheel guy. I drove a sprint car a few times over at Tri State Speedway in Haubstadt, Ind.

My vision was to be an Indy car driver someday. But somewhere along the way I hopped into what we call hobby car, a jalopy, and that seemed to be a lot more fun and a lot more forgiving. So my aspirations kind of went from open wheel racing to more thinking about moving down south and driving stock cars.

I have always been a huge fan of the 500 and followed it from when I was a little kid. Ray and I used to drive by the Speedway but never went in, we just always drove by. I had heard about Gasoline Alley and always had these visions of the races. I remember watching them on TV and the drama from qualifying and Bump Day and everything that goes into making the Indy 500 unique and different. It always intrigued me.

I only went to the Speedway one time when the Indy cars were actually on the track. I went with Richard Petty from Charlotte to Indy and we stood and watched the cars practice. STP had Richard come up and I rode up with him because I'd never been to the Speedway. That's when they were running about 230. I forget who set the track record, but somebody ran 236 that year.

I'll never forget standing on that front straightaway watching those cars come off Turn 4 and they came down that front straightaway and looked like they were floating. The cars came off the corner and you just see them kind of nibbling around as they came down the front straightaway. They were absolutely hauling butt. They'd go by like a screaming eagle and they would turn off into that first turn like they were on a rail. I stood there forever watching those cars. I was fascinated at how fast they were and how quickly they could go around a corner.

Growing up, A.J. Foyt was my hero. I used to drive my stock car and I wore a pair of red golfing gloves and a red bandana that flew out the back, kind of like I saw A.J. do when he would drive a sprint car. That's back when these guys were daredevils. I'd go over to Anderson Speedway and watch the Little 500. I'd seen that race a couple times and I'd go to those dirt track races and watch A.J. and Mario Andretti and Gordon Johncock and all those guys. They'd all run the dirt tracks in Indiana and go to Indy and run the Speedway. That was almost like the training ground, you had to run the dirt cars to get to Indy.

When Roger Penske was letting some of the NASCAR guys come up and drive in his Indy cars, whether it was Donnie or Bobby Allison, Cale Yarborough, or LeeRoy Yarbrough, Roger offered me a ride in an Indy car. It was probably somewhere between 1985 and '89. We were in Michigan for a NASCAR race and I had never even sat in an Indy car.

I think Bill Elliott had taken a car out and made a few laps around the Michigan race track. And Roger asked me, 'Do you want to take the car out?' I went and I got in it. This is when the cars were bad fast and pretty dangerous. At 6'1" I'm a pretty tall guy and I squeezed down in that thing. I remember if I put my feet as far as I could, I think I could have seen my toes sticking out of the front of the car. I thought there's something wrong when the driver is sitting this far forward and your feet feel like they're sticking out of the car.

I was sitting there and was just kind of feeling it to see what I thought. And I'll never forget it, A.J. walked up behind the car and he gave it a shove – he kicked the tire and the car kind of lunged forward a bit. It scared the crap out of me. I hopped out of it and said, 'Thanks, but no thanks. I just don't feel comfortable sitting in that car. I appreciate the offer, but I think I'll pass.'

I just never felt like I would be comfortable if I ever drove one of those cars. Anybody that's been around the Indy cars knew that's when they were dangerous. That's when they caught on fire. As a driver, the biggest fear I ever had was being in a car and have it catch on fire and I couldn't get out of it. I love watching them and have the utmost respect for the guys that drive them, but it wasn't for me.

It's always been one of my favorite races and I can't wait every year to watch it. Just seeing the different guys that have won it through the years and the technology is amazing. Indy is Indy and there's nowhere else like it.

Gasoline Alley

CHAPTER 11

Gasoline Alley

THE OFTEN UNSUNG HEROES BEHIND many Indy 500 memories are the team members: owners, crew chiefs, mechanics, spotters, fabricators, etc. Their home during the month of May is Gasoline Alley, where they work tirelessly throughout the month to prepare (and repair) the race cars.

Russ Brandenburg *was 24 when he worked for Team Lotus in the 1965 Indy 500. He is now a member of the Speedway's Yellow Shirt safety squad.*

I was working as a gofer in 1964 when I heard Lotus was looking for someone to sweep out their garage, so I went over there and helped out.

In 1965 I went back to Andrew Ferguson, the Lotus team manager, and asked if they needed any help. He said sure, pointed to a rack of those famous baggy green overalls. He told me to take one and that I'd be paid $50 a week. That was huge. A lot of people back then volunteered and worked for free, just for an opportunity to get into the track. I was the only American mechanic on the team.

People don't understand what it was like back then. You'd show up about 8 a.m. the Wednesday before qualifying and work pretty much straight through the weekend. I remember falling asleep under the car at one point.

Jimmy Clark was a real introvert, but behind closed doors he was a different person. He was funny and personable. And he was constantly biting his fingernails until there was nothing left. Nothing.

Colin Chapman was one of the smartest people I've ever been around. He was constantly keeping records. Track conditions, temperature, humidity and things like that. Back then not many people did that. Every night when he left he'd say, 'Chaps, I'd like to have these things taken care of before morning.' Then he'd come back in the morning with another list. I was fortunate to work with a group of very dedicated mechanics.

I took the Lotus crew to Speedrome for a figure eight race one night. They were the hit of the program. They went wild and screamed and carried on so that the crowd watched them instead of the race. It was quite a show and they had a ball.

Race day was a blur. I was about the same size as Jimmy, so whenever we moved the car, I would get in to steer it. There were so many people there; we could barely get the car to the track. After the race everyone was running to the winner's circle and I was one of the first to get there.

That night Chapman took us all out to dinner at an Italian restaurant. I have kept several cherished mementos from that month, especially a photo Jimmy signed, 'To Russ, thanks for all the help.'

***Tim Cindric** is the president of Team Penske. He is an Indianapolis native and a graduate of Indiana's Rose-Hulman Institute of Technology.*

My father worked building Indy car engines, mostly for mid-level cars or cars trying to make the race. He never did get to experience winning the 500. Once in a while he got to build qualifying motors, especially in the early 70s. Mark Donohue qualified with some of my father's engines. That's really how my father built the house in Claremont, Ind., where I grew up.

In 1973, when I was five, we moved into a house in Claremont. I lived in that house all the way through college. The carpet in that house was a burnt orange shag carpet. I hated it when I was a kid because I couldn't play with my Hot Wheels on it because they'd get stuck. I had to get one of those oval rugs and put it down and it became the race track for my Hot Wheels. I'd complain all the time about the carpeting in the house. My father would say, 'Look, we aren't changing it because Roger Penske carpeted this house.'

When I was in college we had the same carpeting in the house and there were bare spots, but he wouldn't change it. What had happened is my dad built an engine for Mark Donohue to run in qualifying and he ended up on the front row. Somewhere along the way Roger gave him a bonus as a thank you. He used that money to put that carpet in the house. At that time, carpet was a luxury. I never forgave Roger all those years for the carpet that was in my house.

Before I went to work for Roger, I had an interview with him in New York in 1999. At the time I was working for Bobby Rahal and had never changed jobs before in my life. I wondered if Roger remembered my father, and the first thing he did was ask me about my dad. Then he told me about my dad building engines for him. I thought it was pretty cool that Roger remembered all that stuff. I said, 'Mr. Penske, I'll never forget the carpet that was in my house,' and I told him the story about that orange shag carpet. When I went to work for Roger, the first week working for him, I get a check in the mail. I had just moved into a new house and he said, 'Get yourself some carpeting that you like.' It was pretty cool that he remembered all that.

I think the fact that my father never won an Indianapolis 500 – I had so much respect for what it would be like to win. The first year I went to Indianapolis with Roger was 2001. Just to be at Indy with him was surreal. It was like I made it. I was able to go to Indy and say I worked for Roger Penske. To me, that was everything.

Then to win the race, our first year back at the Speedway (after the CART/IRL split). Helio Castroneves climbed the fence and we're in Victory Lane. It was unbelievable. For Roger, it was his tenth Indy 500 win, but for me it was my first and it was a big deal. Roger threw us all in the pace truck and we got to go around the race track. It was awesome. It was the first time Roger ever finished first and second at Indy. It was my first win at Indy and I called the race for Helio that day. It was unbelievable to do something that Roger had never done there before.

On top of that, on photo day I'd told a story to Roger about my wife's father, Jim Trueman, who had won the Indy 500 in 1986 with Bobby Rahal. I never knew Jim, but I knew of him. In 1986, there used to be an owner's trophy – a bronze Flying Man – that was given to the winning car owner. In our house, we have a pretty cool 1986 car owner's trophy.

I told Roger that my wife Megan teases me about how she has an Indy 500 trophy in her family and I don't. Monday morning after the 2001 race, we're doing photos and it comes to the owner's trophy. Roger and I are standing there for the award. We finish the pictures and he hands me the trophy and says now you have one for your family. So, in our house we now have the 1986 and 2001 Indy 500 owner's trophies.

***Vince Granatelli** is the son of the late Andy Granatelli and was an Indy 500 crew member, chief mechanic and car owner.*

If you win at Indianapolis – it's a great memory. If you go there for forty years and almost win twenty times out of forty – they're not good memories. I hate to be negative, but there aren't a lot of good memories if you don't win. You spend thirty days there doing whatever you can do to win the race and then for one reason or another it doesn't happen.

You get there all excited on May 1st – I don't know how many days they run now, but they used to run from May 1 to 31. So you're there for a minimum of four weeks. After the race, depending on where you finished, you don't say, 'Boy I can't wait to get to Milwaukee.' You only thought about next May.

You don't really forget any year. My first year was '61 and we went there with a Novi, the '56 Curtis chassis with a Novi in it. The car was really fast, but we couldn't get a driver so we couldn't make the show. We wanted Dick Rathmann to drive it, but he was under contract.

Some of the better memories, certainly of the month until the race, was Parnelli (Jones) in '67, with the innovative side-by-side construction turbine car. But Parnelli finished sixth after leading the race by a full lap when a ball bearing failed with only three laps left.

Then 1968 was my first year as chief mechanic, working with Joe Leonard. It was certainly a thrill to be on the pole and we were leading again, but a fuel pump drive shaft broke with nine laps to go.

Those are not memories you forget.

I'd like to give you some good memories. But if I had to say what was the memory I had the most – it was probably walking back from the track after the '68 race, back to the Holiday Inn Northwest, probably about three miles. I remember walking with the crew uniform on like a driver's suit. There wasn't any way to drive out of the track in those days. It was faster to walk. I walked the whole way thinking about how close we came to winning. Of course being my first year as chief mechanic, I thought that would have been sensational to win – sit on the pole and then to win the race. But it wasn't to be.

Those were difficult years because everybody was complaining about the turbines. All we tried to do was to be innovative and come up with something that was better and faster. The '67 car was so far ahead of its time it was a joke. Then we superseded that the following year with the Lotus, which was even more competitive. All to be banned for political reasons – the fight between the tire companies and one thing or another – it got to be pretty political. Not as bad as it is today, but it was pretty political for its day.

It was certainly great for Mario Andretti in '69. He should have won at least seven times. It was exciting for Mario to win – he certainly deserved it.

You've got to remember that the three previous years we should have won the race. We won the race in 1966 with Jim Clark. I think it was a scoring error, but you can't prove it, it's done – it happened. Then with the turbines in 1967 and '68.

So you don't think in 1969 that this is a shoe-in, no matter what. You don't think you're going to win until the checkered flag is up. Until he's pulled into the winner's circle and he's got the wreath – you never know.

***Mark Harder** is an Indiana native who grew up attending the Indy 500 and parlayed his passion into a career in motorsports. The 100th running of the race will be his 44th.*

I have so many positive memories of the Indianapolis 500 that it's difficult to know where to begin. Growing up in the small town of Jasper in southern Indiana, there were two things to look forward to during the long winters – Hoosier Hysteria, the single class high school state basketball tournament in March, and the Indianapolis 500 in May. Growing up in the '60s and '70s, both events had the full attention of the state.

My earliest memories of the Indianapolis 500 were my grade school years. Our family would attend most qualifying weekends and the race. My brother and I would sit in the top row of the Tower Terrace grandstands. This enabled us to watch all the action on the track, as well as see all the crews and cars going out of Gasoline Alley. The excitement of race day is something I'll never forget, and the details of each race were etched in my mind throughout the summer.

The highlight of my early Indy 500 memories was when a small local team based in my hometown entered a car in the 1976 Indy 500 – the Spirit of Indiana Special. It was driven by a family friend, Spike Gehlhausen. On the third day of qualifying, Spike made the race as a rookie. It was spectacular for such a small operation to make the race. The whole town of Jasper rallied around the team, in much the same way a town follows a high school basketball team battling for a state championship. Unfortunately, the thrill of making the race was tempered on the parade lap when the engine expired before the green flag fell.

My college years provided some of my best times at the track. Since classes usually ended around the opening day at the Speedway, I was able to be at the track for almost every practice and qualifying day. I couldn't get enough of all the track activities. In the evening after practice finished, I would figure out how to sneak into the garage area to get closer to the cars and crews. At this point, I knew I wanted a career in motorsports, but was unsure of how to pursue that path. With no mechanical skills, I knew it would have to be on the business side of racing.

That path took me five years from graduating college to landing an opportunity in motorsports – but it was worth the wait. In May of 1990, I joined Shierson Racing to handle sponsor relations. It was a surreal moment, realizing a dream had become a reality.

The timing could not have been better. The first race in my new position would be the 1990 Indy 500. Shierson Racing entered two cars that year, one for Arie Luyendyk and another for Scott Goodyear. Arie was near the top of the timing charts every day of practice and qualified on the front row. Even though he had not yet won a race, you could feel the confidence in both Arie and the team.

Race day in 1990 was a beautiful spring day in Indianapolis. The race ran at a blistering pace and Arie was near the lead for the entire race. On lap 186 he passed Bobby Rahal and went on to win his first of two Indy 500s. The race was over in two hours and 41 minutes, a record that stood until 2013.

Less than 30 days into my new career, I was standing in the winner's circle at Indianapolis Motor Speedway. For someone who grew up idolizing this place, it's something I'll never forget. More importantly, the number of opportunities that originated from Arie's victory has propelled my career for the past 25 years. When I look back to how my career in motorsports has progressed, it definitely originated from that day in 1990.

***Bernie King** was a longtime crew member at Penske Racing and currently oversees the team's collection of historical race cars.*

My first memory was 1985. I was on Danny Sullivan's car when he spun and won. Penske Racing had won before, but that was the first time I had won on a particular car. I used to look after tires and I remember when he spun, we didn't know he had spun. He just came into the pits to change tires and we were all scrambling. That sticks out in my memory.

But in 1987 I was on Al Unser, Sr.'s car and just because we were underdogs with the old March Cosworth and we were behind and all of a sudden we were leading. That stands out the most, the '87 win.

We were running a PC16 chassis and after Danny Ongais crashed, I was part of the group that went back to Pennsylvania to figure out what we had that we could run. We were looking for a third car for Al Unser, Sr. (Ongais's car was destroyed in the crash and he was out of the race with a concussion.)

We were trying to find everything to put together the car which had been on display in a hotel lobby, suspension stuff and things like that. Seeing what we could find to make the car run. Both Rick Mears and Danny had driven it the year before.

Rick and Danny were both running the new Ilmor engine. We were running the older Cosworth engine, but we still knew we had a shot. One thing working for Penske, you know that you have a shot. No matter where you go, you know Roger's going to make sure that he has a competitive car.

It was a pleasure working with Al. He was so relaxed as a driver – driver comfort-wise, seat-wise, pedals, all those sort of things. Al didn't complain about anything. Some of the drivers have their own seats made to fit them. We didn't have an Al Unser seat, so we had to use one of Danny's and padded it out. You'd say to him, 'How's that?' and he'd say, 'Yeah, it's fine.'

We didn't start that well, but with Al, you know you're going to finish. That's the way he was, he'd driven for us before and you had that feeling you're going to finish. You've got a good driver, so as they say, let the race come to you. To me that's what happened – the race came to us.

Yeah, we were surprised we were in the lead, but you know you always have a shot when Roger Penske is involved. You never go to a race thinking you're not going to win when you're part of Team Penske.

***Bernie Marcus** was born in Germany and has worked with Formula One and Indy car teams as a race engine and aerodynamicist. He's worked with Ford Motorsports the past 15 years.*

My most vivid memory is Stefan Johansson qualifying for the 1995 race, even though I was part of the Galles team that won in '92. But the challenge of just qualifying in '95 sticks in my mind like it happened last week.

I had worked with Stefan in Formula One when he drove for Onyx and I was his race engineer. At the beginning of '95, Stefan asked if I would be interested in working with Tony Bettenhausen's team. He wasn't jelling with the engineer there. I knew Bettenhausen was a small, single car team and there wasn't much budget to develop the car, but Stefan talked me into it. I went there more with my heart than with common sense or business sense.

They did have year-old Penskes with Ilmor Mercedes engines. In '94 Penske cleaned up with those cars. They were very, *very* competitive. Bettenhausen had three chassis, basically half the rolling stock from the year before. They also had lots of spares, all the technical information and the setup sheets. My first race was at Nazareth (Pa.). We used Al Unser, Jr.'s setup, tweaked it to suit Stefan and boom, we finished third.

So we went into Indy with fairly high hopes. But when Tony originally did the deal, they were supposed to use the same engine in '95 that Penske had the year before. That unfortunately was ruled out, so we had to go there – Penske too – with the normal V8s we were racing in the CART series. When we started running at the Speedway we could see after the first day the car was dead slow – and so were the new Penskes. We were way down at the bottom of the time sheets.

The first qualifying weekend came and it was clear we weren't going to make it with that car, we were way too slow. We had a meeting Sunday night with Roger (Penske) and he said they were going to get a couple of Reynards to run with Ilmor engines from another team. He wanted to help Tony and Stefan and had arranged for us to get a Reynard with a Ford Cosworth engine and got special dispensation from Ilmor to run a Ford for one race. He even offered to pay the lease price for Tony.

The car we got was basically a year-old Reynard. It took the guys three or four days to strip it down, rebuild it and prep it for the second qualifying weekend. We finally got on the track late Friday and within three laps Stefan was doing 222 mph. We took some wing out and ended up running an easy high 226.

But the next day it got really hot. We went out in the heat and the car was only doing 223s, 224s. Not good. You needed to run 225 to make the show. So we decided to park the car and wait until Sunday.

We went out Sunday morning and ran about 225. Then it got hotter again, so we put the car away and said we'd line up after four o'clock. Stefan ran a high 224 then, which still wasn't good enough. So we aborted that run. We got right back in the box, put new tires on and trimmed the car out some more. He got back on the track with about ten minutes to spare. He made the full run and made the race, bumping out Penske's Emerson Fittipaldi.

So after all that, we barely made the race. It was very popular because we were kind of the underdog. It was also a huge relief for Tony as the sponsor, Amax, was flying in 500-odd customers and executives for the race and it would have been a major problem if the car didn't qualify.

We were very happy and relieved, but at the same time we felt very disappointed and bad for the Penske people. They worked hard and struggled and also tried to help us. But it's racing, and at the end of the day, you've got to do what you've got to do.

***Don Taylor** has worked with a number of Indy 500 race teams.*

For me, A.J. Foyt is the great American hero. Flashing that bright Texas smile, whether at Le Mans, Daytona, or a sprint car race, he is the classic American racer. And his main stage was the Indianapolis Motor Speedway. For many years, primarily in the '60s and '70s, he was *the* star of the Indy 500.

Bob Riley, the legendary American race car designer, is also someone I admire. I have known Bob since our days working in Detroit at Ford. I had done some outside design work for him, and continue to do so today. He had designed several of Foyt's Coyote Indy cars, including the one in which A.J. won his fourth 500.

When the new "ground effects" tunnel cars had success at Indy, Foyt knew he needed a new car. This was before teams started buying production line Marches and Lolas. Indy cars were totally built by hand.

I had been doing some paint schemes for George Bignotti's Indy cars, but my big opportunity came when Bob asked me to help him with the look of the new Coyote's body, to give it some softer lines and fine-tune the basic straight-line shapes he drew.

First step were some color sketches, which A.J. liked, followed by a scale model I built at home using automotive styling clay. The full-size body model was then sculpted in rural Michigan, at a company named Protofab. The chassis was being fabricated in Houston, in A.J.'s shop.

Bob made a trip there to check on progress. Impressed with their skill in handcrafting the tub's thick aluminum outer skin into the specific taper required at the front, per the blueprint, Bob asked crew chief Jack Starne, a slight but strong man, how they had perfected it to fit. The memorable reply, 'We just beat the shit out of it!'

As the body was fitted on the tub, painted in Foyt's familiar orange-tinted red, it needed the vinyl decaling. On my kitchen table sat the iconic, shadowed number 14, the large and small Valvoline decals and the cowboy hat, always on Foyt's cars, to be placed next to the driver's name. I spent many hours hand cutting each with an X-Acto knife.

Predicting how well a new car would perform was less of a science in that era. In this case it was left to Riley's skills and experience, and Foyt's driving. The Coyote's first race was to be at Indy, in 1981, which wouldn't happen today!

The greatest moment for me was Foyt rolling out for his qualifying run, hearing Tom Carnegie's deep-throated, 'And, heeeeee's on it' and standing on edge, listening for every lap's speed to be announced.

When the car came into pit lane for the official qualifying photo, the crew, in their unique red-and-white, Italian restaurant tablecloth-pattern short-sleeved shirts, patron Jim Gilmore, and other team and family members, quickly gathered around the far side of the still hot racer.

Somebody said I should get in the picture too, so I slid in, at the back. And somewhere in the Indianapolis Motor Speedway archives, there is that qualifying photo with my little head looking over Foyt's shoulder.

Did A.J. win his fifth Indy 500? Well no, but he did qualify on the front row and put all on notice that he was still in the game. I felt proud to have played a small role in that magnificent car and in the A.J. Foyt story.

Bob Riley *is a renowned designer/builder of race cars, including the 1977 Coyote A.J. Foyt drove to his fourth Indy 500 victory. He is a member of the Motorsports Hall of Fame of America.*

I'll never forget working with Jim Crawford at the Speedway, especially our first year together in 1988. He was a very talented driver and always had such great spirit, despite the fact his luck never seemed to match up to his outstanding talent.

When I first met him, Jim was known as a nice Scotsman with not much of a record at Indy to write home about. He used a cane to walk following a terrible crash in qualifying the previous year that severely broke both his ankles, one knee and dislocated his feet. I remember taking Jim to see Dr. Terry Trammell. One of Jim's feet was injured so badly that you could hardly recognize that it was a foot.

Through all the constant pain, Jim remained a very engaging person who loved racing at Indy. As long as he was participating at the Speedway, nothing ever seemed to get him down. One year our car lifted off and literally flew in Turn 2 and they had to take Jim to Methodist Hospital. There wasn't anything wrong with him and he just left. The first time we saw him after the crash he was limping into the garage area in hospital pajamas! I guess he had caught a cab.

Jim was completely relaxed at all times and always rapid in the car. He said the only time he ever felt good was when he was in the car. The pain in his ankles and feet must have been very aggravating. Sometimes he would sleep in the car between sessions.

The race in 1988 seemed to finally bring Jim into focus as one of the Speedway's more talented and heroic drivers. He led the race at the halfway point, although under a yellow flag. Eventual winner Rick Mears passed Jim under green, but that wasn't his biggest problem. One of the screws in his ankle began to back out during the race. Amazingly, it didn't slow him down.

He was still a contender for a top-three finish in the late stages, until he radioed in about a left front tire problem. Whatever Jim told us about the car, we believed. He was always quite honest and usually accurate. But in this case, we didn't find a tire problem. I kind of feel he picked up some debris while running his characteristic low line. If it sticks on there long enough you could scrub it off. Or you could crash the car. When he came in, there was a problem with the wheel nut, which cost us some extra time in the pits and we finished sixth. But people admired the fact Jim put so much effort into trying to win despite his injuries and had led the race at the halfway point.

My last year working with Jim was 1994 when my partner Mark Scott and I decided to run a year-old car. We hired Jim, but eventually realized that he just wasn't quite himself. A few years had gone by and he was in a lot of pain.

In practice, we weren't going very well and it looked like we were going to miss the show. We stiffened up the rear springs and shocks, but he kept saying the car was rolling. It was clear we were having difficulties when A.J. Foyt came up and said he would like to try Jim in one of his cars. I thought that was a good idea and it showed how much respect Jim had up and down pit lane. If we got Jim into one of the Foyt cars, and A.J. told him to just drive it, he probably would have made the show.

But Jim wouldn't leave Mark and I. He felt that would have been disloyal. We couldn't get him to leave us. And, we missed the show. It was very, very disappointing.

Jim gave it one more try with another team the following year, then retired to running his deep sea fishing boat out of Florida. He was relatively young – 54 – when he died only a few years later. I'll never forget his spirit and sense of loyalty when it came to racing with him.

***Derrick Walker** is a native of Scotland who has been involved in auto racing since the early 1970s, working with teams such as Porsche and Team Penske in Indy car and Brabham and Penske in Formula One. He later ran his own Indy car team and also served as president of Operations at IndyCar.*

I have a lot of Indy 500 memories and they're all unique in their own way. I've been to the Speedway as a manufacturer – originally I worked for Penske Cars in the U.K. So, I saw things from the perspective of starting to build Indy cars for the first time in Europe. Then I moved to the team side of things and became a manager for Penske. We won a lot of races in those years and had a lot of good years at Indy. Later, I moved to the Porsche Indy car program as general manager and eventually I started my own team.

I had a unique introduction to my first Indy 500 as a team owner in 1991. Looking back, I probably didn't know everything that could potentially happen when you become a team owner, which made it a risky proposition.

I met Willy T. Ribbs at the first race of the year. He wanted to do the Indy 500 – and so did I. Willy had some support from Bill Cosby – a little bit of money. Indy was going to be the first event I could go to with my own organization. So it was logical that we determined we needed each other.

We went to the Speedway with very little money and a very small crew – a handful of ex-Porsche Indy car boys who were all unemployed at the time. They agreed to come and work for nothing and I made the commitment that if we got the team going, I would employ them and pay them back the money they lost by being unemployed.

We bought a car, a Lola that was over a year old and had a Cosworth engine. We went to test and ran it around and it seemed OK. Then we went to Indy for the month of May. We were clearly off the pace with us being a new team and Willy's lack of experience around Indy. It looked as though we were definitely not going to make the show. We went through the first weekend and didn't qualify.

That's when I made the decision that we needed a Buick engine because it was going to have enough power to push us fast enough to get in the show. Most of the early part of the second week we spent converting our car in Gasoline Alley – putting a Buick in the back of it. We bought a couple of Buicks from some guys and they all turned out to be very unreliable and blew up. I was about ready to run out of money and Buick came to our aid and loaned us an engine.

We spent all day trying to get to qualify and Willy by then was convinced that this was probably going to be a tough one. Finally, in the last hour of the second qualifying weekend, we managed to do a masterful job of getting the car in line, which was always a big exercise. You wanted to be positioned to have an opportunity to qualify right at the end, so that if you got quick enough nobody could bump you out.

It took a bit of persuading to get Willy to drive the car, but he did. In the last hour he went out there and ran a 218 or something like that. He came down pit lane acting as though he broke the sound barrier. He had the seat belts unbuckled and he was half out of the car and he was giving it an, 'I'm the man. I'm the guy.' And he was!

I just stood there thinking, 'A few minutes ago it was all but done and now here we are in the race for our first event and we put the first African American driver in the race.' It had been a roller coaster ride during the month – managing the money, trying to get the engine sorted out and getting in the race.

As soon as Willy was in the race, we got our first call from a sponsor and it turned out to McDonald's. This was the first time they had ever sponsored a race car. They gave us a little bit of money to put the "Golden Arches" on Willy's car. We were the first to ever have it on there. Then we got a couple of other little sponsor deals, enough to pay the bills to go to the race.

In the race, the engine blew up right at the start. The whole roller coaster of emotions and effort to get into the 500 just dissipated a couple laps into the race. It was all gone and we were right back to where we started. It was an amazing story.

I look back on it now and it was quite unusual that things worked out the way they did. They don't always work out that way. All of that discussion of getting into it and getting ready and going where Walker Racing had not gone before was a neat experience at the Indy 500. It was a great opportunity to be given that chance and a lot of people helped make that happen.

***Dennis Reinbold** is an Indianapolis native with several auto dealerships in the area. He began fielding cars in the Indianapolis 500 in 2000.*

I grew up around the Indy 500 and went to the race with my friends. When Jim Nabors would sing "Back Home Again in Indiana," I would get goose bumps.

The first time I was going to call the strategy for the race was in 2000. Steve Knapp was driving our race car and I was pretty nervous, especially at the 500. It was my first time doing strategy for an Indy car race. I've done the strategy every race since then that we've participated in, but that was the first time.

On the grid before the race, we were doing the normal radio check. I'm looking around and remember feeling overwhelmed with the crowd and everything. Then I realize that Steve can hear me fine, but we can't hear him. We only had one-way communication. We figured that out right when "Back Home Again in Indiana" started. I was like, 'OK, so much for the nerves. I'm too busy to worry.'

Steve had a scrap piece of paper and Sharpie in his pocket that he pulled out. We just made hand signals – four hand signals. All through the race we were looking to see what hand signal he was giving us and that's how we communicated and adjusted the car the entire 500 miles that day.

One finger was for a push. Two fingers was push/stagger. Three meant the car was loose. And I don't remember what four meant. Every time he went by and gave a hand signal, we had three or four of us on the pit wall looking to figure out what he was trying to communicate to us.

Steve would hold a finger up in the air, or two fingers and we just had to try and figure it out. From the pit stand to see a driver hold a finger up – it's harder than it sounds. It's pretty hard to detect. We confirmed it with him the next time by. It was like, 'Hey Steve, I think I saw you hold up one finger, so the car is pushing right?' And he would give us a thumbs up the next time by.

The car had a push most of the day. We finally dialed that out as the race went on and we didn't get any more hand signals after that point.

That got me past my nerves at the Indy 500 and let me know that, 'Hey, you just have to focus on your job here.' That was a good way to start out to point me in the right direction.

***Jon Beekhuis** grew up in California listening to the Indy 500 broadcast. He started his driving career in Formula cars in Europe before joining CART. He now covers Indy car racing for both ABC and NBC.*

I have a back story from 2012 that got buried in that incredible finish between Dario Franchitti and Takuma Sato. That was the first year there was engine competition between Honda and Chevrolet.

Honda was lacking by maybe a mph or two in practice. When it was time for qualifying, the big guns came out and they got smoked by Chevrolet. I mean it was a two and three mph difference. Scott Dixon and Dario Franchitti ended up qualifying 15th and 16th.

Now me being the technical guy, I spent a lot of time over at Honda and Chevrolet and I remember sitting on multiple occasions with Roger Griffiths, who was then the technical director for Honda. The question was, not just from me, I mean the team owners were asking the same thing, 'Do you guys have anything in reserve?'

He played it poker-faced the whole time and said, 'We're working the best we can and we're hoping that we're going to be able to find something by race day.' I thought that they were in trouble and that they were going to try to use the same configuration for the race.

We now know they knew this entire time they had developed a generation two engine they let no one use until Carb Day. And even though Chip Ganassi had gone into his office on multiple occasions and said we need help, we need more speed, Griffiths kept saying, 'Don't worry, we have engines for you that we'll put in on Carb Day and the 500 and they'll get you where you need to be.'

So on Carb Day, sure enough, number one and two were Franchitti and Dixon. They didn't even run the whole practice, just put them away. Some people thought, 'Oh well, Carb Day is not necessarily indicative of the race.'

So the race fires up and Marco Andretti is the guy to beat, but the Hondas are moving up. He's leading and the time comes for the first pit stops. Marco rolls in, but the top Honda runners didn't pit until two or three laps later. That made bells and whistles go off for anybody technically-minded. That is a big difference and could very well affect the outcome of the race. Not only was Honda keeping up with their power, they had this massive increase in fuel economy. They had found a way to make the engine more efficient.

The incredible thing is that they kept that whole thing under wraps when they didn't want Chevrolet to know what they had – they held their cards very close to their vest. It took incredible discipline to not let anybody have those engines until Carb Day and keep telling them don't worry, you'll be fine.

I think Chevrolet went into the race thinking, 'We've got this thing in the bag.' And I just know the wave of fear that shook pit road after the first pit stops, when they're going, 'You've got to be kidding me. They've just gone two laps longer than anybody else. We're in trouble.'

My understanding was – and this one I don't have confirmed – there was a big meeting in the Penske transporter with Chevrolet after the 500 asking, 'How could this happen?'

So that was one of my favorite technical memories. Of course we know the next year that Chevrolet learned their lesson. They put their hammer down and crushed Honda.

***Roger Griffiths** came from Formula One to join Honda and was in charge of engine development in 2012. He now heads up the Formula E program at Andretti Autosport.*

In 2012, the first four races leading up to Indy hadn't been good for Honda. I was technical director at that time and initiated a new engine development path.

We basically thought Indianapolis was the most important race, so let's build an Indy 500 special. The way the regulations were written, you had to carry the engine into the next round and if it meant sacrificing the next race in Detroit, that was fine, because hopefully, we'd win the 500.

It takes a long time to get the development done, parts made and to get engines built to the right specification. It wasn't going to be made available until Carb Day and obviously that wasn't the best place to introduce a new engine. But it was what it was in terms of when the engines were going to be available. We were prepared to sacrifice qualifying, which is quite a hard thing to do. But at the end of the day, nobody really remembers who sits on the pole, but for sure they remember who wins the race. We all recognized it was an incredibly risky strategy and it could have backfired on us.

We had quite a lot of success during engine development and were showing really good numbers compared to the engine we were racing. But while we had done a lot of work on the dyno, it never really ran in anger on the race track.

It was really hard going through practice and qualifying – I think Josef Newgarden was the only Honda car in the top 10. I remember going through some difficult conversations with Chip (Ganassi) about the relative lack of performance compared to the Chevy engines. I kept telling him, 'You know we have this engine.' But he didn't know the performance improvement that we made.

The engines were delivered and went in the cars for Carb Day and the Target cars were running one-two in the final warm-up. I just remember seeing all the smiles on the Ganassi guys' faces when they were pushing the cars back and they said, 'OK, now we believe you.'

During the race I remember looking up at the scoring tower and watching this march of Hondas coming up through the field. The pit stops cycle through and the Hondas are going a lap or two laps further than the Chevys and thinking that everybody had written us off. It was just such an unbelievable moment for me.

I was in tears at the end of the race. It was the pressure of being back in competition for the first time since 2005 and not having a great start to the 2012 season, then being able to turn it around and just dominate the 500. That was a pretty special moment. Just the immense relief.

Ilmor (maker of the Chevrolet engines) had come prepared for a win and they brought a very nice bottle of Dom Perignon champagne. We all knew each other because we had worked together since 2003 because Ilmor built the previous generation Honda engines.

So they came over and gave me that bottle of champagne. I still have the cork from it to this day.

***Art St. Cyr** is a longtime employee of American Honda and made his first trip to the Indy 500 as the new president of Honda Performance Development in 2012.*

That season (2012) was the first year of renewed competition among engine manufacturers and one of the competitors, Chevrolet, came out of the gate a lot stronger than we anticipated. So we were playing catch up for the first few races of the year and we were pretty far behind.

We knew we had a big power increase coming on our second spec engine and we made the decision to push the development back to give us as much time as possible – so the engine wasn't going to be ready until the race. We had to start the season and go through qualifying on the first spec engine and we didn't qualify particularly well.

We had a management forum at Honda and one of the questions someone asked was, 'What's going on with the Indy effort?' I'm the new president of HPD – I started in April and I'm just really getting my feet wet – and people are already asking, 'What the hell is going on here?' I didn't know how good the new engine was going to be, so I got up there and said, 'You know we had a rough start, but we're working towards it. Practice and qualifying are just that. We feel pretty comfortable with our race spec, but we'll see how it turns out.'

There's nothing quite like being on the grid before the start of the Indy 500. As far as you can see there's people lined up on both sides of the track. So I'm standing around the Target car and some Target executives were there. They're looking at us kind of cross-eyed. They're not very confident.

We started at the back, but by the time 50 laps were booked it was all Hondas in front. So we're feeling pretty good. By the end of the race it's Dario Franchitti, Takuma Sato and Scott Dixon. Takuma got down on the apron and spun – luckily between Dario and Scott. Theoretically Takuma could have taken out both Scott and Dario. It's racing, you never count your chickens before they're hatched.

Afterwards it was very much a feeling of redemption – that we can compete. We just won the Indy 500. That was my very first Indy experience.

My second memory in 2014 is a little more personal. Once the race starts I don't really have anything to do, so I just become a fan at that point. I was with my son, who was 24, and we're watching the race and there was a crash with about nine the laps to go.

We're leading the race at the time – and they threw the red flag. It was a pretty hot day and we were really worried if the engines were going to restart. I'm pacing and my son looks at me and says to just relax, everything will be fine. My son is trying to calm me down.

Thankfully all our cars fired – they start going again and here comes the restart. It turned into a two-person race with the yellow cars – Ryan Hunter-Reay and Helio Castroneves – just going at each other. The other cars on the track might as well not have even been there because everyone was watching those two. They were jockeying back and forth. Every lap they were passing. So we're watching, absolutely enthralled, just thinking this is the greatest race – no matter who won – this is a great race. When Hunter-Reay crossed the finish line in first, my son and I were jumping up and down and high fiving. It was a great memory, especially to have experienced it with my son.

***Lee Orebaugh** has worked at 22 Indy 500s with the teams of Newman/Haas Racing, Chip Ganassi Racing and Rahal Letterman Racing, among others.*

I'm originally from Indianapolis. I used to go to the Speedrome with my dad when he drove. I remember going to the track, sitting in the stands and watching the cars and picking the ones that I thought were the fastest and were going to win. I always thought I was really good at that. Now it's funny that I'm a spotter and get paid to do the same thing I did as a little kid.

The first Indy 500 I actually sat in the grandstands and watched was when Bobby Rahal won in 1986. I sat in Turn 4 where Arie Luyendyk crashed and brought out the last yellow. I then spent many years working with Bobby when he was a driver and then an owner.

A favorite Indy memory was the first and only time I was directly part of a team that won the 500, with Buddy Rice in 2004. That was awesome because you don't get a trifecta at the Speedway very often. We were on the pole. We won the pit stop contest. We led the most laps and we won the race. It was pretty fantastic.

I was spotting in Turn 3 and we were going around for what would be the last lap. It actually ended under rain. The finish wasn't as dramatic as we thought it was going to be. The dramatic part was that we weren't in the lead at one point and the rain was coming. Our strategist had to tell Buddy to get to the front. We'd been passing people all day and were the fastest car out there. We took the lead and then it started raining, maybe two laps later. Then they issued the red and that's when we were the winners.

So, we just won the race and I'm super excited and thinking, 'I'm not missing the celebration that goes on in Victory Lane.' By this time it's starting to rain like crazy. I pack my spotter bag and start running. When you're in Turn 3, you had to go down this skinny, narrow column of stairs to get down from the spotter's stand. The other spotters are kind of letting me go – so I'm passing all these people. Then I have to go down to the bleachers with all these people and after that I have to cross the golf course. I had to jump over fences and I'm heading straight for the Pagoda, that's my beacon. They have some areas blocked off, but I don't care because I'm getting to Victory Lane.

Finally, I get near Victory Lane. I pass all the Yellow Shirts because they don't know who I am – I have a rain coat on and a backpack. I jump over one more fence and the Yellow Shirts are yelling, 'Hey, you can't go in there.' I get to Victory Lane and there's nobody there. I thought, 'Wow, I just missed the whole celebration. That really stinks.'

I start to put my head down and look up to all this flashing going on. Well, they had moved the celebration to the green room. I jumped over another fence. The Yellow Shirts yelled again. I say, 'I'm on the team.' Nobody is going to stop me from getting to the green room. I pop the door open on the green room and all the guys are going, 'Hey Lee.'

There's one drink of milk left in the jug and they hand it over to me and I got to drink the milk out of the jug. That was really cool. Everybody is wet from the rain, and all the team guys are crowded in there. It was pretty awesome. That was the first victory celebration in the green room.

For me, all the people that I've been lucky enough to work with and all the different teams that I've been able to work with at the Speedway is what I really remember most.

Tim Lombardi *joined Team Penske in 1976 and has been the team coordinator for the Indy car program since 1978.*

I think one thing that always stands out in my mind was the year when we didn't qualify for the race – 1995. Emerson Fittipaldi and Al Unser, Jr. were our drivers and we were starting to struggle in qualifying. We tried all kinds of things, even buying cars from Bobby Rahal's team, but things just didn't work out. It was really a huge downer. We had never been in that position before.

I remember the guy on the intercom in the garage area saying something like, 'Will Dr. Kevorkian please go to the Penske garage.' It was probably funny to everyone in the garage area but us, because we were all shocked.

By the end of the next day we had pretty much emptied all the garages. We packed everything up. Loaded the trucks and sent everybody home. I stayed because I still had hotel rooms and tickets, and I had a big Hugo Boss group coming in for the race with hospitality. Basically, the only thing we had left in the garages was one desk, one chair, one telephone and me.

For the next week I was trying to get rid of tickets and hotel rooms. Of course, I had to hang around for the race because I had a group coming in. Halfway through the race I decided to go back to my hotel and grab all my things, and then I left town. I was probably the one that turned the lights out in the garage.

Then we don't come back to Indy for several years. Of course, we had our heads hung down when we walked out of there and it was probably one of the biggest stories in motor racing for a long time.

When we did come back in 2001, it was the year Helio Castroneves won the race and Gil de Ferran finished second. We came back after being away for years and finished first three years in a row. That was pretty stunning to me, that we were down so far in '95 and to come back and win three in a row starting in 2001.

***Mike Hull** began his career with Chip Ganassi Racing in 1992 and is the managing director for the team's Indianapolis-based racing programs.*

Having grown up as an Indy car fan in the days of black-and-white television and radio, for me just getting to go to the Speedway was really special. Then getting to work on race cars at the Speedway was more special. And eventually winning the race multiple times, like we've been able to do, is even more than I can imagine.

I love the history of the Indy 500 and everything about it. The one memory that stands out is from 2010 when Dario Franchitti was still driving for us. We were at a race in Japan and Dario said to me, 'What are you doing when we get back from Japan?' Then he added, 'I'm going to drive Jim Clark's winning Indy 500 car at the Speedway if you want to come out to see it.'

When I was growing up, Jim Clark was one of the people I idolized as a kid. The only time I got to see him race was at Riverside, Calif. in the Rex Mays 300 in November of 1967. In those days you read about everything in the newspaper and you listened to the Indy 500 on the radio. Jim Clark was one of my guys. I read everything I could consume about him and loved everything about him. Dan Gurney was the other driver I followed.

For me, those two race drivers – Clark and Gurney – were separate from all the rest of some pretty special people in Indy car racing.

So, when Dario asked me if I wanted to come out, I said, 'Absolutely I'll be out there.'

It was the most surreal situation I've ever experienced in racing. It was a perfect fall day in Indy – a crystal clear day and in the 50s with a little bit of wind. Dario had a replica Hinchman Jim Clark fire suit and a replica helmet – the whole thing. He came out to the pits and there were just a couple of guys there that had restored Clark's Lotus Ford and were working on the car.

Dario came out – and nobody said a word – it was eerie. It was absolutely silent and he got in the car without saying anything. The mechanic at the front of the car nodded for him to flip up the ignition switch. The guy in the back hit the starter and with one revolution the thing fired right up and Dario drove away. Still nobody had said a word. That car was going around the race track and the sound that Ford engine made was absolutely exquisite. I just stood there and watched and thought it would have been terrific to be at the 1965 Indy 500 to see Jim Clark drive that car. This was the next best thing!

It was a different feeling afterwards because I think Dario felt an enormous obligation almost to his country and to Jim Clark to do what he did on that day. I don't think Dario exhaled until he got out of the car, and I don't think anybody else did either. It was really, really special. I don't really know how to describe it. It's one of the most surreal experiences that I've ever had anywhere in racing. That car and Jim Clark represented one of the reasons I wanted to get involved in Indy car racing.

Now, when somebody asks me about my memories of the Indy 500, I say it was great when Juan Pablo Montoya won the first time for us in 2000. It was great when we followed it up with Scott Dixon winning in 2008 and it was great when we did it with Dario in 2010 and 2012. That very much has been a Chip Ganassi team thing for me because I've worked for Chip for all these years. In reality, what I saw that September day with Dario set the tone for certainly everything I'd done up to that point and everything after.

***Michael Kaltenmark** grew up in Indiana and attended Butler University. After several years handling public relations for Indy car teams, he is now the director of external relations at Butler University.*

I grew up in Wabash, Ind., and we usually watched the 500 on TV or listened to the race on the radio. My brothers and I would come home from church and that's what you would do. It was sort of a rite of passage to summer.

Watching the 500 is how we became Indy car fans. As a kid, I was a huge Rick Mears fan. Of course he won a lot in that bright yellow car and I remember watching and cheering for Mears. When I got older and went to Butler University, I can distinctly remember one day in May walking to class during my freshman year and hearing the race cars at the Speedway. I thought it was awesome that we were close enough to the track that you could hear the hum of the cars.

That rekindled my interest in the sport. When I decided to major in journalism and public relations, I sought out internships in the sport and landed one with Newman/Haas Racing. That's how I got involved and eventually I worked with Vision Racing and other teams.

One story that stands out to me is related to the Indy 500, but didn't actually occur at the Speedway. It was 2006 and I was handling public relations for the Vision Racing team. We traveled to Japan that April for the race at the Twin Ring Motegi circuit. It was about a week-long trip. I enjoyed it because of the chance to travel internationally and I really liked the Japanese culture, the people and the food. Nonetheless, you were away from home and we were usually there during the rainy season. After a while, it became a bit of a grind.

Finally you would get to race day. They really embraced what I would call the Indy car spirit. Before the start of the race they would play and sing "Back Home Again in Indiana." I get chills just thinking about it. The first time I experienced that song there, it overwhelmed me. I definitely got a little misty-eyed and got chills. We were there in April and the month of May was already on your mind.

To me that song just represented something we do in Indianapolis on Memorial Day weekend. It was sort of our thing. But it really transcends boundaries. The Indy 500 is a global event and the scale of it is probably more far-reaching than I can imagine. It sort of opened my eyes right there. It didn't happen at the Speedway, but it still had the feel of the 500 and it was certainly inspired by the 500.

I almost took the song for granted because I did grow up on the banks of the Wabash and my dad would always sing it in the car. I took it for granted, except for race day at the Speedway. It was always a cool tradition. Then to hear it in Japan and be moved that way, it definitely took on a much greater magnitude. It was at a higher caliber in my mind and my heart at that point.

That May, when we got to the 500 and I heard it again, I definitely thought about Motegi. Every time I hear it now, it's a moment for me. I've experienced the song at the Speedway in a couple different ways. It's fun to belt it out with friends in the stands. It's fun to just take it in while I'm standing on the grid before the race. Either way its super moving now and I'm all in on the song.

***Frank Honsowitz** was the manager of Nissan's motorsports programs and is now president and general manager of Ed Pink Engines.*

Unfortunately, it was the project from hell, doing the Infiniti IRL deal.

Nissan approved the Infiniti IRL program in February 1996 – and the first event was January 1997. Eleven months. I had presented it the summer before – the summer of '95. By the end of the year I figured we weren't going to do it. And lo and behold, way too late, they decided to do it.

Nissan Japan had wanted to participate in CART instead of the IRL series. We had to make it clear that the IRL had the Indy 500 and that's what Infiniti wanted to do. So Nissan in Japan scaled down their technology commitment and we had to make up for it by finding people here in the U.S.

It was just brutal. We had no staff, so we had to do the project with contracted labor. Nissan was struggling financially and by the time we went to Indy we'd gone through three budget reductions for the program.

We didn't have a lot of cars, maybe a third of the field, and we didn't have a giant stock of engines. We had guys driving to Cleveland to pick up engines shipped from Southern California because it's faster and cheaper than shipping direct to Indy. It was all pretty painful.

The worst day was Friday before Pole Day, Fast Friday. On Thursday I got called back to Los Angeles to participate in a meeting. Nissan was trying to determine whether they could stay in the IRL or if they wanted to withdraw. So I flew the red eye home Thursday night and did the meeting Friday – then red-eyed back to Indy for Saturday and qualifying. They decided to continue, but reduced the budget again. It was minimal compared to the GM deal. A journalist that knows a hell of a lot made the comment our budget was smaller than GM's hospitality budget.

During May, all the manufacturers had offices inside the Speedway garage area and I think the garage area closed at 8 p.m. or something. But we stayed until 10 literally every night, communicating with Japan and Southern California. So the gates would always be locked when we were ready to leave. My wife Toni was helping one of the teams with PR during the month, so each night I had to boost her over the chain link fence in order to get out of the garage area. She was a real trooper.

Our best finishing car was 12th. We had some failures and some cars had different kinds of problems during the whole deal. But between having to go back home for a meeting about Nissan's commitment, the budget reductions and all the insane hours to get to that point, it just took all the fun out of any enjoyment. I don't think I went to the pit lane until just before the race started.

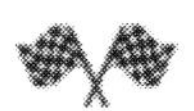

***Cal Wells** formed Precision Preparation, Inc. in 1979 and fielded teams in off-road competition, Indy car racing and NASCAR events.*

The first time I saw the Indy 500 was at a place called Melodyland in Anaheim in the '60s. I went with my dad, who was a big auto racing fan, and we would watch the Indy 500 in black-and-white on a big cube. I was 11 and it really got me hooked.

Indy car racing was something I always wanted to do, but didn't know how to crack the code. I was working with Toyota in off-road racing when they decided they wanted to go Indy car racing. Having raced off-road with Butch and Albert Arciero, we formed Arciero-Wells Racing. We entered the 500 in 1995, the year before Toyota was actually going to begin racing in the 500. We had a deal with Hiro Matsushita to drive the car and Panasonic brought some money. It was really neat because it gave us a year to figure out and work our way through it before Toyota actually started running an engine.

We bought cars and hammered out a deal with Cosworth for engines. That year, Firestone was coming back to the Speedway for the first time in 50 years, or whatever it was. So we did a deal with Firestone too. If I recall, it was just a few of us that did a deal with Firestone – Pat Patrick, Steve Horne, Dale Coyne and us.

We made a huge commitment. We hired a guy who used to be the lead designer at McLaren, Gordon Coppuck. We hired Bob Sprow, who was the crew chief on Rick Mears' car when he won the Indy 500. It was this little group of people. Only a few of us had ever gone Indy car racing before. A couple people the Arcieros knew came to help and we showed up for the month. That was when Indy was truly the month of May.

Firestone was making a big deal about coming back – 50 years. Mario (Andretti) was there as a spokesperson for them. They had all this noise going on. We just didn't pay a lot of attention to it because it became pretty clear that the Firestones were so superior that you were going to be able to gap the field without any issue.

We had done all this stuff just to get the car right. Reynard had come up with a great car. Every Firestone car made the race comfortably. We went out and qualified 10th. I couldn't believe it. It was just one of those things where everything that could go right, did go right. We never hit anything. Nothing ever broke. Nothing ever fell off.

The race starts and there was a crash very early and we barely missed it. We just kept going around all day. At the end of the day, Jacques Villenueve wins it and we finish 10th in our first Indy 500. I couldn't believe it. Frank Arciero had never finished 10th at the Indy 500 because they never had the resources to run competitively. We were thrilled. It was a big moment.

After the race, Al Speyer from Firestone comes around and says, 'Hey, I need you to come to our hospitality tent.' I was surprised because we hadn't talked about it before the race. It was out where the golf course is now and it was big. It was a huge tent and they had something like 10,000 dealers – some huge amount of people.

Now it's maybe 20 minutes after the race and I go find Hiro. Al comes by to get us on this flat bed. It wasn't a golf cart, it was more like a golf cart pick-up truck where you just throw tires on the back. I jump on the back of the cart and I'm bouncing along and Hiro is sitting in the seat. We drive up to this tent and they pull the curtains back. We drive in and this place just erupts. People are standing up and cheering and shouting. When I think about it, I get goose bumps to this day. I said Al, 'What's up?' He said, 'You're the best finisher.' I said, 'What do you mean?' Al then said, 'You guys are our best finisher in our 50th year back at the Indy 500.' I had no idea.

It was a fabulous moment and I'll never forget it, because it was totally unexpected. I had not gone down the finishing list yet to see if any Firestone runners had been ahead of us. There wasn't a contingency prize for it or it wasn't like we wanted to be the best Firestone guy. We wanted to show up and finish – that was our goal. Finish on the lead lap and run well.

To get a top-10 finish at the Indy 500 the first time you show up was huge, but the other huge piece was all these Firestone guys, all these dealers and the reaction when we came in. I still get tingles thinking about it. We were so surprised and it was a really cool moment. It was just spectacular – a surreal moment.

***Lee White** was a member of winning teams in the 24 Hours of Le Mans and the Daytona 24 Hours and many other races. He retired as president of Toyota Racing Development in 2013 after guiding the manufacturer to multiple wins and championships in CART, the IRL and NASCAR, plus a victory in the Indy 500.*

The first time I went to Indy as a competitor I was working for Newman/Haas and was there calling the race for Michael Andretti in 1995. We were leading the race on the 77th lap and he came up to pass a car, brushed the wall and ripped the right suspension off the car, so that destroyed that. Unfortunately, I never won it with Newman/Haas, although we gave it a good shot.

The next time I recall being there I was invited by Chip Ganassi. He was a Toyota team in CART and I was invited by Chip to go to the Indy 500 where they ran an Olds. I vividly recall standing in Juan Pablo Montoya's pits as he won the race in 2000.

The following weekend was the CART race in Milwaukee and Juan Pablo won the race. After the race, I remember standing in his pit and Juan Pablo pulls in, pulls off the helmet that he was wearing – which he wore the weekend before when he won the Indy 500 – and basically said this is for you, and gave me the helmet. It's still in a display case at Toyota Racing Development.

The following year Chip called me again. He had this situation where he was trying to run four cars, but he didn't have enough crew, so he asked me if I would call the race for one of his drivers.

He ran Jimmy Vasser, Bruno Junqueira, Tony Stewart and Nicolas Minassian in the race. I drew the short straw and got Bruno, who didn't speak a word of English, only Portuguese. Somehow he got tangled up in the race and got five laps down. I don't how we managed it with the language problem, but we played the game on pit stops and whatnot, recovered all five laps and finished fifth, on the lead lap.

Since racing is all about winning, I would have to say the 2003 Indy 500 that was won by Roger Penske and Gil de Ferran with a TRD engine, and chassis and aero assistance from TRD, is probably my Indy 500 highlight. In fact, I have a picture on the wall in my man cave of Roger Penske, Gil de Ferran and myself on the yard of bricks on the Monday after the race.

At about that time, we were right in the middle of moving TRD and Toyota into NASCAR. We only had a couple of years left on our contract with the IRL and we were getting close to getting out of that program. Winning that race was a climactic moment, for me at least.

You remember the ones where you're there, pulling the trigger. So I best remember the ones where I was up on the timing stand and working hard to try and win. When you're there as a manufacturer, as opposed to a team member, you're kind of detached from the actual goings on. You're literally watching from the back of the pit boxes – it's different.

But in my 45 years in racing it was all about winning, so you can't say that one win means any less. And without question, that's the one I've got the most pictures of in my man cave.

Janet Guthrie

CHAPTER 12

Ladies

When Janet Guthrie became the first woman to qualify for the Indy 500 in 1977, one of the questions that arose was how Speedway owner Tony Hulman would issue the command to start engines. Since 1945 it had simply been, "Gentlemen start your engines."

Hulman added to the controversy several days before the race, saying that since women didn't actually start the cars – a crewman with a mechanical starter standing behind the car did that – he might continue to say simply, "Gentlemen..."

That's when Kay Bignotti stepped forward. She was the wife of one of Indy's most successful chief mechanics, George Bignotti, and the daughter of three-time Indy 500 winner Louis Meyer. She also held a USAC mechanic's license and offered to start Guthrie's car, an offer that was quickly accepted. Other women's groups criticized Hulman's comments.

A successful businessman whose family fortune owed much to the Clabber Girl line of cooking products, Hulman knew when to cut his losses. He never hesitated when approaching the microphones before the race, stating clearly, "In company with the first lady ever to qualify at Indianapolis, gentlemen start your engines." In subsequent years the call has included "Lady and gentlemen…" or, when appropriate, "Ladies and gentlemen…"

***Janet Guthrie** was the first woman to qualify for the Indy 500 and competed in the race three times. She is a member of the International Motorports Hall of Fame and recently received the Louis Meyer Award for lifetime achievement.*

I think any driver would say that the first time you put a car in that race is an outstanding memory. That was back in the time when you might have 80 or 90 cars entered.

When I first accepted Rolla Vollstedt's invitation to enter the Indianapolis 500 in 1976, the 500 was *the* greatest race in the world. Sure there was Grand Prix and NASCAR was strong, but not nearly as important as Indy. Any racing driver – and by that time I had 13 years of experience in other forms of racing – any racing driver would give their eye teeth for a chance to even attempt to qualify for the Indianapolis 500.

I didn't realize, however, how much antagonism there would be toward a woman in that form of the sport. It actually was a great surprise to me.

At the beginning it was really terrible. Established drivers complained loudly, publicly and at length. 'Women don't have the strength,' they said, 'Women don't have the endurance, women don't have the emotional stability, women are going to endanger our lives.'

Sometimes I could laugh at it, sometimes it made me mad, but the only way to deal with it was on the race track.

We didn't make the field in 1976. A series of mechanical problems kept me from even making a qualifying attempt. We had, however, done well for ourselves at four other Indy car races. I qualified as high as 12th and competed vigorously.

I turned in the fastest speed on opening day in 1977 and was among the fastest drivers on the track the first few days of May. But then I spun and damaged the car trying to get over 190 mph and we struggled with car and engine problems after that. The newspapers were brimming with innuendo that my effort was history as the final day of qualifying approached.

To a driver, a drop into uncompetitive speeds, with its threat of an end to racing, represents a fate worse than death. The most traumatic crash seems but a temporary and annoying inconvenience. Cars and bones can be mended. To a driver, the only thing that matters is getting the speed back again.

Coming out of Turn 4 on the final lap of my qualifying run I could see Rolla and the guys on the crew leaping and waving their arms. I'm not sure whether the lump at the back of my throat was actually my heart, but I am utterly certain I didn't breathe until the yard of bricks at the start/finish flashed under my wheels and the checkered flag swirled overhead.

One minute later I was rolling down pit road and guys on other crews were holding thumbs up, waving and clapping. I was lost in a blizzard of hugs and kisses from Rolla and the guys. The team had held together, we had struggled through fearful adversity, but we had put Rolla's car into the Indianapolis 500.

Nothing in my life would ever be the same.

***Lyn St. James** was an accomplished road racer when she qualified for her first Indy 500. Sports Illustrated named her one of the top "100 Women Athletes of the 20th Century."*

I have so many memories of the Indianapolis 500 it's difficult to pick one. Obviously getting to race in the Indy 500, to win Rookie of the Year honors in 1992, and to qualify and race in seven Indy 500s from 1992 to 2000, those memories will be with me forever.

But one memory that sticks in my mind and truly makes my accomplishments even more meaningful, is attending my first 500 in 1966 with a group of guys from my local gas station in Willoughby, Ohio, along with my mother as chaperone.

After watching the driver's meeting on Saturday and walking outside the fence around Gasoline Alley – because women were not allowed in Gasoline Alley – I desperately wanted a driver's autograph. My buddies were walking around inside and they coerced Mel Kenyon to walk over to the fence to give me an autograph. I was delighted, but shocked when I saw all the burn scars on Mel's face and hands. Years later when I was racing at Indy, I saw Mel in Gasoline Alley. I shared my story of him giving me an autograph in 1966 and he said, 'Yeah, I remember that!'

It's race day 1966 and I have never seen so many people in one place in all my short life. It was the 50th running of the race, so I wore a gold outfit on race day and we sat in Turn 1. At the green flag there's a horrific explosion and cars are crashing everywhere with car parts, tires and wheels flying through the air. The race is halted while they clean everything up and I think about 10 cars were taken out in that crash.

After they got restarted I couldn't believe how fast the cars were going; it was like they were flying. I could hardly tell who was in which car as they flew by, but my buddies started teaching me to identify the car by the sound of the engine. I learned the different sound between the Offy and Ford engines. It was a one-two finish for the Ford engines, with Graham Hill winning in a Lola and Jimmy Clark second in a Lotus.

It was the sounds, the smell, the energy and the excitement that created my love of racing. And while I never said to myself, 'Oh I'm going to do this,' I think it imbedded into my very soul that racing was somehow going to be a part of my life.

Jump ahead to 1992. After I finished the race we were celebrating in the garage in Gasoline Alley and a security guard comes to me and says there's a guy at the gate who says he took you to your first Indy 500. I went to the gate and sure enough it was Dave Froeman, the owner of the gas station who took me to the race in 1966. I was able to let him into our garage and celebrate with us. How cool to be able to share that experience with him!

***Danica Patrick** ran in seven straight Indy 500s beginning in 2005. She was the first woman to lead the 500 and earned Rookie of the Year honors. Her third place in 2009 was the best finish by a woman in the 500. She is the only woman to win an Indy car race.*

Indianapolis Motor Speedway is such a special place and I have so many great memories of my time there. I love driving through the tunnel and coming into the track, even when it's empty, and just seeing the Pagoda.

No matter what car I'm driving, I always feel the track's magnitude and just how special of a place it is. I've always believed that you have to show the track respect and hopefully it will show you the respect back. Especially in an Indy car going 230 mph, the track can bite you pretty big.

One of my most special memories of Indy would have to be my very first start in the Indy 500. The 2005 Indianapolis 500 put me on the map as a driver and that day – May 29, 2005 – was truly a turning point in my career.

The entire month of May in Indy was really special that year. I raced for Rahal Letterman Racing at the time and we started off strong by posting the fastest lap on the opening day of practice. We ended up doing that a few more times that month. It really felt incredible to be in a car capable of those speeds. When it came down to Pole Day, I knew I had a great car. During my qualification attempt, it all nearly came to an end when I had to make a quick maneuver as the car bobbled in Turn 1 on the first lap. Remarkably, I was able to save it and we somehow still ended up qualifying fourth.

When we finally got to race day that Sunday, there was such a great energy at the track. All of the pomp and circumstance around the Indy 500 pre-race ceremonies truly help to make the event one of the greatest spectacles in all of sports.

There were moments of, 'Wow! What the heck is going on?' as I went spinning across the track, ripping my front wing off and then when I stalled it in the pits. But there were also 'Wow!' moments when I took the lead. I have to say it felt very incredible to lead the Indy 500 in my very first start.

The team gambled on fuel late in the race. Then, with just 11 laps to go, I passed Dan Wheldon and found myself up front once again. It almost all worked out. I was just saving so much fuel and trying to make it to the end that I wasn't able to run really low on the track due to older tires and us saving fuel, which ultimately was what allowed Dan to get just a little wing down below me. He didn't have to lift then and was able to get by me. We ended up fourth and while I was disappointed that it ended up the way it did, I led and had a chance to win it, and that's all you can ask for.

I may have not ended up chugging milk in Victory Lane, but my top-five run still turned a lot of heads and life hasn't exactly been the same since that day. I ended up on the cover of *Sports Illustrated* and was on a number of talk shows as a result of my strong performance. It was a bit overwhelming at the time, but I'm forever grateful for my first Indy 500 experience.

***Dr. Jerry Punch** is a television broadcaster for ABC/ESPN.*

I was standing beside Bev Patrick, Danica Patrick's mom, as she stood there with the palms of her hands pressing both cheeks, her fingers covering her eyes as her daughter approached the lead at the Indy 500. Then Danica takes the lead and I'm watching the tears pouring down her mom's face. She was shaking and her hands were trembling as she realized that her little girl had done something that had never been done before – and it's hard to do something at Indianapolis that hasn't been done. Growing up watching her in a go-kart. Listening to her talk at night while hugging her stuffed animals about someday racing at the Indy 500. And suddenly here she was, leading the greatest race drivers in the world in "The Greatest Spectacle in Racing" – that was a pretty special memory.

***Pippa Mann** was born in London in 1983 and was the first British woman to qualify for the Indy 500. She began racing in Europe in 2003 before moving to Indy Lights in 2009 and the 500 two years later.*

My most memorable Indy 500 experience was probably qualifying for my first one. It was 2011 and there were 42 cars competing for the 33 starting spots. I came into the month with only one prior day of driving an Indy car under my belt and driving for one of the smaller teams on the grid – Conquest Racing. The inclement weather that year also limited running to the point where even the experienced guys started to feel like they had their hands tied behind their back. Despite the odds stacked against us, we were looking good and fast enough to qualify in the mid-220s pretty much every time I hit the track.

Then came qualifying.

On Saturday we rolled out for qualifying and we just lost speed. Every run got slower and slower. My teammate had been struggling to find speed the entire month and now we were struggling with both cars. Our garage was tense. I pushed for a new motor as I was convinced the engine had dropped. My team owner was convinced we needed to try something new with the setup. In the end we both won, a new motor went in the back and some big changes would be made to both cars overnight.

I arrived Sunday morning, for the second and last day of qualifying, as it was now a one weekend format. The guys were still working furiously on my car. Warm-up started without me. As the clock counted down, I was strapped into the car. With a mechanic sitting on the nose, we towed out to pit lane, engine being warmed up while we rolled. I got two flying laps before the session went checkered. The new engine felt great. But those changes we had spent all night making? They gave the term "loose" a whole new meaning and there was no time to change them back.

With another band of rain coming in, we had to make it to tech in time to secure our position in line and assure ourselves an opportunity to make our one guaranteed attempt to qualify for the race. We made one change to the car based on what I thought needed the most help and then it was time.

Getting in, I knew I had to stay flat-out into Turn 1 on my first flying lap and every lap thereafter, or we would be going home. I also knew that if my engineer and I were wrong with our one gut instinct change, I would probably experience what it felt like to go backwards at 225 mph when I attempted to go into Turn 1 flat out. That would also mean going home as even if the rain didn't arrive, we didn't have a spare car, and wouldn't have time to fix mine if I bent it.

I distinctly remember heading towards Turn 1 on that first flying lap, determined not to go home because I lifted my foot off the throttle and wondering if that meant I would be going home with my car in pieces. I held my breath. She stuck. The game was on.

I spent the next three and three-quarter laps playing with all the tools I had available in the car, inching more and more speed out of her every time across the start/finish line, while walking on the incredibly narrow tight-rope between "loose is fast" and scrubbing off speed or spinning.

As I came out of Turn 4 on my final lap I ended up sliding to within inches of touching the outside wall. But that final lap was my fastest and when combined into my average, it was the lap that made the difference, the one that got us in the race.

Nine cars didn't make it. Four full-time drivers didn't make it. No other driver with only one day of testing prior to coming in to attempt to run Indy in 2011 made it. But we did. And as a result, on Memorial Day weekend in 2011, I got to start my first Indianapolis 500.

Katherine Legge *competed in the Indy 500 in 2012 and 2013. She is part of an all-female team scheduled to compete in the 500 in 2016.*

When I think of my favorite Indy 500, what comes to mind is when my mum came over from England to watch the race. She hates racing and was so nervous. She spent the entire time pacing the garage. My dad loves racing and comes to most of my races, but my mum, hardly any.

Poor mum grabbed me on rookie orientation day as I got out of the car on pit lane, looked at me dead serious and said, 'But Katherine, they are so fast!'

It was so cool that she got to experience the magic of the Indy 500 and she and my dad did the downtown parade in the car with me. I loved having her there but, poor mum, she was so nervous that day!

Ryan Briscoe

CHAPTER 13

Gentlemen

For those who have never won the Indy 500, and that's about 90 percent of the drivers who have competed in the Memorial Day classic, just qualifying for the race often ranks as the highlight of their racing career. And for those who qualify, capturing the pole is the next best thing to winning the race.

Ryan Briscoe *is an Australian now living in Connecticut who has made 10 Indy 500 starts heading into the 2016 race and earned the pole for the 2012 race.*

I have a lot of great memories from the Indy 500. The one that stands out is getting the pole position. It was more than the moment of getting the pole – that's such a stressful day.

You get the pole and you're just exhausted. But the really cool thing is that for the whole week afterwards, every day you drive into the track, your number is at the top of the pylon. And that was really awesome. You get to have that standing out for everyone to see for a whole week.

Really in today's racing at the 500, it doesn't matter where you start and pole doesn't really give you a big advantage of being able to win the race – but it is a huge achievement. So much effort goes into Pole Day and getting that job done. Getting that pole and then having my number on the pylon every morning as I drove into the track to look at was a great memory.

There was so much recognition for it. Even more than I thought there would be. I've never really talked about it because it's just qualifying and it means nothing towards winning the Indy 500, but it was amazing during the week how much recognition I really did get in the lead up to the race.

I remember having a media day in Charlotte after winning the pole. That's where I lived at the time. So, I got to spend a night at home and we went out to dinner at this Mexican restaurant just around the corner. By coincidence, NASCAR's Kasey Kahne and some of his friends were having dinner there and he just picked up the check for me. I don't really know him – we'd met maybe once or something. He picked up the check and said, 'Hey, congrats on the pole.' I was like, 'Man, that's pretty awesome.'

That year I definitely felt confident we'd have a shot at pole. The car was running really well. I think that was the first year of a knockout format that came down to just nine cars at the end of the day and you've got an hour. I did my lap on my first run of that last hour. Then we sat in line and were waiting to see if we had to go again. It came right down to the wire. I mean, James Hinchcliffe ended up second and his first lap was quicker than my quickest of the four laps. I saw his first lap and it was quite a lot faster than mine. I'm like, 'Here we go – got to do this again.' I remember sitting with my helmet on at the end of pit lane as the next car to go if we had to and I'm sort of following his laps. I'm getting geared up to go and his times just started dropping off and his last lap was slow enough where I ended up beating him. It turned out to be by about nine inches. It was that close at 230 miles an hour. It was a really close fight with him for the pole and we ended up just getting it.

***Ed Carpenter** won two straight pole positions for the Indy 500 in 2013 and 2014. He is the stepson of Tony George of the Hulman-George family, which owns the Speedway.*

The first time I ever drove anything on the track is kind of a unique story. It was in the middle of the winter and my dad and my younger brother and I went out there on snowmobiles. I was about eight or nine. My dad was riding on a fast snowmobile, my little brother was on back, and I was on a little kid version, I think they called it a Kitty Cat. My dad's had so much more horsepower; I think they lapped me a couple of times. But it was pretty cool.

I started racing quarter midgets when I was eight years old. I had some success early on and really enjoyed it. But I can't honestly say I started thinking about competing in the 500 until I was into my teenage years, when I was starting to race USAC and a little bit bigger cars and thinking I'd really like to be out there competing in this race. That's when the mindset shifted to, 'What do I need to do to get there?' I've always been competitive and always wanted to win, but there's a difference from having fun and going out to win, versus trying to build a career path to the 500.

I drove for A.J. Foyt in Indy Lights in 2003 and that was a fun experience. I got to know him when I was young. He and Al Unser, Jr. were my two heroes as a kid. Being able to drive for A.J. at Indy was awesome – just to pick his brain about how to race there and what's important and what's not.

Arie Luyendyk also was working with some of us and there are things I still remember him telling me about what you should be thinking, what you should be looking at on the track, things that have stuck with me. I've been blessed to have been so close to the sport for so long and to have relationships with some of the legends of the sport; to be in a position to ask them questions and soak up some knowledge.

For me, so much about Indy is about respect. That's one of the things those guys taught me. There are times, especially in an Indy Lights car, when it can be an easier place to drive when everything's right. But at the same time, the margin of error is a lot smaller than other tracks we go to.

When you get comfortable or overconfident with that track it can jump out and get you. It happened to me when I was young and it has happened to me as a veteran. When you try to force something – it will really punish you. So having the respect and diligence for me – I try to be consistent every time I go out for the entire month of May, just to make sure it helps keep me focused on what I'm doing on each and every outing.

As long as I'm driving, winning the 500 is at the top of the list. Always has been and always will be. One thing I'm proud of is that 2016 will be my 13th 500 if I am able to qualify. Not sure I ever thought I'd get that many. It's a hard sport to sustain in and to have a career at something that I love, I'm thankful for – for sure. I remember early in my career talking to my dad and thinking it'd be cool to make it to the 100th running and wasn't sure I'd still be doing it at that point, or still have the opportunity to do it, so it's pretty neat to think that I'll be part of that month and part of that history.

***Conor Daly** has worked his way up the racing ranks from a start in karting and has competed in two Indy 500s heading into the 2016 race. He is the son of Derek Daly, a seven-time Indy 500 starter.*

I got back from racing in Europe just in time for the race weekend in 2011 and I went down to the garages to talk with some of the drivers. That was my first year in Indy Lights and I was trying to get deeper into the Indy car world.

I will always remember the position Dan Wheldon was in. He didn't have a ride for the season. You could tell he was so motivated to win, more than ever. I always looked up to Dan, since I met him at his first Indy car race with Panther Racing when I was very young.

Race day was yet another day I couldn't wait for as it was 100 years since the first 500 in 1911. I'd watched every single lap of every Indy 500 from the Tower Terrace Suites, as that's where my mom works, and this race was absolutely awesome. The last few laps were incredible, seeing my friend Bertrand Baguette lead and seeing everyone's fuel strategy go up in flames was crazy. Then, when J.R. Hildebrand came out of Turn 4 and hit the wall, allowing Dan to get the win at the line, the emotion that I, and I think everyone else felt, was overwhelming. Such an incredible piece of history to witness and be a part of. It made me want to get out there and compete someday even more.

I couldn't believe I finally had a chance to drive in the greatest race in the world in 2013. The Indy 500, also my home race, means more to me than anything in the world. I grew up at the track. I've seen many of the highs and lows drivers have gone through in my young life. I finally had a chance to experience it all first person and take the green from the driver's seat and not see it from the Tower Terrace Suites. I'm fairly sure I had goose bumps the entire morning leading up to getting in the car.

One of the funniest parts of that day was the rush to go to the bathroom before the race. Right after all the anthems and songs, the drivers rush to find the nearest bathroom. But Tony Kanaan and I got to the nearest bathroom quite late, so there was a line. We were then brought to a different restroom a little bit further away and they told us to use the women's restroom.

So there I was, in the stall next to Kanaan. I told him there and then that it would be really cool to see him win this race. He told me to enjoy every minute and lap of the day and that I also had a chance at winning. Sure enough, TK won that day and I got through my first Indianapolis 500 with a massive smile on my face – even after two pit fires!

Scott Goodyear *had three second-place finishes in the Indy 500 and is now a race commentator for ABC/ESPN.*

My first visit to the Indy 500 was a total surprise. I was 12 years old and my dad and I were karting in upstate New York.

The next time I went to Indy it was 1989 and I was well along in my career. I felt like I was getting close to being hired to drive an Indy car and having an opportunity to qualify for the 500. I went to watch practice and the first weekend of qualifying so I could get a feel for the place.

What a different perspective watching from the pit lane. Somehow the cars seemed a lot faster watching from the pit lane than they did watching from the grandstand. When I was there, I paid to ride the tour bus so I could get a chance to see what the track looked like and take a few pictures. I was amazed at the size of the track as it didn't seem that big on television or watching the cars go past on the front straight.

I remember coming around Turn 2 on the tour bus and looking down the long back straight. It took forever to get to Turn 3. I was so excited to be on the track, but I wasn't ready for what I saw when we came out of Turn 4 and onto the front straight.

The sight was unbelievable, grandstands on both sides, a front straight that looked like you were driving into a wall of grandstands. It felt like you were heading down a tunnel. And I was just riding the tour bus! My only regret is that I didn't save the ticket stub from my tour bus ride.

My first time driving on the Speedway was an experience I will never forget. I've raced on some pretty famous tracks around the world including Le Mans, Daytona and Sebring and although I remember my first lap at Le Mans driving a Porsche 962, it wasn't as impactful as my first lap at Indy.

When you drive out of the pits at Indy, your surroundings give you a sense of the history of the place. Although it is a major moment for you personally as a driver, you realize you have a tough road ahead of you if you want to become part of the history of the Speedway.

After rookie orientation class and some laps in the pace car as a passenger with Johnny Rutherford behind the wheel, it's now your turn. To say the butterflies in your stomach are active is an understatement. Excited, sure. Questions, plenty. You head out onto the track to get answers.

As if the drive down pit lane wasn't daunting enough, the run around the apron of the track, which they used as a warm up lane in those days, seemed just wide enough for your car. Your job was to keep it below the white line so you didn't allow the right side wheels of your car to creep up onto the track. I kept the car between the lines on the apron in Turn 1 and towards Turn 2, and when I rounded the exit of Turn 2 and drove on the racing surface, Turn 3 seemed so distant.

After running just a few laps at speed, you quickly realize that the straights aren't really all that long when you're driving 230 mph.

Dan Gurney *competed in the Indy 500 from 1962 to 1970, finishing second twice. As owner of All American Racers and builder of the Eagle, he watched his cars win four 500s.*

In 1965 my newly founded company, All American Racers, was gearing up to enter Indy car racing the following year. With funding from the Goodyear Tire & Rubber Company, we were in the process of designing and building our own cars to be entered in the 1966 USAC national championship and, most importantly, the Indy 500.

We were planning to build Eagles for our own team as well as for customers. While trying to put the right personnel together for such a gigantic adventure we decided to buy two Halibrand Shrikes equipped with Ford engines for the 1965 Indy 500 in order to gain valuable experience when the real thing would show up the following year. For this I hired two established drivers, USAC veteran Roger McCluskey and three-time AMA national champion Joe Leonard, who had shown promise on four wheels during a few USAC races the previous season. I saw him as a possible parallel to John Surtees, my competitor on the Formula One circuit, who had won the world championships with bikes and cars.

Joe was a gifted, intelligent and determined racer of the highest quality and I felt his background had prepared him well for the rigors of Indy car racing. But he had a flaw and a big one, very poor eyesight. In order to pass his rookie test, he had to pass a mandatory physical examination and vision test administered by Dr. (Thomas) Hanna, the esteemed medical authority at the Speedway, who worked out of a modest wooden building in the infield of the circuit.

Without passing this test, Joe would not get permission to race. We faced an unexpected dilemma. I took it upon myself to lobby and convince old Doc Hanna to let Joe take his driver's test anyway. It was an uphill battle. Doc Hanna, a contemporary of Tony Hulman and Joe Cloutier, could not let Joe pass without compromising Speedway regulations. But he also had wisdom and he looked at Joe's racing achievements which belied his lack of reasonable vision and tried to find a solution. He came up with some special Coke-bottle glasses for Joe to wear, which enabled him to pass his vision and rookie test with flying colors. We called them the two-and-half-milers. From that day forward, when Joe showed up in Gasoline Alley early in the morning, we greeted him by singing, 'Jose can you see?' to the tune of our national anthem.

George Mack *was one of the world's top kart drivers when he became the second African American to qualify for the Indy 500. He currently is an auto industry executive in Los Angeles.*

My mom and dad allowed me to try all the sports growing up. I was just fair to middling when it came to basketball, football and baseball, which are what most African American kids play in L.A. Then my dad came home with a brand new motorcycle. I was good on a motorcycle, but too aggressive. So my mom told him, 'Listen, I'm all for father and son sports. But this kid is a little bit crazy. Can we put him on something with four wheels?' My motorcycle came up missing and it was replaced by a go-kart.

The whole family jumped on the go-kart bandwagon. I crossed paths with Mark Dinsmore, Buddy Rice, Alex Barron, Tony Stewart, Kevin Harvick, Jamie McMurray and others. We all raced together, beat and banged on each other. For whatever reason, I was able to drive a go-kart really well. I ran the shifter karts in Europe and was the highest finishing American before I put together the Indy car deal.

The Speedway scared the hell out me. It was huge. I had never been on a track that big. It's very intimidating. *Very* intimidating. It was something I had wanted since I was a kid, but now that I was there, I didn't want to screw it up. It's a big leap in power and speed.

Growing a pair of balls big enough to drive the car down into Turn 1 at 230 mph without lifting was very tough. It gets narrow as you head down into Turn 1 and turns into a tunnel. When you're in the car it's like sitting in a bathtub with wheels. You have no vision. You can only see in front of you, that's it. You're blind. It's a leap of faith. Your spotters and your crew are your eyes.

I learned that setting up the car is big. You want that thing to corner as fast as it runs in a straight line. Once you can trust the car, and trust the crew, it becomes a little bit easier.

When I got on the track I was running OK. But we made some changes that made it light in the rear and I backed into Turn 2 going about 215 or 220. I banged my head really good, so I was laid up in the hospital for a week. I had a concussion and vertigo. The team didn't think I was going to be able to qualify because I couldn't really stand up because of the vertigo.

My chiropractor back home in Orange County read I had crashed. He called my cell phone in the hospital and asked if they were giving me a certain pill, exactly what I was taking. He said, 'Don't take those pills! They'll exacerbate your problem.' He said I should find a chiropractor and get adjusted five times a day and if I did that, I would be able to drive. That sounded like a snake oil salesman to me. Some kind of voodoo. But I would try anything, and while I couldn't get adjusted five times a day, I had it done at least twice a day and believe it or not, it helped.

I had to qualify on the last day. If I didn't make it then, that was it. Drivers who had been around for a while were saying, 'If you don't make it, don't worry about it. I didn't make it my first time and I was with a bigger team.' But I was thinking I don't have your last name. I'm a privateer, this is my first shot and I plan on making it, or I'm gonna kill myself trying.

I was still a little woozy, but if I held my head in a certain position, it helped. So we propped my head in the car with padding and it was tilted just the right way. And that's how I qualified the car at 227. I think it was the most consistent four laps of the month.

I miss the competitiveness of racing, but I don't miss the politics. Banging into the wall at 230 doesn't seem very attractive right now either. Ten years ago, that's nothing. But it was a great experience, I'm thankful for the opportunity. We had a chance to make history.

***Simon Pagenaud** has been a regular participant in two of the world's most famous races, the Indy 500 and the 24 Hours of Le Mans, and currently drives an Indy car for Team Penske.*

Coming from Europe, I knew about three races growing up. Being from France, there was the 24 Hours of Le Mans – one of the biggest races in the world. The Monaco Grand Prix was another. And I knew about the Indy 500, which was the oldest race and also the furthest away from where I was at the time, but certainly one of the most famous races.

In 1990, when I was six, I watched my first 24 Hours of Le Mans race. My memory is blurry when I think about the first Indy 500 I remember. Obviously, I knew about the race, but we didn't watch it on TV. However, I do remember reading about it. When I was 17 or 18 and racing in Europe, one of my goals was to come to America. At that time, winning the Indy 500 or winning the Formula One championship were the biggest achievements for a race car driver.

My first time visiting the United States was in 2005, at the end of year. The following year, I went to the Indy 500 for the very first time. I managed to get on the grid and was mesmerized by the event. Even though I run the race now, that's still the case. One day I was on the grid dreaming about being in a race car at the Speedway and then I was starting the Indy 500 on the front row. It was an incredible moment.

It still feels exactly like it did in 2006. What's most intriguing about the Indy 500 is all the emotion. There's a special feeling you get when you're on the race track. You sense the legends that used to drive and compete at the Speedway. It's hard to explain – but you just sense something special.

It's a different kind of race and I don't think there are any other races in the world just like it. When you go race at most tracks, it's just another race. When you go to Indy, it just holds something different and you can't explain it. It's almost like the ghosts of the previous races are still there and they're still watching you. They're still part of the show. It's a very unique ambience that is just one of a kind.

There's one thing about Indy, and I always remember this from TK (Tony Kanaan), who's a good friend. The first year I was there I wasn't too stressed and he was really stressed. TK always gets stressed before an Indy 500. He told me one day that, 'You'll see, the more you do it, the more stressful it gets.' I asked him why. He said, 'Because you get so close to winning you'll want to win it even more the next time. So, it just builds up. There's more stress every year. You'll see – you'll understand.'

He's right. Every year you get more stressed. Every year it means more because you're just printing memories in your head. It's just quite special.

***Will Power** has started on the front row of the Indy 500 three times (2010, 2014 and 2015) and finished as the race runner-up to Team Penske teammate Juan Pablo Montoya in 2015.*

My best memory would actually be driving in the race – because I didn't really watch it before that.

The first time I visited the Speedway was in 2005. I had come over to test for Derrick Walker and was at his shop to make a seat for one of the last races of the season. I was just sitting in the hotel, so I rented a car and went out to the Speedway. I walked through the museum and paid the money for the bus tour. It wasn't like any race track I'd ever seen before. It was just a massive, massive place.

The next year was the first time I ever watched the Indy 500. At the time, I was in Champ Car and we weren't racing that weekend. I actually bought a ticket and sat in the crowd between turns 1 and 2. I got there after the race started and left before it finished. That was when Sam Hornish beat Marco Andretti. I listened to the finish on the radio.

My best memory is probably 2009 when I first drove for Roger Penske. That's the first time I had a really good car – my second year in the 500 and the first year driving for Roger. I was only a part-timer. The car was awesome – good enough to win and in a position to win at the end. I was second to Helio (Castroneves) coming into the last stop. I had passed a bunch of people and got to Helio. I thought I was going to get past him pretty quickly based on how quickly I got past the other people. Then he turned his fuel up and we started racing hard. Then it went yellow – and that was that. There was a pit stop and I got shuffled back to sixth or something like that and we ended up fifth.

Before the race I just remember thinking that I've got to finish this race because this is potentially my last race for Penske and possibly my last race in Indy. I had nothing after that, nothing guaranteed, so I was thinking it could be my last race in an Indy car.

I was starting next to Mario Moraes and Marco Andretti. They were on my row and I was a little bit worried about those guys and the start – not Marco so much, but Moraes was a bit of a maniac. And sure enough, they both crashed. I was sitting back there and they crashed, and I got through that mess. I just remember how good the car was. It was the first time I had such a good car on an oval. The car was so good to drive – it was just solid.

I finished the race thinking, 'Hmm, what's going to happen? Am I going to have a ride or not?' I saw Roger on Monday after the race and he said, 'We'll give you another five races because you did a good job in the 500.'

With Roger, you always have a good car and a chance to win. As you spend more time with the team, you become very aware that it's a hugely important race for him. He's won it more than anyone else and you want to be one of the ones to add to that number.

Graham Rahal *is the son of 1986 Indy 500 champion Bobby Rahal. He made his Indy 500 debut in 2008 at the age of 19 and has started every 500 since.*

I attended the Indy 500 when I was young, but really don't remember much. The earliest story that I actually remember probably happened on race day in 1993 or 1994. I remember watching the race with David Letterman in our family suite. He found it funny to ask me – or really quiz me – about every car and every driver in the race.

My whole life, I've been a super fan of Indy car racing. I knew all the names, knew all the sponsors and knew all the colors. Dave sat there the whole race quizzing me about everybody, but I had it down pretty good. Growing up I was a race brat and always around the race track. I really never went anywhere else.

My favorite memory as a driver would probably be 2015. I finished higher up a couple years before that – I was third in 2011. The difference is, in '15 we were really taking a knife to a gun fight with the Hondas versus the Chevys. To finish in the top five was incredibly rewarding because I had gone through two years at Indy before that where, truthfully, the race cars I had were not very good. During those two years I was not happy and didn't really enjoy it. Every May I was excited because it was the month of May, but the driving part didn't thrill me because the cars were not very good. Then we came back and rebounded – finished in the top five – and it felt like a victory, if not better.

My favorite memory overall has to be when the team won in 2004, because I know the pride that dad and Dave have in the team and their respect for the Indy 500. I was young then, probably 15. It was my first year in open-wheel cars, racing Formula BMW, and I was in Lime Rock, Conn. We had a day off because they don't race Lime Rock on Sunday, you race on Monday. So we sat there and watched the race on the TV in the BMW hospitality tent. I knew Buddy (Rice) had been quick all month, but I didn't talk to dad every day back then. He and I have always been very close, but I didn't have my own phone so I didn't really get to talk to him all the time.

So I was kind of watching from afar. Then I see Buddy's on pole. After that, I see that the team wins the pit stop competition. I'm like, 'This month couldn't get any better.' All of a sudden, the next thing you know, they're the Indy 500 champs. That was a pretty special moment for me and for my family.

I don't remember exactly what I did, but I'm sure yelling or screaming was involved. I'm absolutely sure I did because whether it's you as an individual or your family's team – the Indy 500 is one of a kind. The Indy 500 has shaped my family. It forever changed our name when my dad won. No matter what races you win or how many championships you may win – the Indy 500 is all a lot of people really care about.

The Indy 500 is one of a kind. I've been very fortunate in life to race at Daytona – I've won the Daytona 24 Hours. I've been to the Daytona 500 and to Le Mans and all over the place. And I've been to the Super Bowl and the World Series and all that stuff. In my mind, nothing compares to the Indy 500. It's really as simple as that.

***Sam Schmidt** raced in three Indy 500s before he was badly injured in a testing accident at Walt Disney World Speedway in 2000. He now runs Sam Schmidt Motorsports and established the Sam Schmidt Paralysis Foundation.*

I graduated from USF2000 straight to Indy cars in May 1998, an enormous leap. I only had the experience of racing at Phoenix, a one-mile oval, before coming to Indy. Needless to say, I was scared to death! The smartest thing we did was hire Gary Bettenhausen as a driver coach.

This guy knew every crack of IMS and never needed a computer. He could watch from the wall, see the attitude of the car, look at two tires when you came in and know exactly what the car was doing.

One time Tom Carnegie came over the loud speaker and said, 'Yellow flag for debris.' Gary immediately said 'God damn Frenchman... never could drive!'

Needless to say, it was an interesting month of great chemistry, stories and lots of empty cigarette packets. True old school. With his help, I never had an issue all month and qualified sixth.

***Bill Simpson** drove in the Indy 500, but is best known as a pioneer of racing safety equipment. To prove the effectiveness of his fire proof uniforms he set himself on fire – twice.*

I never thought I'd see Indianapolis Speedway. I was a drag racer.

But when I went there in 1966, I walked into that place and went, 'Holy shit, this is really something.' I made a deal with myself that I was going to end up driving a race car there – which I ultimately did. That was my first experience at the Speedway. I got a lot of good times and a lot of bad times there.

It wasn't until 1974 that I ended up qualifying for the race. That was the highlight of my life. I was sitting in my car and they're singing "Back Home Again in Indiana" and I had tears coming out of my eyes. And I'm thinking, 'Hey wake up, you gotta run this son of a bitch.'

On the parade lap I couldn't believe all the people. My God it was unbelievable. I started the race and it was kind of uneventful, just like any other race really. Once it got going, you were oblivious to what the hell was around you.

I quit driving at the Speedway in '77. I said I didn't want to do this anymore. I want to make stuff and saw a future there. I didn't see a future in driving race cars, other than busting my ass and being six feet in the ground. That's when they started running 200 mph in flat bottom cars, which was a real mother, trust me. If anybody tells you in those days that they weren't scared when they got into one of them things they were lying to you, because they were plenty scary.

The first time I lit myself up was in 1971. I had a new Nomex fire suit. I set myself on fire in Turn 1 – that was the first time I did it – and I got a lukewarm reception. Clarence Cagle, the track superintendent, got really pissed because we did it on the grass. Messed it all up.

Years later I've got a new fire suit and a guy comes to the Speedway with a suit and says mine doesn't do what I say it will, blah, blah, blah. Now whenever someone says something in Gasoline Alley, everyone else knows in about 30 minutes. It's like a bunch of wash maidens out there.

Anyway, this guy's walking around the Speedway telling people that I'm full of shit and I'm a liar. I step outside the garage and here he comes walking down the alley. I said, 'Hey man, why the hell are you telling people that I'm a liar?' He said, 'I don't believe in your stuff and I have a fire suit that is far superior,' and all this bullshit about it being light years better. So I challenged him to a burn-off.

He goes 'What's a burn-off?' I said, 'I'm going to get a fire suit from somebody' – I ended up borrowing Pancho Carter's because I didn't have one – 'and I'll meet you across the street in the parking lot of a building I own. I'll put my fire suit on and you take your shit over there and we'll sit down in a chair and we'll get someone to pour gasoline on each one of us, light the mother and we'll see how long we can sit there until we say uncle.'

He looked at me and he said, 'You're crazy.' I said, 'I've been told that before, but I'm telling you, that's what we need to do to settle this whole issue.' He says, 'OK.'

Well that went through the garage area like a lightning rod. So I go over there after they close the race track and there are a thousand people in that parking lot. Cameras. ESPN.

Tom Sheldon, the guy that runs my suite, bought two one gallon gasoline cans and they were each half full. He had two chairs set up and he had a big old clock in the center of it.

Only the other guy's not there. I look at Tom and all the people and asked, 'What the hell you think we should do? He said, 'You better set yourself on fire.'

So I did.

When I got done doing that, there wasn't any doubt about my suit. Everybody at the Speedway wore a Simpson uniform. Everybody. We never saw that other guy again. I don't know; he just disappeared into the sunset.

1964 Indy 500

CHAPTER 14

Tragedy

TRAGEDY HAS BEEN AS MUCH a part of the Indy 500 as triumph. Seventy men have won the 500 and nearly that many drivers, riding mechanics, crew members, track workers and spectators have lost their lives during the race, practice or testing. The death rate reached a peak during the 1950s and 1960s when drivers developed, in the words of Dan Gurney, "...a World War II mentality, sooner or later you were gonna get it."

Three-time Indy 500 winner Bobby Unser put it another way: "A race driver's life in those days wasn't considered to be a very long. Roughly 50 percent of the drivers died in racing accidents. That's just the way it was. And it was an acceptable thing. That's the scary part. All race drivers, racing people, they accepted it. And I did too. Was I right in doing that, I don't know. But I'd do it again tomorrow."

Two races often stand out in people's memories, 1964 and 1973. In 1964 Dave MacDonald and Eddie Sachs were killed in a fiery second lap crash that also involved Unser, Johnny Rutherford and Ronnie Duman. It remains the only accident in Speedway to claim the lives of two drivers.

In 1973 driver Art Pollard was killed in practice on the morning of Pole Day qualifying. In the race, a wild accident as the field received the green flag put Salt Walther and several fans in the hospital with burns and stopped the event before even a lap had been completed. Rain mercifully washed out the remainder of the day. When the race was finally restarted two days later, Swede Savage, who was battling for the lead, lost control and was badly burned in a horrific crash. He would eventually die from complications caused by the burns. A crewman, Armando Teran, who started running towards the accident, was hit and killed by an emergency vehicle also responding to the crash.

Paul Pfanner *is the president and CEO of Racer Media & Marketing, Inc. and founder of RACER Magazine and RACER.com.*

The 1964 Indianapolis 500 will always be remembered as the last year a front-engine roadster won at the Brickyard and for the tragic accident that stopped the race for the first time in its long history.

Few remember it was also the first Indy 500 to be televised live. It wasn't shown via a traditional TV network. It was shown live in hundreds of theaters across America via closed-circuit TV.

So early on the morning of Saturday, May 30, 1964, I sat in a darkened theater in El Monte, Calif., with my father, a lifelong racing fan and aerospace pro who was deeply involved in the early days of the Apollo program. The weekend before, he'd surprised me by announcing we were going to see the Indy 500 at a theater near our home in Whittier.

I wasn't into cars and had no idea what the Indy 500 was, but my father found a TV show on the Saturday before, previewing the race. Jimmy Clark and his low, sleek and futuristic Lotus-Ford captured my attention and the roadsters of A.J. Foyt and Parnelli Jones seemed to me to be relics from another era. Eddie Sachs was interviewed and was a funny guy who made me laugh and care about him, but I had already found a favorite in Clark and felt a growing sense I was in for something special.

It changed my life.

That spring Saturday morning my dad and I witnessed a life-and-death drama unfold in real time. I saw things I'd never seen or experienced before as my young eyes stared into the riveting low-resolution black-and-white video projected crudely on a big screen. To a nine-year-old boy who knew nothing at all about racing, it was exotic, heroic, terrifying, mesmerizing and effortlessly memorable. Just two minutes into the race, it also became my first direct exposure to death and its aftermath. It was all very real and I learned that day that life had risks and extreme consequences on both ends of the human scale. It remains deeply personal and stands forever in my psyche as the origin of my life-defining passion for racing.

The nine-year-old boy who was transfixed by all that happened on that day still lives in my heart and stokes my passion. I fell in love with the dark beauty of our sport and the mystery of racing that still attracts me and still leaves me in awe of those who risk everything to chase their dreams at Indianapolis Motor Speedway.

I found myself in Whittier awhile back, standing over the headstone of *David G. MacDonald, Beloved Husband and Father, 1936 - 1964.* Twin checkered flags etched between the dates gave the only hint of his life and his death in the sport he loved. My late father's grave lies only 1,200 feet north of MacDonald's and in the placid silence broken only by the whispers of these ghosts from my childhood, I wondered how those affected by that horrible day had found the strength and courage to move forward. I also considered that, because of that blackest of days, a shared destiny led me to becoming the man I am today and doing what I do now.

Jim Dilamarter *worked with teams that won three Indy 500s and finished second twice between 1965 and 1973. He still works for Parnelli Jones outside of racing.*

In 1966 I started the month working with John Mecom's team on Jackie Stewart's car when it was decided to move me to teammate Graham Hill's car on Carb Day. I was bummed. From Jackie Stewart to Graham Hill! Wow! No offense Graham, Jackie was just a damn good driver. I liked him personally; he was my kind of guy. Hill was more somber, even though he was a funny, funny man. But he didn't seem to be real aggressive.

Jackie was way out in front in the race with about 10 laps to go and I'm sitting there feeling sorry for myself. All of sudden, Jackie's engine starts to lose oil pressure and he pulls off. Hill, who was running a distant second, takes over the lead and wins the race. I was in total shock. My disappointment and disillusionment turned to joy in less than 10 laps.

That was in stark contrast to 1973. First, Art Pollard, the godfather of my daughter and a great friend of my family, was killed in practice.

I had retired from being a crew chief and became the team manager. One of my jobs in that role was to handle the sign board for our driver, Al Unser, along pit wall. That's where I was when Swede Savage hit the wall coming out of Turn 4. It was right after a pit stop and his car was full of fuel, about 75 gallons, and it went off like a bomb. I saw the explosion on the front straightaway and froze. The kid next to me was Armando Teran and he was signaling for one of the other STP cars, the team Savage drove for.

Al was coming down pit road when the accident happened. When they waved the red flag I walked across pit road into our pit. We all started arguing. Al was ticked off and said he shouldn't have been brought into the pits. He was afraid he would be a lap down when they restarted the race. We were arguing he was gonna be OK.

All of a sudden this shoe comes flying through the air and hits me in the shin. I looked up just in time to see the poor kid with STP getting hit by a fire truck going the wrong way on pit road. He evidently had stayed at the wall a lot longer than I did before he ran onto pit road.

It killed him instantly. I was shocked, but we didn't stop arguing. We saw this kid get killed, but didn't even stop arguing about a pit stop.

A few minutes later I thought to myself, 'We must be animals. This isn't a place for humans if you see somebody get killed and you just ignore it.' That's when I thought, 'I don't think I want to do this anymore.'

That was essentially the last time I had anything to do with the actual running of a race car at Indianapolis. It just took it all out of me. I didn't want to be a person like that, who is so intense on winning a race that someone else's life didn't even matter. Give me another job. Give me a desk job.

Over the years I softened up a little bit and did have a little to do with the cars, but I didn't have my heart in it. That incident finished me.

Vince Granatelli *was the chief mechanic on the car of Graham McRae in 1973, a teammate of Swede Savage. Armando Teran was a member of his team. He quit racing afterwards, but returned to Indy in 1987.*

I remember sitting in Turn 4 where the accident happened, sitting on the outside wall and being completely dejected. We didn't know we were going to lose Swede for sure – but we knew that we lost Armando Teran. I remember Dan Gurney coming up to me and telling me this is the business we're in, move on, you're not going to change things. He was very close to Swede Savage, but saw the feelings that I had and wanted to console me. He had the compassion to see that I was hurting and came by. He helped me get through it.

Wally Dallenbach, Sr. *competed in 180 Indy car events, including 13 Indy 500s. He served as chief steward of CART from 1981 through 2004 and is credited with helping to improve racing safety during that period.*

I came to Indianapolis in '73 without a ride. Dan Gurney asked me what I was running and when I said I didn't have a ride he said, 'I've got a brand new Eagle sitting back in the garage in California. If you want to wait until the second weekend, I'll get it out here and put you in it.'

That turned out to be a really ugly year. I was good friends with Art Pollard, we'd been teammates and we were close. But Art lost control of his car in Turn 1 while practicing on the morning of Pole Day and was killed.

The rest of the week we just sat around and finally the car showed up. It was like a dream come true. I never felt a car that handled so good as that '73 Eagle. I got in the car and qualified 20th.

The records will show all the crap that went on that year. We had the first lap crash with Salt Walther. I started behind Walther, so it all happened right in front of me. He was forced over into Jerry Grant, who was right up against the wall. His right two wheels got between the left two wheels of Grant. He ran over one and it flipped him into the fence and it tore the car to pieces. I got doused with fuel and I caught on fire. I spun the car, but it spun straight down the straightaway. I couldn't see anything because the flames had screwed up my mask.

I finally slowed down to a point where I steered it to the grass. Then along comes Salt Walther, upside down, sliding and in a few flames. His two feet are hanging out of the car and it looked pretty bad. So I jumped out of my car and ran over to help the firemen.

I remember having on a brand new pair of Nomex gloves and grabbing the turbocharger because it was the only thing I could grab – the car was torn up so bad. We flipped the car over and then I walked away, because I didn't want to see him. I thought it was going to be worse – but it was bad enough.

When we restarted the race I had a magneto failure. I came in and jumped out of the car because they had to pull the seat to get to the magneto.

I was standing behind the pit wall waiting for them to fix the car and that's when Swede Savage came out of Turn 4, lost it and drilled the infield wall. Swede and I were friends. He confided in me a little because I drove the 40 car in '72 and now he was in the 40 car.

There I am watching all this and I see this guy flying through the air and he lands right in front of our pit. As it turned out, he was my right rear wheel guy (Armando Teran) from the year before. He got hit by a fire truck going the wrong way and it threw him about 70 to 80 feet in the air. I looked at him and he was motionless.

Some of the memories are heartbreaking and some of them are very rewarding. There are things I was able to do as chief steward and I became a campaigner for safety on both sides of the guard rail, so to speak. I got things done where other people kind of were blown off – what do you know, you never drove a car. So a lot of things got done and safety issues got corrected.

We built one of the best safety teams in the history of racing. We tried to think about the next disaster and plan for it the best we could with what we had.

***Mike Harris** was the longtime Associated Press motorsports writer.*

The 1973 Indianapolis 500 is widely regarded as the most depressing race in the event's lengthy history. It certainly was for me, in my nearly 50 years of covering the race. After two years of working in the pits and one writing sidebars, it was my first time writing the main story for The Associated Press from the open-air press box that hung under the second deck over the start-finish line.

Even before race day, things turned grim. Veteran racer Art Pollard was killed in practice on the morning of Pole Day. Until that moment, the month of May had been fun and exciting for me, and ripe with anticipation. I had only covered the 500 since 1970, but I had gotten to know Pollard fairly well and had enjoyed a nice chat with him just before he climbed into his car for that fateful run. After that, a black cloud seemed to hang over the track for the rest of the month.

The wet weather that had hampered practice and qualifying continued on race day and the start of the 500 was delayed for four hours. Finally, the green flag waved and the cars took off. But seconds later there was a horrendous fiery 11-car crash on the main straightaway in which David "Salt" Walther was badly burned and flaming fuel and debris injured several spectators. Before the track could be cleaned up, rain fell again and the race was postponed to the next day.

The rain continued and the only excitement on the seemingly interminable second day was keeping track of which truck among those trying to dry the track was leading the most laps and watching the occasional streaker run across the race surface.

Finally, after another wet morning on the third day, the clouds parted and the sun shone through long enough to get the race going. Then tragedy struck again. Swede Savage, who had pitted just two laps earlier, crashed on lap 59 and his car was enveloped in flames. He was badly burned and died several weeks later in a Michigan hospital. Meanwhile, Armando Teran, a crew member on the car driven by Savage's teammate Graham McRae, started running up pit lane toward the crash scene in Turn 4.

I was writing a quick lead about Savage's horrifying crash as my editor, Darrell Christian, later the AP's sports editor, gathered and fed me information on what was going on. Suddenly, I heard a loud and eerie thump and looked up and across the track in time to see Teran's body flying through the air. He had been struck by a fire truck on pit lane. Teran was pronounced dead later that afternoon.

Christian kept feeding me information and I kept writing lead after lead as more details of the crashes and the injuries became available. Finally, after about an hour, with the race about to restart, Christian patted me on the arm and said, 'Hey, take a breath. We're caught up as much as we can be at this point.'

I sat back and realized that the front of my shirt was soaking wet. Then I realized that I had been crying, the tears streaming down my face and onto my chest as I continued to write. It was without question the worst hour of my working life.

Eventually, rain cut the race short, with Gordon Johncock, another Savage teammate, winning without much joy. I was told I had done a good job in the face of the tragedies and the weather, but it was definitely the worst few days in my career.

***Dr. Stephen Olvey** grew up in Indianapolis and attended the University of Indiana School of Medicine. He was CART medical director from 1978 to 2003 and is the author of "Rapid Response: My Inside Story as a Motor Racing Life Saver." He remains a consultant to IndyCar on head injuries.*

I developed a love for the Indy 500 way back. When I was 10 or 11, I started listening to the radio broadcast and I had developed a real admiration for Bill Vukovich. The first year that I went to the race was the year he crashed and I still, to this day, remember the black smoke rising up from the back straightaway.

My father, brother and I were sitting in Grandstand C along the front straight. There was this black cloud of smoke rising from the area of the back stretch. I distinctly remember Tom Carnegie saying he had been mortally wounded. I looked at my father and said, 'Oh good, he's only wounded.' My father, who was a physician, had to explain to me that meant he had died. I was quite upset, but it did not diminish my love for the sport.

Back then, roughly one out of seven drivers died every year. It seemed like every two weeks, sometimes more often than that, the news would come on Monday morning about one of the Indy drivers that had died over the weekend. I hate to say it, but I think you realize that it was something that came with the territory and that it was going to happen. But the fact there were drivers willing to take that risk, to do what they enjoyed doing the most, I soon began to appreciate that. I felt that I understood how that could be.

I was always kind of a thrill seeker – not at all to that extent of course – but I used to do things that were fairly risky and you got kind of a rush out of it, to be honest. You think back and that was really a dumb thing to do, but while you're doing it, you were really enjoying it. It felt like you were really living. So I felt I had an understanding and I knew he died – it's the old cliché – I knew he died doing the thing that he loved to do most and that's nothing to knock. It beats lying around a nursing home and dying of old age.

Gordon Smiley's crash was the worst I have ever seen and the hardest thing I've ever had to deal with. I was between turns 1 and 2 in the rescue truck. We got our signal to dispatch and we knew the only car on the track was Gordon's. We didn't know anything else until we got partially through the third turn and it was appalling to see all the debris. There was debris everywhere and it was difficult for us to discern where the driver was because there was a large amount of stuff, which later turned out to be the motor, which had separated from the tub.

What was left of the tub was sitting on the race track with nothing else – virtually nothing else attached to it – but we realized that's where Gordon was. So we stopped the truck and I got out and ran to the scene. When I arrived at the scene I looked into the cockpit of the car and here's the driver with the top of his head gone – no helmet. The helmet was found later quite a ways from the scene. It had come off early in the course of the crash

This all got to me horribly later, but when you're in critical care you do what you have to do. About all we could do was cover him up with a blanket – we knew he was dead. We didn't want any pictures being taken or anybody seeing because the whole thing was live on television. So we covered him, got him out of the car, which was not difficult because there wasn't much of the vehicle left, and put him in the ambulance. One of the hardest things I've had to do was the ride in the ambulance with him. I think every bone in his body was broken and it was a very difficult thing to do..

But the hardest thing is to explain to a wife or family that their driver didn't make it. I've had to do that too many times through the years. After 25 years doing Indy car racing, that's the toughest thing by far.

***Dr. Jerry Punch** has worked on various motorsports broadcasts.*

Motorsports is the ultimate reality series because it is about life and, unfortunately at times, death. There's no reality series that can mimic the emotions that a family or a driver or an event will deliver over two to four hours of television.

I was standing and talking with Larry Curry and John Menard in front of the Menard garage one morning while practice was going on – just talking about going downtown to some function – and someone says their driver, Scott Brayton, had been in an accident.

I'm standing there and my phone rings from ABC and they say this is a bad deal. So John – I'm not talking I'm just listening – John turns to Larry and says to go pick up Scotty at the infield hospital, because they've got to go somewhere.

I looked up and I must have had this white as a sheet look on my face, and I said, 'You're not going to pick him up, you've got to go – you got to – this is not good.' And Curry, suddenly the blood drains out of his face and he jumps in the golf cart and they take off and we know what the result was.

They had a memorial service a few days later on the front stretch. They had a table set up on pit road and the drivers were all sitting in the Pagoda stands and they brought his family and his little girl out. I've seen some gut-wrenching things, but the little girl, I don't know how old she was at the time, she was tiny, and I don't think she had any idea what was going on or what this was about.

But there was a table sitting there with some pictures of Scott on it and the little girl, as she walks up to take her seat, runs over and grabs a picture off the table and gives it a kiss – gives her daddy a kiss. To understand what the little girl had just lost, there were guys who were legends in the sport in the stands that were in tears. And so was I.

Rick Mears

CHAPTER 15

Triumph

WINNING THE INDY 500 RANKS at the top of any race driver's list of achievements and trumps all other accomplishments. Nearly all say the victory changed their life forever. For those that have won it more than once, it is often their last victory that stands out.

***Parnelli Jones** was a rookie in 1962 when he became the first driver to qualify at an average speed of more than 150 mph. He won the 500 in 1963 driving for J.C. Agajanian.*

My oldest son P.J. was born April 23, 1969, so he was a little over a month old when we took him back to Indy for the race that year. When we saw the Borg-Warner Trophy, we pulled the top off and set him inside and took a picture. That's one of those personal highlights that I really remember. We've been looking for that picture ever since. We've got it somewhere, just haven't been able to find it.

Of course once you become a winner there, it's just nice to come back every year and be part of the Speedway and to be recognized. I wouldn't miss it for anything.

When you're coming up through racing, Indianapolis is your ultimate goal. I had always listened to it on the radio and finally got an opportunity to be part of it. It was really something. I was there in 1960 when Jim Hurtubise almost hit the 150 mark. I was in the pits when he finished his run and he said, 'That ain't nothing, wait until Parnelli gets here.' That was a big boost for me because suddenly some of the owners and other promoters started noticing me.

I should have won three or four times. My rookie year in 1961 I led the race for 27 laps, had a chance to win and then lost a cylinder. Came back the next year and was the first to run 150 mph, was long gone in the race and lost the brakes. Made two pit stops without any brakes or brains.

Then I came back in '63 and won. In '64 I was leading when my car caught fire. I had a chance to win that one. I finished second in '65 when Jimmy Clark won and in '67, when I drove the turbine car, I came within three laps of winning. I had a great career there, I just only won one race. Of course the real ultimate goal is to win. I was fortunate to do that.

The one where I was long gone and leading the race and lost the brakes was a real heartbreaker for me, mainly because I hadn't won it yet. When I drove the turbine car, I felt as much for Andy Granatelli as I did for myself. Stupid me, if I had just taken it a little easier going out of the pits, we'd have won it hands down.

It's not quite the same winning as a car owner as it is winning the race as a driver. We won a couple of times with Al Unser, in '70 and '71, and they were big thrills for me too. I guess you could they were second best.

***Jim Clark** won the 1965 Indy 500 driving a Lotus-Ford, the first rear-engine car to win the race. He was the Formula One World Champion in 1963 and 1965. The following is from his autobiography, "Jim Clark at the Wheel" and was written prior to his '65 win. He was killed while racing in a Formula Two event in Germany in 1968.*

To me, Indianapolis is almost indescribable, big and impressive, with quite the longest grandstands I have ever seen. It is one big holiday fair and motor race rolled into one, a national institution, with the circuit almost a shrine. I was totally unprepared for it.

The whole scene was a mass of color, because these Indy cars are really gaudy. Added to this were the crowds, bands and the whole ballyhoo which is Indianapolis. It is noisy, spectacular, and reminds you of what the history books say about ancient Rome.

All around me were these giant race cars. I was well back in the field (at the start) and there was nothing but smoke, dust and roar of engines around me. It was all rather unreal.

***Graham Hill** won the 1966 Indy 500 as a rookie driving for John Mecom. He was a two-time Formula One World Champion and is the only driver to win the Triple Crown of motorsports, the Indy 500, Monaco Grand Prix and 24 Hours of Le Mans. He died when the plane he was piloting crashed in 1975. The following is from "Graham" by Graham Hill with Neil Ewart.*

They make a tremendous fuss about the winner at Indianapolis. There's a black-and-white checkered carpet and girls and television cameras and all that jazz – and a great glass of milk they make you drink.

The incredible thing is that within minutes they presented me with a newspaper with the headline – GRAHAM HILL THE WINNER – across the front page complete with photographs. I don't know how they managed it, but I was terribly impressed. When the prize-giving came round they capped it by giving me the actual metal printer's plate of that front page and it's something I have treasured ever since.

Johnny Rutherford *was a rookie in the 1963 Indy 500. He competed in the race 23 times, winning in 1974, 1976 and 1980.*

I won the national sprint car championship in 1965, but early the next year I crashed and broke both arms in a sprint car race at Eldora (Ohio) and was out for the season. I knew that it was going to be hard to get anything decent after that until I proved myself. It was a struggle and I ran for several people at the Speedway, but I never finished the race until '73 when I got a chance to go to work for McLaren.

Gordon Johncock had been driving for them. He didn't fit them and they didn't fit him. Herb Porter helped me get that ride. They brought the car to the Speedway in late January or February and we tested it, the M16 McLaren. The car was not good and we struggled. The thing pushed the front end terribly. We ran for three days and we just couldn't get it to stop, so they went back to Detroit with the car and worked on it and got it ready. When we came back to Indianapolis, I got in the car and went out and they had fixed the front-end problem.

It had front wings and a rear wing the size of a picnic table. It really had a lot of downforce and McLaren figured out how to counteract that with high horsepower. Roger Bailey had built a fire-breathing engine. It was strong.

I went out to qualify and set a new track record. I was the first one to go 200 unofficially in practice and then set a new track record of 199 mph on my fastest lap and 198 mph for my four-lap average.

It was just a chance to be with a great team. I spent seven years with McLaren and won two Indy 500s in '74 and '76, and finished second in '75. In that race we had made our pit stop and were ready to go to the end. Then the rains came. Bobby Unser, who was driving for Dan Gurney, had stayed out and he won the race and I finished second. I've always thought if it hadn't rained, I would have been the first to win three races in a row at the Speedway, but it didn't happen that way. It was a good run.

Indianapolis was like a magnet for me. I loved every aspect of the Speedway. When I retired I thought, 'What in the world am I going to be doing? How can I find life after racing?' I did the pace car program and enjoyed that part of it because I was still up close and personal. I knew what was going on and still had a chance to lead a few races. The Indianapolis Motor Speedway was a great part of my life and I'm still involved – have been ever since.

Rick Mears *is one of three drivers to collect four Indy 500 wins (1979, 1984, 1988 and 1991). Driving for Roger Penske, he started from the 500 pole six times and earned three series championships.*

Off the top of my head, there are three things about the Indy 500 that are all pretty close to being my favorite memory. Obviously it's winning at Indy – but which one.

The first win has its place because of being the first. So, it ranks right up there. Another thing that ranks highly was my first pole position in 1979. It was only my second year at Indy and it surprised everybody – including me. That was my first-ever pole, not just at Indy, but anywhere in an Indy car. Seeing the smiles on everybody's faces when I came down pit lane after that run was pretty gratifying.

However, the fourth win is really the one – if I had to pick just one memory – it would be the fourth win. That first win in '79 – it was only our second year there. It was like, 'Wow, OK we won it. We won another race. Let's go on and win the next one.' I didn't understand at that time how difficult it is to do. I didn't grow up around Indy and never dreamed of being at Indy – that was way out of my league. I hadn't really studied Indianapolis or the history of it and although I did appreciate it, not as much as I did later.

Then you start looking at it and saying, 'Man, not too many people run here to begin with and very few have won – and even fewer have won more than once.' What are the odds of winning again? They're getting greater all the time. Then you win the second one and it makes it pretty exciting, but you go on another couple years and you don't win it again. The same process happens. You're more appreciative and you understand it more. You look around and now there are only a few guys that have won it more than twice, so the odds are greater that you aren't going to do it again. When the third one happens, it raises the level again.

After the third one, only two guys had won it four times. What are the odds of that happening again? It's getting later in your career and you don't know how much longer you're going to run. When that fourth one happens it just goes to the top of the list because of all those things involved.

One thing that helped put it on top was the way it happened – with Michael Andretti and I having a shootout at the end. I would go into every race pretty much the same way, especially at Indy. I always spent the first half of the race getting to the second half. Working with the race car and reading the track conditions. Seeing who your competitors for the win are going to be and using them as your yardstick. Figuring out where you need to have your car at the end of the race after the last stop and have it the best it can be for the shootout – if it materializes. In the other three races a shootout never materialized. It came close once, but the shootout never really happened. That's really the most gratifying way to win one – to win any race.

The fourth one boiled down to the end after the last stop. Michael had been the strongest guy all day long. He was still running and he hadn't had any problems. He was the guy I'd been watching and measuring against what I was going to need. When it came to that last restart, we had a little traffic and he got by me. I thought, 'OK, here we go. It's time to go.' Then I was able to come around and get by him on the very next lap on the outside in Turn 1. It was unknown territory – the speeds we were running at that point. That was the fastest we'd been into (Turn) 1 all day. Then Mario (Andretti) had a problem and stopped on the track. It created a yellow and we had another restart. We were able to hold Michael off on that next restart and stretched it out again. We had a better car and started getting away from him. It was a matter of just don't make any mistakes and get it to the end.

I knew we had him covered – but you never know until it's over because anything can happen. The pressure starts building the last couple of laps. At this point in time, especially towards the end of my career, it's almost unbelievable that you're going to win Indy again. But until you come off of (Turn) 4 and get past pit entry, you're still not done. Once I get past pit entry, I can ricochet home the rest of the way no matter what happens. But before pit entry, something could break and you could hit the end of pit wall and not make it to the finish line. Once I was by pit in, then it really hit home. It was hard to contain the emotions on the cool off lap.

What's the first thing you think about? Initially, it's that you've won. Then you think about the whole team. You can picture pit lane and Roger, your guys and family – and how excited everyone is. What it means to everybody. All of that is going through your mind. And then being the fourth win – it hits in there too. But, that really comes a little bit later. Once you get into Victory Lane and you're holding up the four fingers for the photographers and all of that, that's when the fourth win starts adding in to it. And it just builds from there. I remember my first win – I was excited, but maybe it was a week later when it really sunk in. The fourth win, with all the progression of everything throughout the years, it hit home a little quicker.

Having the opportunity to drive for Roger and staying with that team is what made it happen, because they gave me the tools I needed as a driver to be successful.

Jon Beekhuis *has been to the Indy 500 as a fan, driver and broadcaster.*

My favorite memory of the Indy 500, from a fan and a driver standpoint, I would immediately have to say is 1991, Rick Mears making that incredibly aggressive move around the outside of Michael Andretti in Turn 1. I wouldn't be the first to pick that one out, but just from a driver's standpoint, the commitment and the bravery that kind of move took – and the way those two respected each other, even though they wanted so desperately to beat each other – is one of the moments that shows how hard people push for the Indy 500.

Danny Sullivan *won 17 Indy car races, including the 1985 Indy 500. He was the CART champion in 1988.*

To win the 500 and to beat Mario Andretti and the other competitors in the field, which was really intense, is very special. But to spin part way through the race, then go on to win it, added that extra little pizzazz. It's something that has carried forward with me. Everybody says, 'Oh, spin to win, spin to win – oh yeah, we remember that race.'

So for me it's fairly easy, that's the biggest memory for me at Indy.

There were a lot of factors leading up to the spin. I was always so close behind Mario coming down the front straightaway that I couldn't read the pit board and I couldn't see the scoring tower because of the buffeting. I thought there weren't many laps left – I thought we only had about 25 laps left.

I was quicker off turns 3 and 4 than I was off 1 and 2, hence the reason I was trying to pass him going into 1. I got a draft and went in there with him, and of course Mario doesn't like to be passed at any time, particularly in the 500. I got a good run on him, but

Mario just kind of came down and took me almost to the grass. Down to the apron, just enough to trip the car when I came back up on the track.

Luckily for me, I was further around the corner; otherwise I would have had an angle that for sure would have taken me to the wall. I turned a little bit more around the corner and it just tripped the car. I tried to correct it and it wasn't going to work, so the spin occurred. I thought, 'Oh shit, I just get the lead at the Indianapolis 500 and now I'm going to crash.' I was really angry at myself. Then all of the sudden the smoke cleared coming out of the spin and there were the Turn 2 suites.

I got it started and took off. I radioed Derrick Walker and said, 'Hey the yellow is for me, the yellow is for me. I'm OK, I didn't hit anything, everything's good.' Remember, they didn't have the live feed back then. That was the last year before we had a live broadcast.

I came in and changed four tires and came back out. At that stage I just thought, 'Boy I was lucky and now I've got to catch Mario and pass him in the same spot,' because that's where my car was quicker.

But prior to that, Tom Sneva and Howdy Holmes got tangled up and I just missed hitting Sneva in Turn 1 – I mean by inches. I thought, 'I'm having a lucky day here,' but I still didn't think I was about to win the race.

I had to catch Mario, and of course now it's getting closer to the end of the race and he was going to be even tougher to pass. But I got it done. Then one of the Whittingtons had a crash and brought out a yellow. I looked in my mirror and there was another car and then Michael Andretti and then Mario. I thought Michael's not going to hold Mario up, so I've got to really make a great restart.

They restarted us with four laps to go. If I'd had a hammer I would have broken the mirrors in my car. I didn't want to be tempted to look back and see Mario right behind me. When I restarted I just thought, 'OK, be smooth as you can. No quick movements. Hit all your marks. Make sure you're on your line. Stay focused. Look dead ahead.'

I think my fastest lap of the race was my second to the last lap. I was so nervous and I didn't want thinking about winning it to creep in and jinx me.

The only time I thought I was going to win the Indy 500 was when I was about 100 yards from the finish line. I took a look and Mario was a couple of seconds back and I thought even if it blows up right now, he can't catch me. But I never ever thought, 'I'm going to win it,' until I was 100 yards away from the finish line.

So if you ask what was my most memorable time at Indy, that was it. But it's so much more. The Hulmans, meeting people and fans, the parties and the parade, the Yellow Shirts, the Speedway Motel, the history of the competitors – from A.J., the Unsers,

Gordon Johncock and my peers, Bobby Rahal and Rick Mears. The list just goes on and on.

They weren't all good memories. I had a crash there and broke my arm. But it was a major part of my life. And when I look back on it, I wouldn't trade any of it.

Bobby Rahal *is the 1986 Indy 500 champion and a three-time IndyCar champion (1986, 1987 and 1992). He is currently fielding an entry for his son Graham.*

What's my best Indy 500 memory? Well, I suppose somebody would say, 'It must have been the year you won.' Clearly that was a pretty good day. Particularly given the fact that there were so many instances where we had races that were going very well and then we didn't finish for whatever reason.

So I think you just have to say that 1986 win, but part of that story is Jim Trueman, my team owner. I mean it was such an amazing sequence of events. The original race date was Jim's 51st birthday and of course he was on death's door even at that point. Then the race got delayed a weekend. And then to win the race.

Before we went to Indy that year, I sat down with Jim in his office in Columbus (Ohio) and he basically said, 'You know I'm not going to be here next year, so let's make sure we win this thing.' Not that I felt any huge amount of pressure outside of what I would normally feel, but clearly everybody knew that this was it as far as he was concerned.

I tell people I still don't recall seeing the checkered flag. Those last two laps I thought we were going to run out of fuel. If I had a whip, you would have seen me whip the side of the car like a horse. I was running on the back straight, literally saying, 'Don't leave me. Don't leave me. Don't run out of fuel.' On the last lap, we set the fastest lap of the race.

When you win you think of so many things – but you really don't know what to feel. It's the Indy 500. With all due respect, it's not the Portland 200 – which is a great race to win, having done that. But, this is the Indy 500 and it really immortalizes you. When you first do it, you really don't have a clue. You think you know what the impact will be on your life, but you really don't know.

When you cross that finish line, maybe the first thing you feel is relief. Obviously, you feel a tremendous amount of joy too. That was only my fifth year. Some guys have been to the Speedway for years and years and never won it, or had to wait years before they did win it. When you look at where we started in 1982 as a team and then four years later winning the race – it was a pretty amazing learning curve.

You'll never have to answer the questions, 'When are you going to win the Indy 500? Is this the year you win the Indy 500?' Your life changes professionally and it changes personally. There are probably just a handful of sports events that have that impact – maybe the Kentucky Derby or the Masters in golf. So, when you do cross that finish line – I think the biggest feeling was just tremendous joy.

I came in and it was the first year they had the elevated winner's circle. We had adopted a little girl in January of that year and I held her up like a trophy in Victory Lane. There are still questions about who's the youngest person ever in Victory Lane at Indy – and it's Michaela Rahal, age three months or something like that.

Then there's Jim. I was being interviewed on TV and he was right there. I started to choke up. I think I said, 'I knew my greatest days would be with Jim.' Then they asked Jim about the race. If you look at the TV interview, they ask him and his voice is hoarse and he says, 'He drove a great race. The best race he ever drove.'

At that time, everything is coming at you so fast – your emotions internally and everything from outside. I was just trying to keep it all under control.

Now I'm never introduced as a three-time Indy car champion. I'm always introduced as the 1986 Indy 500 champ, and that demonstrates the importance of the place. They go, 'Oh yeah, the 1986 Indy 500, and by the way he won three Indy car championships.' The championships are always a sideline.

***Arie Luyendyk** is a native of Holland and a two-time winner of the Indy 500 (1990 and 1997). He established one (237.498 mph) and four-lap (236.986 mph) track records in 1996.*

As a kid growing up, I would read the British magazine *Autosport*. They always wrote about the Indy 500 because Jim Clark was driving there, and he was competitive and winning. I remember reading about Indy and looking at the pictures, including the crashes and of the people who had died. To me, Indianapolis was like, 'Wow, those guys are something else.'

When I started racing, I remember going to the Lola factory to pick up my Formula 3 car. While I was there, I noticed they were building a car for Al Unser, Sr. for the Indy 500. It was enormous compared to the Formula 3 car. The engine was just huge and the thing was so impressive. As a young guy, I thought there's no way I could ever drive one of those cars. I was literally scared just looking at it. But years later I was driving a Super Vee car in America and then I took a step and was driving Indy cars.

One memory that stands out is when I arrived at the Speedway. The first driver I ran into was Mario (Andretti). Nobody gave much advice back then, not like now when we give the young guys a lot of advice. But Mario said to me, 'Just take it easy. This place will bite you.' It was like a warning shot from Mario not to approach Indy like any other track – it takes time to learn it. I remember that vividly.

I was a road racer from my early beginnings in Europe. I had to learn to drive the ovals and I really took a liking to them. They suited me really well – especially the high speed ovals like Indy. It was made for me, or I was made for Indy. I knew how to go fast – and knew how to slow down when necessary. I didn't have many crashes there compared to a lot of other guys. I was just lucky. Indy became my specialty, and it happened to be the most important race for Indy cars, so that was good for me.

My favorite moment at the Speedway was winning the race for the first time in 1990 and everything that goes along with winning it. The recognition and notoriety you get, along with the respect from the fans. The fans are another thing that is special about Indy. They're really behind the drivers. Not just behind me or any other one driver, the fans just love the Indy 500.

Another exciting time for me is Pole Day. If you end up on the pole – in my eyes it's always a big deal. It was always a big challenge because there's a difference at Indy between racing and getting the ultimate speed out of your car. It entails setting it up a certain way, running very little downforce and driving on the edge. I always enjoyed qualifying at Indy and loved taking the thing as fast as it could go. For me it was always a highlight to get pole position.

The Speedway lives a life of its own, and so does the race track. It's a track that's obviously built from concrete, steel and asphalt, but it kind of has a human nature to it. More people have lost at the Speedway than have won there. More people have walked away disappointed than feeling great about what they did that day. That's just the nature of the beast – you can only have one winner on race day.

***Kenny Brack** was born in Sweden and won the 1999 Indy 500.*

My first year with AJ Foyt Racing in 1998, we lost the 500 because of fuel mileage. That's the year A.J. smashed the laptop computer on the pit stand. But we went on to win the championship. As soon as the season was over, we focused on Indianapolis. In November we got the new Dallara (chassis) and the entire team gathered around it. I said, 'This is the tub that will win the Indianapolis 500 in May.'

I walked and crawled every inch of the track and even the grass to get ready. You couldn't have a better guy than A.J. He had a wealth of knowledge. That was before everything was done by computer. You'd still look at the flags in Turn 1 for help with the setup. No one knew more than A.J.

The race came down to fuel economy again. With 12 laps to go we could run full fuel and we were pretty certain Robby Gordon couldn't make it to the finish. But if there was a yellow flag, you never know. We finally passed Robby with a little more than a lap to go and A.J. starts yelling on the radio, 'We won baby, we won it,' or something like that. I asked if I had taken the checkered flag and when he said no, I said, 'Then shut the fuck up until we do.'

In the garage afterwards, the King of Sweden called to congratulate me. A.J. was in a hurry to go and when someone told him who I was talking to, he yelled, 'Tell him the King of Texas is waiting.'

A few years later I died in Texas after a crash, at least for a few seconds, before they revived me. It was the highest level of g-forces ever recorded in a crash. It took me 18 months to work myself back into shape. I turned down a couple of rides for Indy in 2005 that I figured weren't right for me. But when Buddy Rice, who had replaced me at Rahal Racing, was hurt, I agreed to fill in for him.

We posted the fastest time in qualifying that year at Indy and it was an emotional experience for me. It showed me I had come back. A.J. came over to congratulate me and I don't think he could have been happier if I was driving for him.

We dropped out of the race and the next night at the banquet Mario Andretti asked me if I wanted to race the following week for the Newman/Haas team. I thought about it a couple of days and decided to retire. I didn't have the energy or determination it takes to run at the front every week. Drivers have a "best-by-date" and at 39, with a new baby, I had reached mine.

I never regretted retiring. It was a Hollywood ending to my career – IRL champion, 500 winner, coming back from the highest g-force crash and then turning the fastest qualifying time at Indianapolis.

***Juan Pablo Montoya** has recorded a pair of Indy 500 wins driving for team owners Chip Ganassi (2000) and Roger Penske (2015).*

If you mention the Indy 500 to me, the first memory that comes to my mind is when Roberto Guerrero was on the pole and spun out on cold tires.

I was watching that race with my dad in Colombia. It was painful to watch. Roberto's father was my dad's best friend and his younger brother is one of my best friends. It was pretty tough to watch and tough to swallow, to be honest with you. I remember everybody saying that the temperatures were too low and it was a big deal. He just lost it warming up the tires. I was 17 and I really didn't understand the meaning of the Indy 500.

I remember it was heartbreaking for my dad. His jaw just dropped to the ground when it happened. Roberto's father had been really excited about that race. He said they were really happy how fast Roberto was in race trim, and that he was going to crush the field.

My first visit to the Speedway was in October 1998. I had just won the Formula 3000 championship and made a deal to come race with Chip (Ganassi). At that time the team's shop was on 38th street and CART wasn't racing at the Speedway, so we were just talking about the 500. One day I was at the shop for a seat fitting and asked, 'Where's the Speedway?' They said it's like four blocks away. I remember saying, 'This is the middle of the city. What do you mean it's four blocks?'

I came through the museum and took the bus ride around the track, and that was my first time at the Speedway. The first thing I noticed was how long and flat the straights were. And the tight corners. It's completely different.

People (foreign drivers) have no idea what the oval is all about. That's why most of them come here and struggle, because their mindset is completely opposite to where they need to be. The cocky ones come and have massive shunts and some just never get up to speed. The careful ones come in and, you always tell them, you got to have some understeer. But, the level of understeer that you need – that's the key thing.

Personally, I think the more you do Indy – the more you appreciate it. The first time, I didn't care too much about it. The second time it was really nice to be back. And last year (2015), apart from the win, it was just a really nice month and I really enjoyed it. There was a group of us that did a little bike riding every morning and then we'd practice in the afternoon. It was a nice month and things just clicked. There wasn't too much pressure or anything.

I've been very lucky and very blessed. I mean, I work hard. I've worked really hard all my life. I think people would kill to drive for just one of the teams I've raced for, if you think about it. You know the Penske experience for me has been better than you could even imagine.

When you experience Indy with Roger Penske it's very different. You learn to appreciate what the Indy 500 is. They have a lot of respect for the Speedway. They have a lot of respect for the series and the whole history behind it, and it's a pleasure to be a part of something like that.

***Helio Castroneves** has three wins (2001, 2002 and 2009) and four pole positions (2003, 2007, 2009 and 2010) in 15 Indy 500 starts for Team Penske.*

It has been spectacular for me to win three Indy 500s.

The first win was awesome because I planned everything by talking with the big names at the Speedway – Rick Mears, Al Unser, Sr., and even Al Unser, Jr. I had good conversations with all those guys and everything I planned for the race was according to what they said – and it worked out pretty good.

That first year driving in the 500 was actually my first time ever seeing the race live. I'd watched the race before on TV, but the first time I drove in the race was my first time seeing the race. Needless to say, I liked my first time at the Speedway.

Climbing the fence at Indy after that first win was breaking all the protocol. I did not intend to do that, but it was such a moment of joy and I felt the fans wanted to see that. It turned out to be a perfect scenario after a magical race. People don't realize that the way you celebrate is also a way to make the race even more special. Climbing the fence with my crew and mechanics and team members just showed that it's really not an individual sport, even though I'm the one driving the car. It's a team sport and without them I wouldn't be able to do what I did – win the Indy 500.

In 2000 I had climbed the fence after a win. It was already part of my routine for winning a race, but a lot of people didn't see it until I was winning the Indy 500. It became more well-known because of that first race at Indy.

Along with the three wins, one other thing that I really remember was my 2003 pole position. It was my first pole at the 500. The weather that day was very brutal. It was very difficult conditions – the whole day it was like 40 degrees. The weather had changed completely, especially the temperature. It was cold and really windy.

My teammate Gil de Ferran and I were like, 'OK, this is going to be very difficult.' I think Tony (Kanaan) put together a tremendous lap. I was like, 'Man, this is going to be hard, but I'm going to take it on. Go big or go home.' We were able to catch the pole position under those terrible conditions. Afterwards, I remember Rick coming up to me and saying, 'Man, that was impressive.' For Rick Mears – the king of qualifying – to come over and say that to me was impressive. It meant a lot to me.

That was probably one of my favorite moments at the Indy 500. We kept the flag that was flying from the Pagoda that day. It was all ripped and showed that it was a very brutal day. But, despite those conditions, we were able to secure that pole position and that I'll never forget.

***Gil de Ferran** won the 2003 Indianapolis 500 and was a two-time series champion (2000 and 2001). He recorded his two titles and his Indy 500 win driving for Team Penske.*

My strongest memory of the Indy 500, or the one that left the deepest mark on me, was actually the year I won the race in 2003. The reason is because it was a real emotional roller coaster in a sense – all the events leading up to the 500 and then the race itself.

You probably have to first go back a few months before that May. In October of the previous year, I had an accident at Chicagoland Speedway. It was one of the biggest accidents of my career and I ended up in the hospital with a concussion. Basically, the whole weekend was wiped out. If I recall correctly, I was leading the championship at the time, but had to miss the last race of the year and finished in third place. It took me over a month to get over that whole thing.

At the start of the 2003 season, I finished second in the first race at Homestead (Fla.). We went to Phoenix for the second race of the year and I was running well. Late in the race I was looking to get by Michael (Andretti) and we got together and ended up in the wall. It was another enormous accident – a hospital job. Again it was a concussion. I also broke vertebrae and had to miss the next race, which was Japan. The thing that took me the longest to recover from was the concussion – it was not very much fun.

I got cleared to drive just before the opening day of practice for the Indy 500. That day was possibly the worst day I ever had in a race car. It was just awful. My timing was completely wrong. I was driving horrible. I was slow. The car was surprising me all the time – which normally wasn't the case. Nothing was flowing. All that happened after I told Roger (Penske) I was fine.

Psychologically I was fine and physically I was fine, but I was thinking, 'Oh no. This is it. I can't drive anymore.' My abilities, however little they were, had obviously been left somewhere in a wall in Phoenix. I was very introspective. It was me – it wasn't the car. I was not driving well. I left the track early and thought, 'OK, my career is over. We're done.' That evening was not very nice.

The next morning I woke up and thought, 'Let's give it another go and see what happens.' I went out to the Speedway and we took the car out right at the beginning of practice. There were a lot of cars out and I remember thinking, 'It's just not working for me.' We went back to the garage. Then the sun came out and the track started getting hot. Everybody went back to their garages. But I'm like, 'OK, let's try this again.' I just kept running laps and slowly it started to come back to me and I finished the day on a high. We were relatively fast, I was feeling a lot more comfortable and I just decided to take one step at a time. As the week progressed, I got more confident and was feeling better. At that point, everything seemed back to normal.

Before qualifying, I had several moments in the warm up. By the time qualifying was going on and we were in line, I already had so many moments, I think there was somebody helping me not to hit the wall. Eventually I just decided to put a lot of wing in the car and run a safe lap. The tension was too much. I just couldn't deal with it anymore. I just wanted to put the thing in the race. I knew we had a good race car and we ended up qualifying 10th.

In the race the car was good. We were running a bit more wing than Helio (Castroneves), who was running up front. Early in the race, I found myself running in the top four or five. It was a good position to be in and everything was fine.

During one of the early yellows, I had an issue with my neck. I was trying to warm up the tires, but was having cramps in my shoulders. My shoulders were cramping like crazy and I couldn't warm up the tires. I could just about drive the car, but swinging the car left and right, left and right – it was super painful. I was thinking, 'That's all I need now. I'm going to quit halfway through the race.' Then, I said to myself, 'Calm down. Relax your shoulders.' We decided to keep going. I made a couple good restarts and found myself behind Helio who was leading the race. Now I'm thinking 'I can win this thing.'

Two years earlier in the 500, I was dominating the race and Helio passed me in the pits and I couldn't get him back. I was desperate to get him back and running so close to him that I burned up the right front tire to the point there was really no hope of passing him. It was a strategic mistake of mine.

This time around, I knew if I did the same thing – ride on his behind – I'd end up burning my tires and not being able to pass him again. I elected to just do some 'slow cooking' and wait for opportunities – traffic, yellows, restarts or whatever. There were a couple opportunities with traffic where I would drop back and when I saw traffic coming I would try to close up to him. It didn't work a couple times and then one time it worked. I went by him and was able to keep him behind me as long as I went flat all the way around.

It was a case of putting my head down and not lifting – and then we had several restarts. Going into the restarts, even though the tire pressures were down a little bit, I had to go flat out. We played this game of cat-and-mouse over several restarts. I tried to outsmart him like mad. I would start early or I would start late and then use every trick in the book to keep him behind me. Obviously I did and that was one of my greatest single triumphs behind the wheel of a racing car.

When I was in the lead, I started daydreaming. It's a common problem and some drivers would admit to it. When you're close to a big accomplishment, you do start daydreaming like when you're leading the race or about to win the championship. That's usually when you make a mistake. I was almost screaming at myself, 'Stop daydreaming. Just focus on driving. The result will come if you drive well. Pretend you're not leading the Indy 500 with 10 laps to go. Just drive the thing.' I was talking to myself, going through the turns and getting in a rhythm-making zone. It's interesting because if you see me crossing the finish line I don't even raise my hands because I'm just going through my check list of stuff to do.

Roger said, 'Checkered flag.' Roger was always very matter-of-fact on the radio. He said 'Checkered flag, you won.' I'm like, 'I what? Really?' It took me quite a while to break out of that sort of robotic mindset that I was in. I was completely overcome with emotion because of everything leading up to the race. I was trying very hard to keep it all bottled up and not let it affect my performance in a negative way.

That whole month was memorable because of everything that led up to it – from me thinking my career was over to eventually culminating two weeks later with one of the biggest wins of my career.

I always remember something Rick Mears told me in the aftermath of that race. Rick was such a huge part of the team. He pulled me aside and said, 'Hey man, well done. Congratulations. You don't realize what happened to you, but it will come to you in due course.' I didn't actually understand what he meant by that. I was like, 'OK Rick. Thanks.' He was so right though, as he usually is. It was very much like that. In fact, I would say several years later that feeling kind of grows on you. It's hard to explain, but it grows on you.

Buddy Rice *won the 2004 Indy 500 driving for Rahal Letterman Racing.*

The year that we won was the first time David Letterman had his name with Bobby Rahal as a team owner, so that was a big deal for us. It was crazy because of all the weather delays we had. We started late, had stoppages and then everything was crazy at the end when the race got shortened by the storm.

The whole victory celebration and everything was in the garages underneath the grandstands. We didn't do the normal ceremony. To be down there and have everybody condensed and packed in there, it was crazy. The rain and all the tornadoes around – a bunch of people won't forget that one.

Because it was so compacted, it made it more intense for the people that were there. Obviously it would have been great to be outside and do the normal ceremony, but I've always been, I guess, a little bit different. So it's kind of nice – kind of funky – that it ends up being the way we won, how it happened was so different. So that was really cool.

We weren't considered the number one contender going into the month. We weren't considered a lot of things, but that was the first time anybody had swept pole position, pit stop competition and the race since Rick Mears in '91.

We had to come back through the field after a stall in the pits. We'd been moving forward, but not at a big clip. I don't remember exactly where we were – about seventh or eighth. Finally Scott Roembke on the box said, 'Hey, the rains are coming. We gotta get going and we gotta go *now*.' We stopped saving fuel – we knew we were going to have to stop again no matter what before the rain came. We went full wick on the fuel and I switched up some stuff on the car – on the bars and stuff. It was like qualifying all the way to the end. As hard as you can run to get back to the front. We were coming fast and the car was hooked up. We were just like ripping through everybody.

We actually made the pass for the lead on a pit stop. I had a blistering in and out – my in and out lap was mega and the boys did a good pit stop and we got out and we were like way gone on everybody. We were technically running second when we came out, but it ended up being a pass for the lead because Adrian Fernandez was out of fuel after another couple of laps and that was it – it was over with because the rains came.

It's a mixed feeling when the rain starts. You're driving fast, you know the rain is starting and you know that's not a good thing around that place. Your natural instinct is to back out of it, but you're leading. You can't crash, you can't back off, and the rain really starts coming. They start telling you to back down and then the yellow comes out. We still had to circulate a couple more laps while it was super wet.

Like I said, the celebration was so tight and compact and everybody was so close together that it had a different feeling than being out in the open air with everybody. It was pretty cool.

When you pull into Indianapolis, you get this rush, like the feeling you get going into a historical place. The one thing that I really liked that year was that there'd be a bunch of former drivers at Bobby's hospitality place and they'd hang out and tell stories about all the stuff that happened back in the day. It was really cool to sit and listen to all those stories. It's really neat, I just like the historical value – I like everything about it – it's a cool place and you've got to have every facet to be able to win.

Sam Hornish, Jr. *grew up in Ohio and won the 2006 Indianapolis 500, edging Marco Andretti by 0.0635 seconds, in the first last lap pass for victory in Indy 500 history.*

When I signed the contract to go to work for Roger (Penske), I felt he was hiring me to win a championship and I was signing on to win an Indianapolis 500. We both achieved what we were looking to do. I would have liked to win some more Indy 500s and championships, but getting the opportunity to drive one of those cars was above and beyond anything. It's pretty unbelievable to drive for Roger.

We felt like 2006 was our race to lose. We started the season on equal footing with everybody having a Honda. We felt like the previous two years, that's what kept us from winning the race – we didn't have the horsepower we needed. We were the fastest every day of the month, except for one day when we were second. That was the last day of practice when we were doing drafting runs to try and figure out fuel mileage.

Looking back at that race, I wasn't going to put myself in a bad position until it counted. And that was obviously going to be the end of the race. We ran in the top three all day. We didn't lead a lot of laps, saved fuel when we needed and we figured out when our last pit stop was going to be. Then the fuel pump got stuck on the pit stop and that put us back – we had to do a drive through penalty.

All the times that Roger had to calm me down on the radio, I felt like I had to calm him down that day. You know Roger is about as cool a customer as you're going to find. I said, 'This isn't over yet. Those guys have run hard, they all have to pit again. As long as we're ahead of them when they start pitting,' – meaning staying on the lead lap – 'they're going to cycle through and we're going to come out ahead of them.' We went to a conserve mode and started saving fuel and people started pitting. I was thinking, 'This is really going to work out the way that we want.'

And then the yellow flag comes out. I'm like, 'Man, I don't know if it can happen now.' Marco (Andretti) was on pit road when the yellow came out and with everybody slowing down, he gets back out first and there are a bunch of people ahead of me. I was fourth in position on the race track, but ninth in line.

I knew that getting past Scott Dixon on the restart was really going to be important for me to win the race. Dan Wheldon was right behind me. As we were coming through Turn 4, Dixon didn't get a good start and I had to check up a bit. When I turned, Wheldon was there, I think straddling the white line and probably with two wheels in the grass. We actually touched. Neither one of us lifted, but it just worked out that maybe he turned a little bit more and maybe I turned a little bit less, as we got to the corner. That was really where I feel like, in a lot of ways, where we won the race – the restart we had.

I was able to get around Dixon and about two other lapped cars by the time we got to Turn 1. I had Marco and Michael (Andretti) ahead of me. I had raced with Michael before and knew he would be difficult to pass. When I did, I was like, 'Man, this could happen. I might be able to win this thing.'

I caught Marco, but wasn't really intending to pass him on lap 198. I got a good run and ended up getting to the inside of him, but it wasn't far enough to where I felt like I could justify the position, so I had to get out of it. I thought I cost myself the race right there. Downshifted a couple gears. Got a good draft and through turns 1 and 2 and I'm like, 'I might get there.' In Turn 3 it was, 'I'm going to get there,' and by Turn 4 I thought I might run over him by the time I got to the exit of the corner.

The car was a little tight, pushing a little bit coming off the corner. I was like, 'Keep your foot in it.' Came pretty close to brushing the wall at exit. I was going to let him make the first move and drive up his gear box until he did. He went to the inside and when he went to check his mirrors I was already there. There was not really anything he could do about it. I couldn't believe it had actually happened.

I watch the replay now and I'm like, 'One of these times I might not get there.' It was just awesome, the way that it worked out. It was, at that time, the only pass on the last lap to win the race – that was really cool.

I feel sometimes people don't realize how big it is until you get to do all the Victory Lane things and you're on the media tour. That's really when you understand how big a race you just won. When I won, it felt like somebody has just taken 1,000 pounds off my shoulders.

It's hard to imagine that you can grow up in a small town in northwest Ohio and have the dream that you want to just go to the Indianapolis 500 and qualify for the race. To win with one of the most prolific teams there's ever been there, is just amazing.

***Scott Dixon** captured the checkered flag in the 2008 Indy 500 and is a four-time Indy car series champion (2003, 2008, 2013 and 2015).*

Well, I'm sure everybody talks about their win – and it's probably my biggest memory just because it's so unreal.

I think it was just so surreal. I still went through Turn 1 flat – didn't even see the checkered flag and was still racing until they came on the radio and said we had won the race. It instantly turns into a feeling of wanting to get back to see my wife and the team and everybody that helps get you to that point. Even weeks after the race you still kind of don't believe it. It's insane to be on a short list of 68 or 69 people who have won the race, and to be part of what this year will be its 100th anniversary.

The hardest part for me was actually during the race. We had such a good month. We were the fastest car in most of the practice sessions, we started from the pole and the whole month had gone really smoothly. So, the whole time during the 200 laps I was thinking, 'Did I hear something? Is that the engine? Did I just feel something?' That was actually the most disappointing part. The whole time I was thinking something's going to go wrong – until I knew we had actually won.

It was just a massive sense of relief – like a bunch of weight was lifted off your shoulders. The first emotion I felt was, 'Wow, we actually got to the finish and we won the race.' After that, I think my emotions changed.

I think the joy – the joy came once I saw my wife Emma, once I saw Chip (Ganassi) and once I saw all the team guys – that's the pure joy. But, you're still in shock a little bit too. I think it's really surreal because you want to get back to the pits and then you're rolling the car to the winner's circle.

Then you're putting the wreath on. It's things you've seen before on TV for many years. The driver putting on the wreath and drinking the milk – but you're actually doing it. It just feels really insane. You're always questioning, 'Am I actually drinking the milk?' Then going out and kissing the bricks. It's the repetition of things that you've seen thousands of times before during the month of May because there are endless video feeds of previous victories. Then you're in that situation. You're having flashbacks to where it all started in go-kart racing to other milestones getting to this point. You see your career sort of in a bit of a flash and you're like, 'We just won the Indy 500.'

I think it was all a bit of a blur. You do the race. You talk to the media. Then you go out with everybody from the team. You're up at six the next morning for photos. Then we went straight to New York, then to Texas and right back to New York. After that you go to the next race in Milwaukee. Then you go right after that to the next race in Texas. So, for three weeks, you're kind of on a massive high and you're running on adrenaline, but you still haven't had that moment. It wasn't until after the Texas race and we had a week off that I finally sat back at home and was like, 'Yeah, that's cool.' It finally sunk in, but it took a while – for me at least it did.

***Tony Kanaan** won the 2013 Indianapolis 500 for Chip Ganassi Racing after 11 attempts.*

My best memory of the Indy 500 is, obviously, when I won. But, not just because of the win.

It was a special year in many ways. Alex Zanardi was back at the Indy 500 for the first time (since he was badly injured in a 2001 crash in Germany). He was there because Chip (Ganassi) had got him his old race car – and he was there to receive it.

It was funny because Zanardi had never actually watched the 500 live, and he came to see me before the race. He brought the Paralympics hand-cycling gold medal that he won the year before (2012) to show me and he said, 'You should rub this because it brings you luck.' And I did, right before the race, and I ended up winning the race. Apart from the win being very special – something I'd been trying for a long time – that was one of the great memories of the win as well.

When we first got to the Speedway that May I decided to really enjoy my time. It was the last year of my contract. I didn't know if I was going to get a new contract or not. Things started to get a little bit more difficult on the sponsorship side. So I decided to enjoy Indy in a different way that year because I didn't know if I was going to come back the following year.

I woke up race morning a lot less stressed than I had been in the past – the prior 11 years – and maybe that helped. Instead of saying, 'I don't know if I'm coming back,' I decided to really enjoy everything about the race. I probably never enjoyed it in a way that I should have because you always put that pressure on yourself – it's the 500 and you want to win.

But that year I just relaxed and started to enjoy it more – from looking at how many people were at the track to the driver introductions to the pre-race ceremonies. It was just a lot more relaxed. A feeling I haven't been able to duplicate or replicate any race morning since, especially at the 500.

It was surreal crossing the finish line. I was sobbing. It was a promise that I made to my dad when he passed 25 years ago – to win the Indy 500. I couldn't really think straight. Once I got to pit lane – seeing every single member from all the different teams clapping and giving me thumbs up – that was extremely touching because I wasn't expecting that either. It rarely happens. The only other time I remember seeing it was when Dale (Earnhardt) Sr. won at Daytona. I felt very humbled and was thinking, 'Look what's happening to me.' Then hearing the crowd and how the crowd reacted – standing there screaming my name. It was like, 'Man, this is unbelievable.'

When I actually got to the winner's circle, so many people came to talk to me that I didn't have time to process anything. It was just a bunch of people talking to me and kissing me. I have no idea if you ask me who was there. I probably have to go back and watch the video to see who said, 'Congratulations.'

Later that afternoon, Zanardi came to see me and he said, 'I told you about the medal.' And with that, I actually gave him my winning Indy 500 helmet. He got extremely emotional. I'm a very emotional guy, but seeing Alex dropping tears because I had won the race and given him my helmet, it was very special.

***Ryan Hunter-Reay** won the 2014 Indy 500 and was the 2012 Indy car series champion while driving for Andretti Autosport.*

Oh man, the best memory of my career is winning Indy. The fight to the finish was really the highlight. The red flag and then a final shootout between me and Helio (Castroneves). We were passing each other on every lap to the end.

I remember on the last restart thinking, 'This is it. This is the moment of your career. You can either take all of it right now and change your career forever, or be disappointed for a long time.' I'm glad it turned out the way it did. It was the second closest finish in Indy 500 history. To get an American flag back on top at Indy was a proud moment, and I took a lot of pride in that.

On Carb Day we had the car out there in race trim and I felt that we were good – we had good balance in the car. Considering the weather hadn't changed much on race day, I knew we had a good shot that morning. Even though I only qualified 19th, we came through the field and by the halfway point were in the lead.

After crossing the finish line, it felt like I was out of the car. I couldn't even feel myself sitting down. That's how elated I was. It was just unbelievable. All kinds of emotions came over me on the cool down lap. Your whole life, and really your whole career, flashes through your memory because of everything you ever worked for to get to this point.

My family was there along with all the sponsors that have been with me for many years. It was unbelievable. It was great to get to the winner's circle and see my kid – my son, who was two years old at the time – wearing a uniform that matched mine. That was fantastic. Those memories I'll never forget.

The enormity of the whole thing doesn't sink in right away. It can't just because there's so much going on. You're doing this interview and that interview. You're up until two in the morning after winning the race. The next morning you have to wake up at five to do more interviews. Then it's right on to the race the next weekend. It sets in over time. One day you're standing next to the Borg-Warner trophy with your face on it taking pictures and you get what occurred. But, the enormity of the whole situation didn't really sink in for me until the off-season.

It's a career-changer – a career-definer, for sure. You're now in a different club. I still have a lot of work to do in my career, but your first Indy 500 win puts you in that different club.

Acknowledgements

WITHOUT THE SUPPORT AND ENCOURAGEMENT of our wives, E.J. Garner and Emily Spiegel, we would never have undertaken this project. Family has always played a key role in our lives, and thanks from Art to Bonnie, Bill, Jim, Sylvia, Anna, Emma and Katy. Marc would like to thank Merrill, Andrea, Peter, Ben, Eva, Eddie, Kate and Sam.

Dan Boyd provided much of the photography for this book, along with Mike Levitt from LAT. Jonathan Ingram, in addition to providing us with his 500 memory, also served as our copy editor. An established author of such titles as *The Art of Race Car Design* and *America's Hottest Racer, Danica Patrick* among others, Jonathan helped with the consistency and continuity that can sometimes be a challenge with more than 150 entries from multiple sources.

You don't put together that many memories without an incredible amount of help. In addition to those agreeing to share their stories, to whom we owe a debt of gratitude, there are many others who helped arrange interviews, had suggestions as to who we should talk to and helped us make those connections. No matter how many we mention here, we're sure to miss some.

Among those we turned to repeatedly for contact information, recommendations and assistance with interviews were Tom Blattler, Anne Fornoro, Andy Hall, David Hovis, Robin Miller, Steve Shunck, Doug Stokes, Lynzy Stover and Les Unger. Others who helped us make connections include, Mike Arning, Chris Biby, Barbara Burns, Wendy Belk, Van Colley, Rory Connellan, Julie Cordes, Amy Crook, Dan Cotter, Michael Jordan, Julie Klausner, Ron Kantowski, Kathy Lauterbach, Mai Lindstrom, Haley Moore, Annette Randall, Patty Reid, Teri Thomas and Cal Wells.

About the authors

Art Garner is the author of *Black Noon, The Year They Stopped the Indy 500,* winner of the Motor Press Guild's Book of the Year award and a finalist for the PEN/ESPN award for literary sports writing. He spent more than 35 years in automotive public relations. He lives in Olympia, Wash., with his wife, E.J. Follow him on Twitter: @artpgarner

Marc B. Spiegel earned the Jim Chapman Award for excellence in motorsports public relations as determined by a vote of national media while working in the CART Indy Car series. He has more than 25 years of experience in the business of sports marketing and public relations. He lives in Charlotte, N.C., with his wife Emily.

32815613R10129

Made in the USA
San Bernardino, CA
16 April 2016